D0752216

Adobe®

Camera Raw

S T U D I O ▪ S K I L L S

By Charlotte K. Lowrie

Kevin Ames • Ellen Anon • John Paul Caponigro • Bob Coates
Seán Duggan • Macduff Everton • Katrin Eismann • Rob Sheppard
Eddie Tapp • David H. Wells

Wiley Publishing, Inc.

Adobe® Camera Raw Studio Skills

Published by
Wiley Publishing, Inc.
111 River Street
Hoboken, N.J. 07030
www.wiley.com

Copyright © 2006 by Wiley Publishing, Inc., Indianapolis, Indiana

Library of Congress Control Number: 2006925873

ISBN-13: 978-0-471-78264-3
ISBN-10: 0-471-78264-5

Manufactured in the United States of America

10 9 8 7 6 5 4 3 2 1

1K/QV/QX/QW/IN

Published by Wiley Publishing, Inc., Indianapolis, Indiana
Published simultaneously in Canada

No part of this publication may be reproduced, stored in a retrieval system or transmitted in any form or by any means, electronic, mechanical, photocopying, recording, scanning or otherwise, except as permitted under Sections 107 or 108 of the 1976 United States Copyright Act, without either the prior written permission of the Publisher, or authorization through payment of the appropriate per-copy fee to the Copyright Clearance Center, 222 Rosewood Drive, Danvers, MA 01923, (978) 750-8400, fax (978) 646-8600, or on the web at www.copyright.com. Requests to the Publisher for permission should be addressed to the Legal Department, Wiley Publishing, Inc., 10475 Crosspoint Blvd., Indianapolis, IN 46256, (317) 572-3447, fax (317) 572-4355, or online at http://www.wiley.com/go/permissions.

LIMIT OF LIABILITY/DISCLAIMER OF WARRANTY: THE PUBLISHER AND THE AUTHOR MAKE NO REPRESENTATIONS OR WARRANTIES WITH RESPECT TO THE ACCURACY OR COMPLETENESS OF THE CONTENTS OF THIS WORK AND SPECIFICALLY DISCLAIM ALL WARRANTIES, INCLUDING WITHOUT LIMITATION WARRANTIES OF FITNESS FOR A PARTICULAR PURPOSE. NO WARRANTY MAY BE CREATED OR EXTENDED BY SALES OR PROMOTIONAL MATERIALS. THE ADVICE AND STRATEGIES CONTAINED HEREIN MAY NOT BE SUITABLE FOR EVERY SITUATION. THIS WORK IS SOLD WITH THE UNDERSTANDING THAT THE PUBLISHER IS NOT ENGAGED IN RENDERING LEGAL, ACCOUNTING, OR OTHER PROFESSIONAL SERVICES. IF PROFESSIONAL ASSISTANCE IS REQUIRED, THE SERVICES OF A COMPETENT PROFESSIONAL PERSON SHOULD BE SOUGHT. NEITHER THE PUBLISHER NOR THE AUTHOR SHALL BE LIABLE FOR DAMAGES ARISING HERE FROM. THE FACT THAT AN ORGANIZATION OR WEBSITE IS REFERRED TO IN THIS WORK AS A CITATION AND/OR A POTENTIAL SOURCE OF FURTHER INFORMATION DOES NOT MEAN THAT THE AUTHOR OR THE PUBLISHER ENDORSES THE INFORMATION THE ORGANIZATION OR WEBSITE MAY PROVIDE OR RECOMMENDATIONS IT MAY MAKE. FURTHER, READERS SHOULD BE AWARE THAT INTERNET WEBSITES LISTED IN THIS WORK MAY HAVE CHANGED OR DISAPPEARED BETWEEN WHEN THIS WORK WAS WRITTEN AND WHEN IT IS READ.

For general information on our other products and services or to obtain technical support please contact our Customer Care Department within the U.S. at (800) 762-2974, outside the U.S. at (317) 572-3993 or fax (317) 572-4002.

Trademarks: Wiley, the Wiley Publishing logo, Unofficial Guide and all related trademarks, logos, and trade dress are trademarks or registered trademarks of John Wiley & Sons, Inc. and/or its affiliates. Photoshop is a registered trademark of Adobe Systems Incorporated in the United States and/or other countries. All other trademarks are the property of their respective owners. Wiley Publishing, Inc. is not associated with any product or vendor mentioned in this book.

Wiley also publishes its books in a variety of electronic formats. Some content that appears in print may not be available in electronic books. For more information about Wiley products, please visit our Web site at www.wiley.com.

Credits

Acquisitions Editor
Michael Roney

Project Editor
Cricket Krengel

Technical Editor
Michael Guncheon

Copy Editor
Paula Lowell

Editorial Manager
Robyn B. Siesky

Business Manager
Amy Knies

**Vice President & Group
Executive Publisher**
Richard Swadley

Vice President & Publisher
Barry Pruett

Project Coordinators
Adrienne Martinez
Jennifer Theriot

Graphics and Production Specialists
Jennifer Click
Carrie A. Foster
Lauren Goddard
Heather Pope
Amanda Spagnuolo

Quality Control Technicians
Joe Niesen

Proofreading
Leeann Harney

Indexing
Lynnzee Elze

Cover Designer
Ryan Sneed

Book Interior Design
Elizabeth Brooks

Acknowledgments

Many fine qualities distinguish photography as an industry, but perhaps none as much as the willingness of photographers to freely and patiently share their knowledge with eager students.

This book is a confirmation of that unique quality.

On the following pages, some of the best photographers in the nation share techniques with you that they've perfected through hours of personal study and practice. This book is dedicated to those contributors and to all photographers who so graciously share their art and passion with others.

Introduction

Welcome to *Adobe Camera Raw Studio Skills*. This book offers a one-of-a-kind collection of RAW image processing techniques and insights from some of the top professional photographers in the nation. The photographers featured in this book, some of whom are pioneers of digital photography and RAW image capture, share their personal image-processing insights— all of which you can use to add professional polish to your images.

RAW Capture: The New Frontier of Photography

If you're new to RAW capture and processing, think of RAW capture as the second wave in the revolution of digital photography. By having control over the RAW image information, photographers gain unprecedented control during capture and post-processing by using programs such as Adobe Camera Raw.

Legends in photography, including Ansel Adams, looked forward to today's technology as a means of gaining greater technical control and creative interpretation over images. In 1980, Ansel Adams wrote, "In the electronic age, I am sure that scanning techniques will be developed to achieve prints of extraordinary subtlety from the original negative scores. If I could return in 20 years or so I would hope to see astounding interpretations of my most expressive images. It is true no one could print my negatives as I did, but they might well get more out of them by electronic means. Image quality is not the product of a machine but of the person who directs the machine, and there are no limits to imagination and expression." (Ansel Adams, *An Autobiography*).

Early adopters of RAW capture and processing see it as the new frontier of photography.

George Lepp, professional nature and wildlife photographer and founder of the popular Lepp Institute (www.leppinstitute.com/LeppInstitute/index.htm) in California, is one of the early adopters of not only digital photography, but also the complementary technologies that surround it such as inkjet printing. For Lepp, RAW capture and processing is equivalent to regaining the control that photographers had in the black-and-white darkroom. "We've taken back the control of the second half of the image. I can do things that I never dreamt that I could do before. I make 44- x 90-inch prints in my office of a quality that I never dreamt that I could do, and they last 100–200 years. The colors are vibrant. I never was happy with the prints being made for me. And I'm doing it all myself."

Lepp, a Canon Explorer of Light and author of three photography books, believes that the new technologies are affecting the way that professional photographers work. "Those who are embracing new technology are excited about it. Those who are not embracing it are finding it to be the opposite. Not only is it dragging those people down in the sense that they don't want to get involved in it, but they see other people doing work that might be better than theirs because they do have the technology."

Begin with A Good RAW Image

RAW capture is exciting because photographers have unprecedented control over image data from capture to print, and that means they can control not only the quality of the image, but also the mood, color, and creative interpretation of the image.

While this book offers valuable insights into processing RAW images for the best possible results, the techniques in the book assume that

▶ You are using RAW capture on your digital SLR, and,

▶ That the RAW images are properly exposed.

If you're accustomed to JPEG capture, you may question the advantage of switching to RAW. Simply stated, RAW capture is the single best way to preserve all the bits captured in the image with the ability to control how the bits are interpreted. RAW images offer far richer data depth and file stability during conversion and editing. In contrast, JPEG capture mode pre-processes images and discards large amounts of image data along the way. The result leaves little if any wiggle room to correct exposure, white balance, contrast, and saturation during image editing.

The second assumption is that you begin with a well-exposed RAW image. Good exposure is as important with digital photography as it is with film because it offers significantly more latitude and stability during processing. But what does good digital exposure mean?

A good exposure of RAW files ensures that the camera captures the maximum number of brightness levels that your camera can deliver. During conversion, tonal mapping, or gamma encoding, assigns linear tonal levels to perceived brightness—resulting in an image that resembles what we saw with the human eye. Without going into the details of gamma encoding, it's important to know that digital capture devotes a relatively large number of image pixels to highlights and fewer to shadows. In fact, in digital imaging, the first f-stop of brightness accounts for half of all the tonal levels in the image.

This characteristic has practical implications for traditional exposure guidelines. For example, exposing for the shadows sacrifices half or more of the possible levels of brightness that the camera can capture. At the same time, underexposure captures relatively few dark levels. If you subsequently brighten the image during editing, the limited numbers of levels must be redistributed across the tonal spectrum. Visualize this process as a rubber band being stretched. As the band is stretched, small holes analogous to breaks between tonal levels appear. This stretching creates gaps between tonal ranges that show up as posterization in the final print. In addition, underexposure magnifies noise in shadow areas. For example, figure IN-1 shows gaps in the histogram of an 8-bit JPEG image. Even with a non-aggressive curve applied, the tonal levels have been lost, as shown by the gaps. The spikes show compression.

The general rule for good digital exposure is to expose for the highlights and develop for the shadows. In fact, slightly overexposing images is better. When tonal mapping is applied, the file has significantly more bits that can be redistributed to the midtones and darker tones where the human eye is most sensitive to changes. If highlights are overexposed, programs such as Adobe Camera Raw can recover anywhere from one-fourth to a full f-stop of highlight detail during image conversion. In figure IN-2, a negative Exposure value of 1.95 initiates Camera Raw's highlight recovery feature to recover the brightest highlights in the waterfall. In short, a modest overexposure delivers the best image that a digital camera can produce.

►IN.1

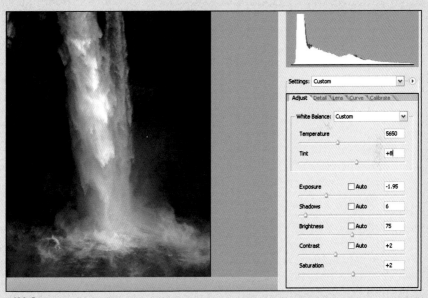

►IN.2

If you have a collection of well-exposed RAW images, you're ready to take advantage of the all techniques and insights that *Camera Raw Studio Skills* has to offer.

Contents

Section 2: Image Processing Techniques

About the Author

Charlotte K. Lowrie

Seattle, WA
charlotte@wordsandphotos.org
www.wordsandphotos.org

Specialty and clients

Editorial and stock photography

Microsoft, National Association for the Self-Employed, *Quill* magazine, private clients, and various stock agencies.

Techniques in this book

Charlotte Lowrie is a freelance editorial and stock photographer and an award-winning writer based in the Seattle, Washington area. Her writing and photography have appeared in magazines including *Popular Photography & Imaging*. She is the author of two books: the best-seller *Canon Digital Rebel Digital Field Guide* and *Teach Yourself Visually Digital Photography, Second Edition*. Charlotte also teaches photography classes at BetterPhoto.com. She was the managing editor of the discontinued MSN Photos Web site for more than four years and served as the managing editor of Double Exposure magazine for a year. She is also a featured photographer on www.takegreatpictures.com.

Contributors

Kevin Ames

Atlanta, GA
kevin@amesphoto.com
www.amesphoto.com

Clients

The *Wall Street Journal*, *Time Magazine*, as well as numerous other magazines, brochures, and catalogs for clients including Westin Hotels, AT&T, Carter's Atlanta, Spanx, and La-Z-Boy.

Techniques in this book

Kevin is a recognized leader in the fast evolving world of digital photography and post-production.

In addition to his full-time commercial studio, Kevin has spoken at numerous national events for the Professional Photographers of America. He is a Photoshop World Dream Team instructor for NAPP. He has presented classes at international conferences in Canada, Ireland, and Italy. Domestically he has spoken at Photo Plus East, the NAB Post-Production Conference, the Mac Design Conference.

He writes for *Photoshop User* magazine. His articles and reviews have appeared in *Studio Photography and Design*, *Photo Electronic Imaging*, *Professional Photographer*, and *Digital Output*, among others.

He is the author of *Photoshop CS: the Art of Photographing Women* and *Digital SLR Photography with Photoshop CS2 All-In-One For Dummies*, both from Wiley. He is also a co-author of the *Photoshop World Dream Team Instructors Book* from Peachpit Press.

Kevin is a Certified Professional Photographer, Certified Electronic Imager, Photographic Craftsman, and an Approved Photographic Instructor. Kevin is a member of ASMP, NAPP, PIDA, and PPA.

Ellen Anon

Erie, PA
ellenanon@mac.com
www.sunbearphoto.com

Specialty and Clients

Nature and outdoor photography

Inner Reflections Calendars, Canon Europe, McDonalds, and the Erie Zoo. Fine art images are currently available at Glass Growers Gallery. Images are represented by Mega Press stock agency.

Techniques in this book

Ellen loves to photograph anything outdoors as well as various types of macro subjects and seeks to create images that go beyond simple documentation to evoke emotional reactions. She believes that photography is a two-step process. The first step is creating the image in the camera, and the second step is optimizing the image and presenting it to create the most impact.

Ellen freelances as a photographer, writer, and instructor. Currently she co-leads some of Arthur Morris's larger photo tours to Florida and New Mexico. In addition she leads Photoshop workshops for Joe and Mary Ann McDonald as well as her own Photoshop in the Field Workshops.

Recently she co-authored *Photoshop for Nature Photographers: A Workshop in a Book* with Tim Grey and she is currently writing *Aperture Expose: The Mac Photographer's Guide to Taming the Workflow* with her son, Josh Anon. Her writing and images have appeared in numerous publications including, *Shutterbug*, *Nature's Best*, *Mother Earth*, *eDigital Photo*, *Apogee*, and *Popular Photography*.

John Paul Caponigro

Caponigro Arts
73 Cross Road
Cushing, ME 04563
info@johnpaulcaponigro.com
www.johnpaulcaponigro.com

  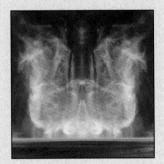

Clients

Adobe, Apple, Canon, Colorbyte, Epson, GretagMacBeth, Kodak, LowePro, and Sony.

Technique in this book

John Paul Caponigro combines his background in painting with traditional and alternative photographic processes using the digital platform. He is respected internationally as one of the most prominent artists working with digital media processes. Exhibited internationally, his work resides in numerous private and public collections including Princeton University, the Estée Lauder collection, and the Smithsonian.

John Paul's primary focus is the natural world. The wastelands he photographs are breathtakingly beautiful, yet the conspicuous absences found within them add an unusual complexity and social relevance when issues surrounding the environment, the medium of photography and its changing nature as well as his practice within it, and their mutual interaction are considered. Many viewers find his work profoundly spiritual.

John Paul teaches primarily in his studio or on location and occasionally at prominent workshops including The Santa Fe Photographic Workshops and The Maine Photographic Workshops. He lectures frequently at universities, museums, and conferences.

John Paul's work has been published widely. Reviews have appeared in numerous periodicals and books including *Art News* and *The Ansel Adams Guide*. He is a contributing editor for *Camera Arts* and *View Camera* and a columnist for *PhotoTechniques* and *Digital Photo Pro*. His book, *Adobe Photoshop Master Class* (Adobe Press, 2003) is now in its second edition.

John Paul is a Canon Explorer of Light and an Epson's Stylus Pro. You can subscribe@johnpaulcaponigro.com for his free enews, Insights, latest news including new tips, techniques, and reviews.

Bob Coates

Bob Coates Photography, Inc.
PMB 508 2370 W. Hwy 89A Suite 11
Sedona, AZ 86336
928-284-0200 or toll free 877-746-8646
bob@bcphotography.com
www.bcphotography.com
www.bcweddingphoto.com

Specialty

Weddings and portrait photography

Techniques in this book

Bob Coates Photography, Inc. "Specializes in not Specializing" so that they can come up with interesting new ways of photographing subjects. Bob believes that combining the techniques of different types of photography leads to new ways of capturing images.

People who hire Bob Coates Photography, Inc. do it not just for the expertise, but for the experience brought to the job. Bob is the author of many articles for professional photography magazines as well as the books *Photographer's Guide to Wedding Album Design* and *Sales and Strategies and Techniques for Digital Photographers*. He also produces Photoshop training CDs and DVDs through Software Cinema.

Bob has presented programs from Hawaii to the Virgin Islands and is available for workshops tailored to your needs from two hours to two days on Photoshop training, marketing, and other photography-related subjects.

Coates is a member of Professional Photographers of America (PPA), Arizona PPA, Wedding and Portrait Photographers International (WPPI), National Association of Photoshop Professionals (NAPP), and the Sedona Wedding Professionals Association.

Seán Duggan

Grass Valley, CA
sean@seanduggan.com
www.seanduggan.com

Specialty

Fine-art photography

Techniques in this book

Seán Duggan is a fine-art photographer, author, and educator. In his photographs, he looks for the extraordinary in the ordinary. He searches for scenes and moments that are capable of transcending the literal representation of time and place to become images that are interpretive and enigmatic, rich with metaphor, symbolism, and subtle mystery.

Equally at home with low- and high-tech approaches, his visual toolkit includes cameras ranging from a custom-built pinhole camera and plastic toy cameras, to digital SLRs and advanced Photoshop techniques. His photographs have been exhibited at the Monterey Peninsula Museum of Art, the Center for Photographic Art in Carmel, California, and at galleries and in exhibitions throughout California.

Seán is a co-author of *Real World Digital Photography* and *Photoshop CS Artistry, Mastering the Digital Image*. He teaches classes on digital photography and Photoshop at the Academy of Art University in San Francisco and the University of California, Santa Cruz Extension in Silicon Valley. He has also taught workshops at the Santa Fe Workshops, Maine Photographic Workshops, Palm Beach Photographic Workshops, and the Lepp Institute of Digital Imaging.

You can see more of his work at www.seanduggan.com. His photo blog, www.f1point4.com, features a regularly updated collection of images and musings on photography, digital imaging, and the creative process.

Macduff Everton

126 E. Haley Street, Suite A18
Santa Barbara, CA 93101
www.macduffeverton.com
www.macduffeverton.com/stock

Specialty and Clients

Editorial—*Condé Nast Traveler, Fortune, GEO, House and Garden, Islands, Men's Journal, National Geographic Traveler, Sophisticated Traveler, New Yorker, O: The Oprah Magazine, Smithsonian,* and *Virtuoso Life.*

Advertising—Atlantis, Ritz Carlton, Phat Farm, IBM, Epson, Nature Conservancy, Kodak, Celebrity Cruises, Goldman Sachs, Ameriprise, Apple, Mexico Tourism, American Airlines, Outward Bound, Rolex, Leica, and Lincoln Navigator.

Technique in this book

Macduff Everton gives a sense of place, whether it's portraits of individuals or of a landscape. He is a contributing editor at *National Geographic Traveler, Islands Magazine,* and *Virtuoso Life.* An early champion of his work, Andy Grundberg, wrote, "Macduff Everton updates travel photography in the same way that Ansel Adams updated nineteenth century photography of the West. He captures strange and eloquent moments in which time, and the world, seem to stand still."

His black-and-white documentation in the Yucatan of individuals and their families over 20 years resulted in the seminal publication, *The Modern Maya—A Culture in Transition* (University of New Mexico Press, Albuquerque, 1991). Currently Macduff is working on an update to *The Modern Maya* that chronicles their changing lives over 35 years.

Everton exhibits his photos nationally and internationally. He is a popular instructor at Santa Fe Workshops, Toscana Photographic Workshop, and Mountain Light Gallery Workshop.

Macduff enjoys working with his wife, Mary Heebner, an abstract painter and writer. Their two very different visions of a place often inform each other's work. They collaborated on *The Western Horizon*, Abrams, 2000.

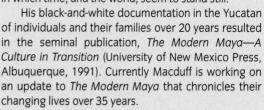

Katrin Eismann

katrin@photoshopdiva.com
www.katrineismann.com

Clients

Apple Computer, Adobe Systems, DxO Labs, Eastman Kodak, Nikon USA, Fuji Film, U.S. Navy, and World Press Photo

Techniques in this book

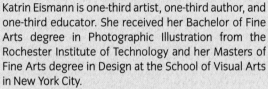

Katrin Eismann is one-third artist, one-third author, and one-third educator. She received her Bachelor of Fine Arts degree in Photographic Illustration from the Rochester Institute of Technology and her Masters of Fine Arts degree in Design at the School of Visual Arts in New York City.

Katrin co-authored *Adobe Photoshop Studio Secrets* and *Real World Digital Photography* and authored *Photoshop Restoration and Retouching* and *Photoshop Masking & Compositing,* both of which have been translated into six languages. She is a featured columnist in *Photoshop User* and *American Photo* magazines and is a popular speaker at the Photo Marketing Association (PMA), American Society of Media Photographers (ASMP), Professional Photographers of America (PPA), PhotoExpo, and Photoshop User conferences. Her images have been featured in numerous books and magazines, as well as at group and solo exhibits. She is on the facility of the School of Visual Arts where she teaches in both the graduate Photography and Related Media and the undergraduate Computer Art programs.

Katrin spends a great deal of time in airports waiting for flights to domestic and international destinations to fulfill a busy and rewarding consulting and teaching schedule.

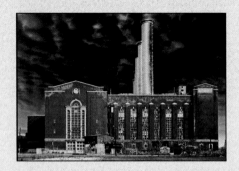

Rob Sheppard

robsheppard@wernerpublishing.com
www.robsheppardphoto.com

Specialty and Clients

Nature and editorial photography.

Minnesota Department of Transportation, Norwest Banks (now Wells Fargo), Pillsbury, 3M, General Mills, Lutheran Brotherhood, Ciba-Geigy, Anderson Windows, the *National Geographic* magazine, and *The Farmer*, *Outdoor Photographer*, and *PCPhoto* magazines.

Techniques in this book

Rob Sheppard has had a long-time and nationally recognized commitment to helping photographers connect with digital imaging technology. He was one of the small group of people who started *PCPhoto* magazine nearly eight years ago to bring the digital world to photographers on their terms. He is the editor of *PCPhoto* as well as *Outdoor Photographer* magazines (second only to *Popular Photography* in circulation), group editorial director of all Werner Publication photo magazines (*PCPhoto*, *Outdoor Photographer*, and *Digital Photo Pro*) and is the author/photographer of over a dozen photo books, including *Adobe® Camera Raw for Digital Photographers Only*.

He also writes a column in *Outdoor Photographer* called "Digital Horizons" and teaches around the country, including workshops for the Palm Beach Photographic Centre, Santa Fe Photography and Digital Workshops, Digital Landscape Workshop Series, and the Great American Photography Workshop group.

As a professional photographer, Rob worked for many years in Minnesota (before moving to Los Angeles) doing work for a variety of clients. His photography has been published in many magazines, ranging from *National Geographic* to *The Farmer*.

Eddie Tapp

Atlanta, GA
etapp@aol.com
www.eddietapp.com

Specialty and Clients

Advertising and editorial photography

Epson, Eastman Kodak, Foveon, Polaroid, Apple Computer, The Society for Imaging Science and Technology, Dynacolor Graphics, Marathon Press, H&H Color Lab, CPQ Color Lab, PhotoLogic (Ireland), PGC (Japan), D.O.D., D.O.E., U.S. Army, U.S. Navy, and other government agencies along with a list of photographic studio operations.

Techniques in this book

Eddie Tapp is an award-winning photographer, lecturer, consultant, and author on digital imaging issues. Eddie has been actively involved in educating and consulting corporations, studios, and agencies in the applications of digital imaging workflow, color management, pre-press, and digital photography globally through workshops, seminars, on-site consulting, and training.

He is Director of the Institute of Visual Arts in Maui, Hawaii. Eddie is an Explorer of Light with Canon USA and is on the Photoshop Dream Team with NAPP. He served six years as the Chairman of the Committee on Digital and Advanced Imaging for the Professional Photographers of America (PPA) where he holds the Master of Photography, Master of Electronic Imaging and Photographic Craftsman degrees, is an Approved Photographic Instructor, and is a Certified Professional Photographer. He also is the Commercial Council representative to PPA for the GPPA.

His articles have appeared in The *Professional Photographer*, *Photo Electronic Imaging*, *Infoto* magazine, *Southern Exposure Digital Capture*, and others. Eddie served on Adobe's Photoshop beta team for Photoshop releases 6, 7, CS, and CS2. He has also served as print judge at many professional photographic competitions.

David H. Wells

Providence, RI
david@davidhwells.com
www.davidhwells.com

Class and workshop schedule:
www.davidhwells.com/PublishedWork/Workshops/FutureClasses/0.htm

Specialty and Clients

Editorial photography

Aramco World, *Chicago Tribune*, *Geo Magazine*, *Life Magazine*, *Los Angeles Times Magazine*, *National Geographic* Publications, *Newsweek Magazine*, the *New York Times Magazine*, *Philadelphia Inquirer Sunday Magazine*, *Time*, *U.S. News & World Report*, and the *Washington Post Magazine*.

Techniques in this book

David H. Wells is a freelance photojournalist and photo-educator. David has taught classes and workshops at the University of Pennsylvania, Syracuse University, the University of the Arts, the International Center for Photography in New York City, the Maine Photographic Workshops, and the Rochester Institute of Technology. His teaching topics range from photo essays and understanding light and color, to stock photography basics and digital photography and workflow.

David has received a Fulbright fellowship to India and grants from Nikon/N.P.P.A., the Pennsylvania Council on the Arts, the MacArthur Foundation's Program of Research and Writing on International Peace, the New Jersey Council on the Arts, and the Rhode Island State Council on the Arts. David's photographs have been exhibited nationally and overseas. Portfolios of his work have been published in *American Photographer*, *Camera and Darkroom*, *Camera Arts*, *Nikon World*, *Photo District News*, *Photo Magazine* (France), *Photographers International* (Taiwan), *Photo Techniques*, and *Zoom* (Italy).

Section 1

Workflow and Image Evaluation

Time-Saving Adobe Bridge Strategies

Chapter 01

In this chapter

Techniques for Batch File Renaming in Adobe Bridge

Contributor: David H. Wells ■ **Specialty:** Photojournalism and Editorial
Primary Tool Used: Batch Rename in Bridge

As image collections grow, using a file-naming strategy that helps narrow the search for images can save significant time. The first step is to create a naming strategy that is useful throughout multiple image collections, and then use Bridge's Batch Rename feature to automate file naming. Another advantage of using Bridge is that it helps automate backup by allowing you to create a backup copy of renamed files in a separate folder.

1

In Adobe Bridge, open the folder that contains the images you want to rename. Then select the images that you want to rename. If a folder contains images of different subjects, places, or assignments, select only one group of similar images to rename. You may want to create subfolders to group images by subject, location, or assignment either before or during the renaming process.

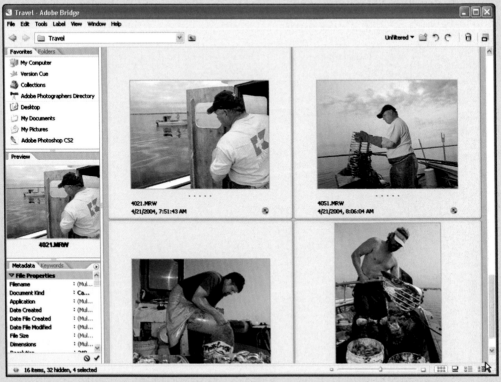

▶1.1

▶ Tip
To navigate complex file directories quickly, choose Window ➤ Workspace, and then choose File Navigator. To gain additional space to view the file structure, drag the vertical divider bar between the Folders and content panes in Bridge to widen the Folders panel.

▶ Note
Although you can also use the earlier versions of Photoshop's Batch dialog box to rename files, they require that you run an action on the files and save them. In Bridge, you can simply rename the files without running an action or saving the RAW files.

2

Choose Tools ➤ Batch Rename. Bridge displays the Batch Rename dialog box. In the Destination Folder section, you can choose among three options. Your choice of folder depends in part on the workflow and backup process that you've established. For example, if your first workflow step is to create a backup of RAW images with a naming system, you can choose Copy or Move to other folder. The options are as follows:

- **Rename in same folder.** This is the option to use if you aren't backing up images and simply want to rename the files.
- **Move to other folder.** When you choose this option, Bridge displays a Browse button for you to choose the folder or create a new folder.
- **Copy to other folder.** If you want to back up the original files, this option accomplishes both the backup and the renaming in a single step.

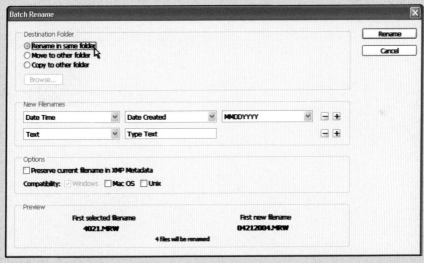

▶1.2

3

In the New Filenames section, Bridge offers a set of options with drop-down menus. Here you can implement a universal file-naming strategy that you can apply to current, existing, and future images.

In the first drop-down menu, you can choose Text, New Extension, Current Filename, Preserved Filename, Sequence Number, Sequence Letter, Date Time, or Metadata. If you want to include the date and time, choose Date Time in the first option box. In the second option box, choose any option except Yesterday; then in the third option box choose HHMMSS (Hour, Minute, Second) or HHMM (Hour, Minute). Bridge inserts the option you chose in the filename.

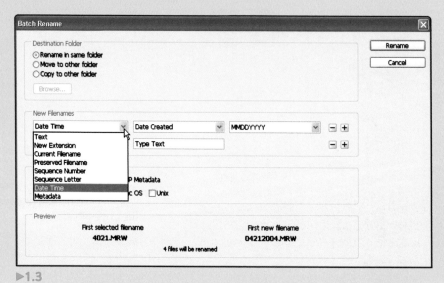

▶1.3

4

Choose the options you want, and then click the plus sign at the right to add more filename fields. Bridge displays additional selection boxes based on the selection made in the first option box on the first row.

Tip ▶ If you choose an option that includes a sequence number, Bridge automatically increments the number for each file that is renamed.

Try selecting different options until you get the set of fields you need to implement your preferred file-naming strategy. At the bottom of the Batch Rename dialog box, Bridge previews a sample of the file-name as you build it.

Batch Rename

Destination Folder

- ◉ Rename in same folder
- ○ Move to other folder
- ○ Copy to other folder

Browse...

Rename

Cancel

New Filenames

| Date Time ▾ | Date Created ▾ | MMDDYYYY ▾ | − + |
| Text ▾ | quahog | | − + |

Options

☐ Preserve current filename in XMP Metadata

Compatibility: ☑ Windows ☐ Mac OS ☐ Unix

Preview

First selected filename
4021.MRW

First new filename
04212004quahog.MRW

4 files will be renamed

▶1.4

5

Select the Preserve current filename in XMP Metadata option to retain the existing filename. If you have not edited the files in Camera Raw then choose this option to retain the original filename. If you've edited the files in Camera Raw, the filename gets embedded with the Camera Raw settings. But because restoring original filenames from XMP sidecar files is difficult, preserving the original filename is a good idea. If you need to undo renaming, you can choose the Batch Rename command, and then choose Preserved Filename to return to the original filenames. However, many photographers rename and make a copy of the original files as a first step in the workflow. In that scenario as well, turning on the Preserve current filename in XMP Metadata option is best.

X-Ref For more information on XMP sidecar files and setting Bridge preferences, see Appendix A.

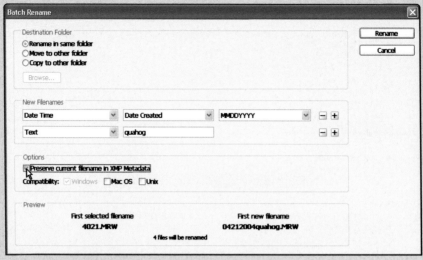

▶1.5

6

Choose the operating systems that you want the images to be compatible with. The current operating system is selected by default and cannot be deselected.

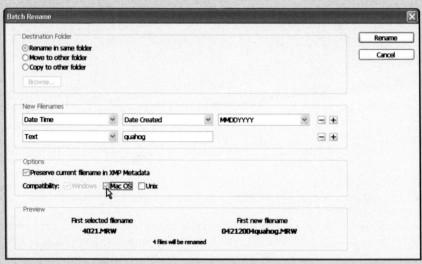

▶1.6

Click Rename. Bridge displays a message saying that it will save the updated metadata in the XMP sidecar file rather than in the original RAW file. If you later copy the file to another computer or to disk, be sure to copy the XMP file along with the image file.

Click OK in the Batch Rename dialog box. Bridge applies the modified filenames.

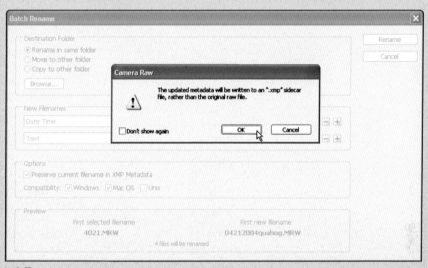

►1.7

Create a File-Naming Strategy

The camera gives each image a unique name and number. Usually the camera uses the date as a starting point, and then it adds a number for each image. However, with some cameras, you can choose to name files continuously or to restart numbering with each new session. In the latter scenario, you can end up with duplicate filenames. To avoid duplicate names, use the continuous numbering option on your camera. This system has the added advantage of tracking the camera's actuations, or number of total shots. Additionally, if you want to know the number of images per shoot, you can use continuous numbering coupled with some simple math to track the number of the camera's actuations.

After you get the files on the computer, be sure to rename files using a consistent naming convention that is universal throughout your system of shooting, archiving, processing, printing, and disseminating images. It can be as simple as the month, year, the location where the images were made, and the original filename. In this example, images from India made in December of 2005 would start with 1205India followed by the image number generated by the camera. The final filename would be something like 112005India3723.ORF. To view your files, choose View ➤ Sort, and then sort the files by date and order that you want.

Customize Bridge Workspaces

Contributor: Charlotte Lowrie ▪ **Specialty:** Editorial and Stock
Primary Tool Used: Adobe Bridge Workspace

Depending on the phase of the workflow, being able to view images in folders in different ways is helpful. For example, during image selection, seeing images at a large size is important, but when it's time to add metadata, having an enlarged view of the Metadata panel in Bridge is more important to work most efficiently. This technique shows you how to switch among and customize Bridge workspaces to facilitate different phases of the image workflow.

1

In Adobe Bridge, choose Window ➤ Workspace, and then choose one of these options:

- **Lightbox.** Choosing this view hides the left panels in Bridge and displays only the image thumbnails. This view is equivalent to an electronic contact sheet.

- **File Navigator.** Choosing this workspace removes the left-pane image Preview, Metadata, and Keywords tabs and creates a spacious area in which to navigate among Favorites (pre-populated by Adobe) and Folders on various drives.

- **Metadata Focus.** Choosing this workspace narrows the left-hand panes to Favorites, Metadata, and Keywords.

- **Filmstrip Focus.** Choosing this workspace hides the left-hand panels, displays the selected image at the maximum display size of 512 pixels, and displays the other images in the folder as a filmstrip along the bottom of the window.

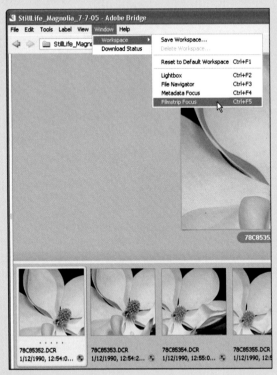

▶1.8

Tip

To display the left panel when it is hidden or to enlarge or shrink its size, drag the horizontal bar between the panels. You can also use the display buttons to the right of the status bar to modify the size and arrangement of image previews and to display or hide metadata.

2

To resize the left panel panes horizontally, drag the horizontal divider bar located between panels up and down. For example, if you want a larger area to work with in the Metadata workspace, drag the horizontal divider bar between the Favorites and Metadata panels to the top to hide the Favorites panel. The horizontal divider bar remains accessible so that you can quickly reconfigure the panels as you work.

> **Tip**
>
> Bridge displays up to three icons under thumbnails to indicate the status of the image. Icons show whether an image has been edited in Camera Raw and the settings preserved, an image has been cropped in Camera Raw, or the image is open in Photoshop.

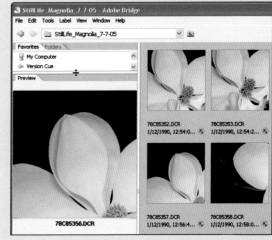

►1.9

3

After you have a workspace pane modified as you want, drag the Thumbnail size slider to change the size of the thumbnail display.

When creating a workspace for the image-selection phase of the workflow, enlarge the thumbnails to a medium or large size so you can see a series of similar images at a large enough size to make selection decisions. Saving the modified workspace saves the preview size as well.

> **Tip**
>
> If a specific workspace view isn't adequate, you can also open additional Bridge windows and adjust the displays and workspaces to compare images in different windows. To open a new Bridge window, choose File ► New Window. Then size the windows for side-by-side viewing.

►1.10

4

Click a display button in the lower right to select the type of display you want in the content area. The choices are, from left to right: Thumbnails view, Filmstrip view, Details view, or Versions and Alternates view.

▶ **Note**

Some redundancy exists between the Filmstrip workspace and the Filmstrip display button. The noticeable difference is that the Filmstrip workspace automatically displays filmstrip thumbnails at the maximum size and overrides smaller sizes you've chosen using the Filmstrip display button. Regardless, you can resize thumbnails with the Thumbnail size slider.

78C85357.DCR
1/12/1990, 12:56:41 PM

3:32 PI

▶1.11

To save a modified workspace, choose Window ➤ Workspace ➤ Save Workspace to open the Save Workspace dialog box. Type a name in the Name field. If you don't want Bridge to position the workspace in the current position, you can deselect the Save Window Location as Part of Workspace check box. Click Save in the Save Workspace dialog box.

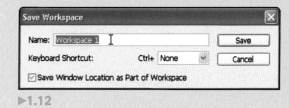

▶1.12

Tip

To reduce the size of the Bridge window, click the Switch to Compact Mode button on the toolbar. Bridge becomes a small window that stays on top of other open windows. To reduce Bridge further, try Ultra-Compact Mode, which you can select after you select Compact Mode. In Ultra-Compact Mode, Bridge is displayed as a floating bar that you can drag and dock anywhere on the screen.

SB Sidebar

Take Advantage of Bridge Preferences

In a perfect world, when you change options in the Bridge Preferences dialog box, your changes would be saved with customized workspaces, but such is not the case. Instead, display options in the Preferences dialog box apply to all workspaces and displays. To check out the options available in Bridge Preferences, choose Edit ➤ Preferences(Bridge on a Mac) ➤ Preferences.

In the General section of the Bridge Preferences dialog box, you can set the background color in the Content pane from white to varying shades of gray to black. The changes you make apply to all Bridge displays and workspaces.

A careful review of all the Bridge Preference options is worthwhile. In the Advanced section of the Preferences dialog box, you can choose to use centralized cache or distributed cache files. If you routinely back up files on disk, using a distributed cache allows you to burn the cache files to the disk rather than having to export a centralized cache to the disk. For additional information, be sure to check out the details in Appendix A.

Save Time Using Metadata Templates

Contributor: David H. Wells ■ **Specialty:** Photojournalism and Editorial
Primary Tool Used: Photoshop File Info Templates

Metadata provides the foundation for organizing, finding, and tracking images and modifications you make to the images in Bridge. And the metadata that you add stays with files as you create variations of them. This technique shows you how to create a template to automate the process of adding metadata and append the template to all or some of the files in a folder.

1

Open a blank file in Photoshop CS2. The name, dimensions, resolution, and other details of the new file are not important because the file is only used to create a metadata template. Once you have created the metadata template, you can delete this file.

Choose File ➤ File Info. Photoshop displays an Untitled dialog box. If you typed a name for the new file, the dialog box is titled with the name you typed. On the left of the dialog box is a list of categories, most of which offer fields where you can add metadata. However, not all categories have editable fields. To make the template most useful, identify the categories and the fields that have the broadest application for all the files that you create or for all or most of the files in the current folder. The most likely categories are Description, IPTC Contact, IPTC Content, IPTC Image, IPTC Status, and Origin.

> **Note**
> Metadata describes an image, including the filename, date, resolution, and exposure (EXIF) information. Bridge also includes IPTC Core fields.

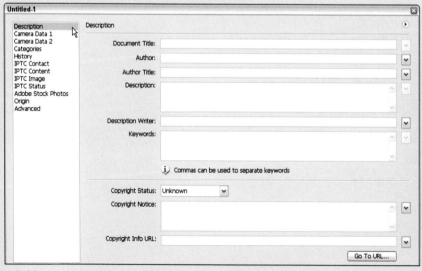

▶1.13

2

As you choose categories at the left, fill in the fields that apply to the images.

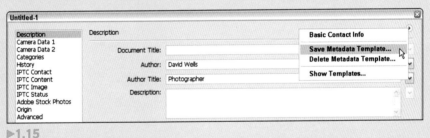

▶1.14

3

Click the Menu button at the upper right of the dialog box, and then choose Save Metadata Template (1.15). Photoshop displays the Save Metadata Template dialog box.

▶1.15

4

Type a name for the template in the Save Metadata Template dialog box and click Save. Click OK to close the new file dialog box.

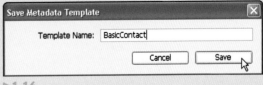

▶1.16

Tip ▶ It's unlikely that a single template will fit all the images that you work with. You can create multiple templates that fit your most common shooting scenarios, and then append multiple templates to files. Alternatively, you can also create temporary templates that contain the metadata information for a single shoot.

5

In Bridge, switch to the folder of images to which you want to apply the metadata template. Select the images you want to apply the metadata template to. To select all images, press Ctrl/⌘+A.

▶1.17

6

Choose Tools ➤ Append Metadata, and then choose the name of the template containing the metadata you created in the previous steps. Click OK to append the metadata. Bridge appends the template to the files.

Bridge appends the metadata only to fields where no metadata currently exists. This ensures that no existing information is overwritten. The beauty of this technique is that you can go back to existing folders and append one or more metadata templates to images in the folders.

In Bridge, you can also choose File ➤ File Info to view and change metadata for individual files or to edit the information in the Metadata panel. There may be differences between the field labels (names) in the Metadata panel and those in the File Info dialog box in Bridge. However, the underlying XMP property is the same—simply a different view.

▶1.18

Add Keywords

Contributor: Charlotte Lowrie ■ **Specialty:** Editorial and Stock
Primary Tool Used: The Synchronize option for batch processing

One of the most powerful features of Adobe CS2 is its search capability. Keywords can be an integral part of the search criteria provided that you add keywords via the Bridge Keywords panel. As with adding other metadata, Bridge offers ways to add keywords and keyword sets to multiple files simultaneously, making this task relatively pain-free.

1

The keyword sets, or categories, and keywords provided by Bridge are, at best, a starting place for creating more useful keywords. To change the name of an existing keyword set, right-click the keyword set name, and then choose Rename. Bridge displays an edit box where you can type a new name. You can repeat this renaming process for the individual keywords under the keyword set name.

> **Note**
> Keywords added in Bridge are distinct from keywords you add to XMP metadata via the File ➤ File Info command.

> **Tip**
> Entering keywords is easier if you switch to the Metadata Focus workspace. (Choose Window ➤ Workspace ➤ Metadata Focus.) Bridge separates the Metadata and Keywords tabs and provides a larger workspace for entering keywords.

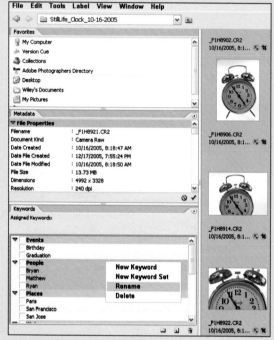

▶1.19

2

To create a keyword set, choose the New Keyword Set button at the bottom of the Keywords panel. Type a name for the keyword set in the Keywords Set field, and then press Enter.

> **Tip**
>
> Consider adding keyword sets with keywords that fit the photography you shoot most often. If you shoot landscapes, create a Mountainscapes set and add individual keywords. Or create a keyword set with keywords that apply to a specific shoot. This approach is effective for images with a common subject.

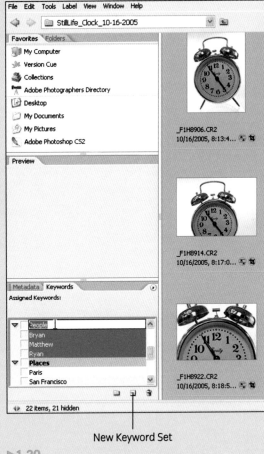

New Keyword Set

▶1.20

3

To add a new keyword, choose the Keyword set to which you want to add a new keyword. Then choose the New Keyword button at the bottom of the Keywords panel. Type the new keyword and press Enter.

Repeat this step for all the keywords you want to add to a keyword set.

> **Tip**
>
> You can quickly rearrange keywords by dragging a keyword from one keyword set to another. Also, if you want to delete a keyword or keyword set, select it and click the Delete Keyword icon at the bottom of the Keywords panel (it looks like a trash can).

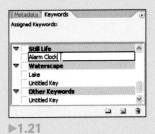

▶1.21

4

To apply a keyword, select one or more images. Select the check box to the left of the keyword you want to add. Bridge displays a message asking whether you want to apply edits to multiple files. Click Yes in the dialog box that appears (if you only select one image, the dialog box does not appear). Bridge adds a check mark next to the keyword and adds the keyword to the sidecar XMP file of the image or images selected.

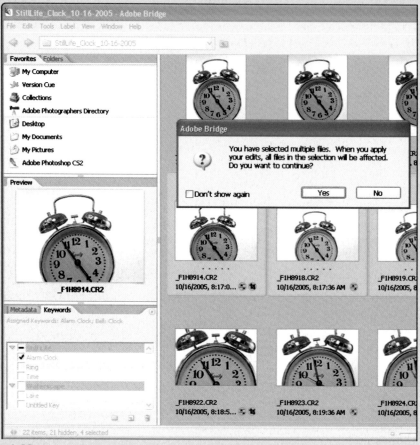

▶1.22

More About Keywords

Although keyword fields are available in File Info fields, keywords added in the File Info dialog box are added as XMP keywords and are distinct from keywords added in the Keywords panel in Bridge. Keywords added in the File Info dialog box are displayed in Version Cue files in the Other Metadata section of the File Info dialog box. And from a workflow standpoint, adding keywords in the Bridge Keywords panel, where you can create sets of keywords and apply all or part of them to one or more images simultaneously, is more efficient. If you rename a keyword, however, the original name continues to appear in the files you've applied it to. To apply the changed name, select the files and apply the changed keyword name by checking it in the keyword panel.

You can ensure that keywords persist by adding the keyword to the Other Keywords category. Then just right-click to display the context menu, and choose Make Persistent.

Because keywords are important in the ability to find and retrieve files, creating a consistent strategy for keywords is a good idea. The advantage is clear. When a client or stock agency asks for existing lifestyle imagery of a 20's-something woman drinking coffee with friends, you can search for and retrieve all the files in your library that fit the description based on your consistent and careful keyword implementation. And, after Bridge finds the images, you can save the search criteria and results in a Collection. You can find out more about image Collections in Chapter 3.

It's All About Making the Work Flow

Chapter 02

In this chapter

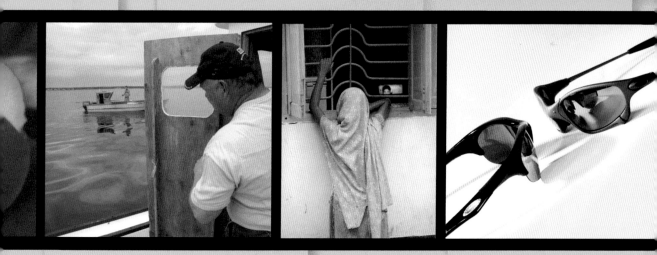

One Photographer's Workflow

Contributor: David H. Wells ■ **Specialty:** Editorial and Stock
Primary Tool Used: Various

Workflow is a buzzword with as many different approaches as there are photographers. This technique provides a workflow overview from an editorial photographer's point of view, and covers everything from backing up images and registering them with the Library of Congress to delivering images to the client.

1

After you finish an assignment and download files to the computer, the first steps in the workflow are to sort files from a shoot, and then select the best images. In Bridge, select all the images in the folder, and then choose View ➤ Sort ➤ By Filename.

If you follow a date-plus-place naming convention (see the sidebar later in this technique), you can quickly sort images by the dates used in the filenames.

Choose Edit ➤ Deselect All, and then begin the selection process. Choose Window ➤ Workspace ➤ Filmstrip Focus. Scroll through the images selecting any image you want to rate. When you select an image, stars appear under the thumbnail. Click to select a star rating from one to five stars.

▶2.1

Tip ▶ Registering images with the Library of Congress protects the copyright to your images and is an important part of the workflow. The copyright gives you the right to control use of your images for your lifetime plus 70 years. The annual fee for bulk image registration is $30. For more information, visit www.editorial photo.com/copyright/.

Once you finish rating the images, you can view the top-rated images. Click the Unfiltered arrow at the top-right side of the Bridge window, and then choose the rating level for the images you want to display. For example, you can choose to display images rated with three or more stars, or only the images rated with five stars.

Select all the top-rated images that you want to process, and choose File ➤ Open in Camera Raw.

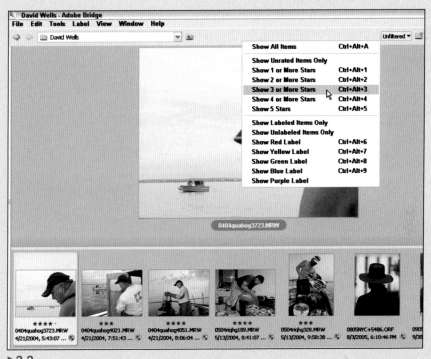

▶2.2

3

In Camera Raw, choose Select All➤Save [selected number of] Images. In the Save Options dialog box, choose JPEG from the Format drop-down menu, and click Save.

Now you have a set of JPEGs of the best selects to show to the client. Though you may now have only a small set of selected images for the client or end user's review, registering the entire shoot with the Library of Congress is best, as you do later in the technique.

You can present the JPEG images to the client on a disc or on a Web site for selection.

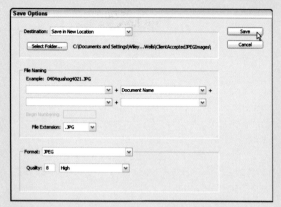

➤2.3

Tip

You can also use the Image Processor batch action on the Photoshop ➤ Tools menu in Bridge to save files in JPEG format. For more information, see "Automate Aspects of the Workflow" later in this chapter.

X-Ref

For more information on presenting images to clients, see Chapter 7.

4

After the client makes the selections, create subfolders to separate selected images from rejected images by file type. You may want to switch to the File Navigator workspace. Then choose File➤New Folder and type the name for the first folder. Continue to create and name folders as needed to categorize accepted and rejected images by file type. Then separate the images into the folders.

If you maintain an ongoing master collection of images in a database or asset management program, add a set of JPEGs to the main image database.

Note

You can create additional subfolders to categorize images with recognizable or obscured faces and whether or not the images have model releases.

Tip

For disseminating images as stock photography through multiple agents, create a tracking sheet listing the name of the image set, model releases, dates, quantities of images sent to and returned from the agency, number of images selected and kept, and number of similar images discarded (for agencies requiring exclusivity).

➤2.4

5

To send images for copyright registration (which you should do before any dissemination of images), you'll make a contact sheet of all images in the folder. Open the folder that contains all of the images. Choose Tools ➤ Photoshop ➤ Contact Sheet II. Photoshop opens and displays the Contact Sheet II dialog box.

In the Document section, choose the options you want for the contact sheet.

For bulk copyright registration, you can make a 4- × 6-inch print at 240 or 300 PPI with no more than 12 images on each sheet. The Library of Congress requires that each print be at least the size of a postage stamp, and having 2 images per sheet generally meets that requirement.

Select these options:

- Set the document size to 4" x 5". The final printing size will be 4" × 6", but using this size leaves an extra inch for adding your contact information to the contact sheet later in the process.

- If it isn't already selected, select the Flatten All Layers option.

- Choose the layout you prefer from the Place drop-down menu. The across first option works well.

- If you select Rotate For Best Fit, Photoshop rotates vertical images. Generally, turning off this option is best so that vertical images aren't rotated.

- Verify that the Use Filename As Caption option is selected, and then choose the Font and Font Size (you may need to choose a 6- or 8-point font size, especially if you use long filenames).

Note ▶ You can begin the process of registering images with the Library of Congress at anytime during the first few steps.

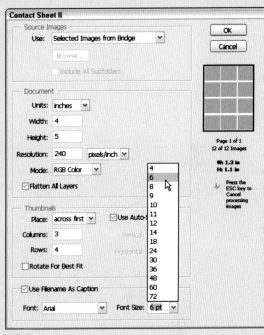

▶2.5

6

After you set the options in the Contact Sheet II dialog box, click OK. Photoshop opens and sizes the images, and then displays the contact sheet.

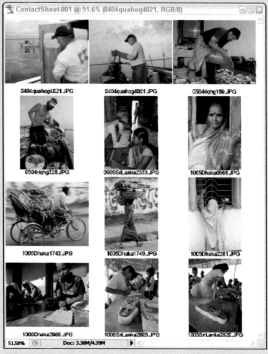

▶2.6

7

Next, add your contact information to each contact sheet. To add extra space to the canvas for contact information, choose Image ➤ Canvas Size. In the Canvas Size dialog box, change the size to a Width of 4 inches, and a Height of 6 inches. This places extra space at the top of the contact sheet.

Tip

The best way to add contact information to contact sheets is to create a Photoshop action that will do the work automatically after the action is recorded.

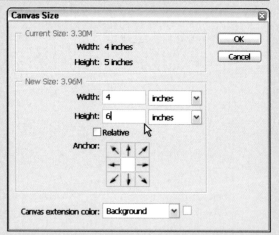

▶2.7

8

In Photoshop, select the Type tool. At the top of the contact sheet type your contact information, including:

- (c) your name
- Street address
- City, state, and ZIP code
- Area code and telephone number
- E-mail address
- Web site URL

Be sure to leave some space between the edges of the canvas and the text so that part of the text doesn't get cropped off during printing.

> **Note**
> You may want to create a new folder for the contact sheets. You might use a name such as ProofsWithCopyrightInfo or an abbreviation or derivation of that name.

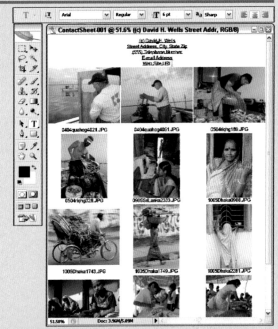

▶2.8

9

Choose Layer ➤ Flatten Image, and then save the file in TIFF format.

> **Note**
> If you make prints through a photo lab that uses TIFFs, you can automate the process of converting TIFFs to JPEGs with a Photoshop action.

Print two copies of the contact sheet — one for your records and one for the Library of Congress. Then package the contact sheets and registration form, with a check to bulk register the unpublished images.

> **Tip**
> Ensure that the registration form, check, and deposit copies, or contact sheets, arrive at the Library of Congress before the CD arrives to the client. Send the package using a controlled carrier, verify arrival, and print the signature verification. File the verification with your copy of the registration and contact sheets.

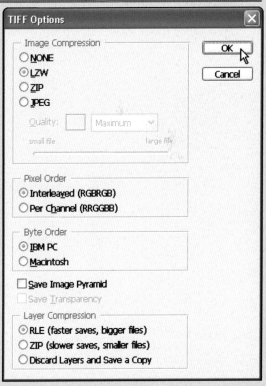

▶2.9

10

After presenting the selected images to the client and getting the file specifications for client-selected images, you can add captions to the RAW images in Bridge. Select the image and type the caption information in the appropriate IPTC field in the Bridge Metadata panel.

Tip

With the final selects identified, burn those important selected images to high-quality CDs such as archive-quality Gold Foil CDs. Label the CDs using the same naming convention as discussed in the sidebar later in this technique, and store the CDs, ideally in a bank safe-deposit box.

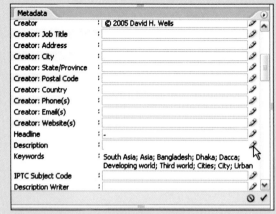

Metadata	
Creator	: © 2005 David H. Wells
Creator: Job Title	:
Creator: Address	:
Creator: City	:
Creator: State/Province	:
Creator: Postal Code	:
Creator: Country	:
Creator: Phone(s)	:
Creator: Email(s)	:
Creator: Website(s)	:
Headline	: -
Description	:
Keywords	: South Asia; Asia; Bangladesh; Dhaka; Dacca; Developing world; Third world; Cities; City; Urban
IPTC Subject Code	:
Description Writer	:

▶2.10

11

Process the RAW versions of the client-selected files in Camera Raw. Follow your normal workflow for correcting color and tonality. Adjust the resolution as necessary to meet client specifications.

X-Ref

See Chapter 4 for more on processing RAW files.

After the client approves the corrected images, deliver them via CD or by uploading them to the client's server. It is also a good practice to update the tracking sheet (mentioned earlier) with the quantities sent, dates, and so on, and print a contact sheet showing image names of client-selected images. This can be attached to the tracking sheet for you records.

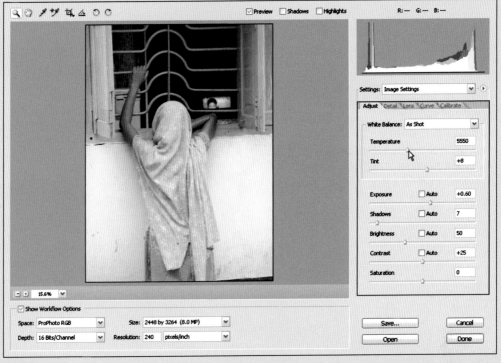

►2.11

SB Sidebar

Workflow Begins on the Road

Workflow should begin on the road with shooting and judicious in-camera editing. As memory cards fill up, you can transfer their contents to a portable storage device such as a FlashTrax or to a laptop. Depending on the device, you can name the folders of images using a convention such as date (mmyy) and place; for example, 1103Cal. Later, when you download images to the main computer, you can apply the same naming convention to individual images for consistency, such as 1103Cal followed by the original filename (image number) from the camera.

Once home, group images into groups or folders of images that will fit on a single CD. Make as many groups or folders as necessary to backup all your images. Burn two CDs of each group or folder. Be sure to name the folder within the CD and on the outside of each CD with the same date and place convention/file-naming strategy discussed earlier. (Remember to only write on the center of the CDs.) After you burn the duplicate CDs, you can delete the unedited sets of images from the portable storage device.

As insurance, carry one set of CDs with you while traveling and ship the other set to your home or studio address.

Working with the Digital Negative Format

Contributor: Charlotte Lowrie ■ **Specialty:** Editorial and Stock
Primary Tool Used: Save as DNG

With the introduction of Adobe's Digital Negative (DNG) format, the option now exists for what many photographers see as the best archive format currently available. DNG can store the original RAW data within the file allowing for the original proprietary image to be extracted at a later time. DNG also allows you to store a JPEG preview within the file making it easy for clients to quickly preview the image.

1

After making image adjustments to one or multiple images in Camera Raw, click Save. Camera Raw displays the Save Options dialog box.

To save the file in a different folder, click the Destination drop-down menu, and choose Save in New Location. Camera Raw displays the Select Destination dialog box. Navigate to the folder in which you want to save the images. If you don't want to save in a different location, make no changes in the Destination section (Save in Same Location).

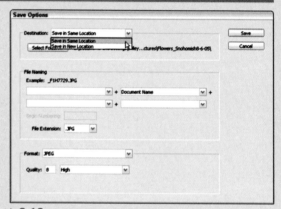

▶2.12

2

If you haven't already renamed files, type a name for the processed images under the File Naming section.

> **X-Ref**
> The same options are available in the Save Options dialog box as you get when choosing Tools ▶ Batch Rename. For details on using the Batch Rename command, see Chapter 1.

▶2.13

3

In the File Extension option box, choose .DNG. If you prefer lowercase file extensions, click the File Extension option box drop-down arrow, and then choose the lowercase .dng option.

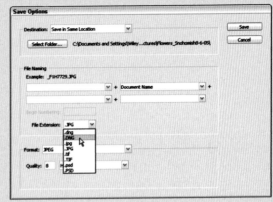

►2.14

4

If it isn't already selected, choose Digital Negative from the Format drop-down menu.

> **Note**
>
> Saving images in DNG format means that Camera Raw doesn't need to write a separate sidecar XMP file to store the image adjustments that you make. Instead, with DNG, the settings are stored directly in the DNG file. DNG makes file backup easier because you don't have to remember to copy the XMP files along with the image files to the backup disc.

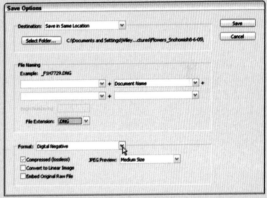

►2.15

5

Select any of the following options based on your specific needs in the Format section:

- **Compressed (lossless):** Compresses the image with no loss of image data.
- **Convert to Linear Image:** Stores the image in an interpolated format.
- **Embed Original Raw File:** Embeds the original RAW data within the DNG file. You can extract the file to reprocess the image; for example, if future versions of Camera Raw offer the ability to do more with the original image. This option is also a good choice for archiving the original RAW bits along with maintaining the current conversion settings.

►2.16

From the JPEG Preview option box, click the drop-down menu to select whether to save a JPEG preview at Medium Size or Full Size, or you can also choose None.

If you save a JPEG preview and, if you have set Camera Raw Preferences to update embedded JPEG previews, then Camera Raw updates the image preview in Bridge after you save the DNG file. Otherwise, the image preview in Bridge is not updated unless you Export Settings from the Camera Raw menu.

Click Save to apply the options.

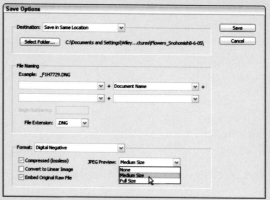

►2.17

Note

If you choose to save a Full Size JPEG preview, Camera Raw embeds both a full- and a medium-size preview. This feature offers other programs the ability to extract the size they need for thumbnails without parsing the RAW data.

SB Sidebar

The Pros and Cons of DNG

With the introduction of the Digital Negative format (DNG), Adobe aims to create a universal industry-standard format for RAW images. The success of DNG depends on its acceptance and adoption by camera manufacturers and other software companies. Currently RAW file formats are proprietary, which means that each camera manufacturer has its own RAW format that can be displayed and converted using its conversion program. Conversely, a universally accepted file format such as TIFF allows images to be displayed and edited on virtually any computer using commercially available image-editing programs.

Proprietary formats also make RAW images more susceptible to obsolescence. As technology advances, there is no assurance that proprietary RAW formats will be supported as newer formats are released.

However, Adobe's Camera Raw plug-in not only reads but also converts virtually every proprietary RAW format. But to do this, Adobe engineers do some reverse engineering to interpret and display the images—a situation that will continue unless camera companies give companies such as Adobe access to RAW data.

A universally accepted, industry-standard format such as DNG would also offer greater assurance that today's RAW files will be usable years or even decades from now. Unlike camera companies that have not committed to backwards compatibility for their proprietary RAW formats, Adobe has firmly committed to supporting DNG as a supported format now and into the future.

An industry standard format would also give RAW files the same portability that TIFF and JPEG files currently enjoy. As a result, photographers could hand off RAW images to editors, stock photo agencies, and clients with confidence that the files have the same universal readability that TIFF files enjoy.

You can learn more about DNG on the Adobe Web site at www.adobe.com/products/dng/main. html.

Automate Aspects of the Workflow

Contributor: Charlotte Lowrie ■ **Specialty:** Editorial and Stock
Primary Tool Used: Image Processor

Most Photoshop users are familiar with actions that automate a series of tasks. The same concept is used with the Photoshop preset actions in Bridge that you can use with RAW files.

This technique spotlights the Image Processor action that can, among other things, make quick work of converting a batch of edited RAW files to JPEG format for initial client review. It also offers the option of including either a Photoshop preset action or a custom action on files in Bridge.

1

In Bridge, group the images that you want to convert to JPEG, TIFF, or PSD format in a folder or subfolder. Be sure that the images have Image Settings selected in the Camera Raw Settings menu so that the adjustments you've made in Camera Raw are used in the action.

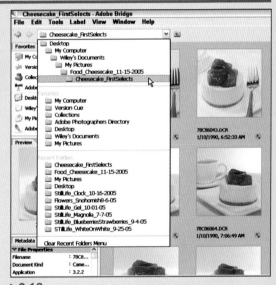

►2.18

2

In Bridge, choose Tools ➤ Photoshop ➤ Image Processor. The Image Processor dialog box appears in Photoshop. This dialog box goes step-by-step through the choices you need to make for automated image processing.

In step 1 of the Image Processor dialog box, you select the images to process. Be sure that the Open first image to apply setting check box is deselected. If this check box is turned on, the Camera Raw dialog box will open and remain open for you to make changes, thus interrupting the action. In general, skip opening the Camera Raw dialog box entirely throughout your selections.

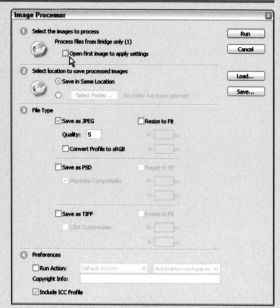

►2.19

3

In step 2 of the dialog box, Select location to save processed images, you can save the image in the same folder or choose another folder. The Select Folder option displays the Browse For Folder dialog box where you can navigate to another folder, or click Make New Folder to create and name a new folder in which to save processed images.

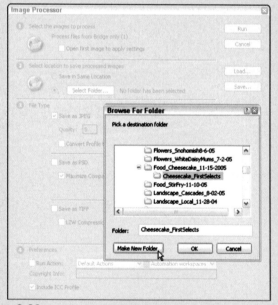

►2.20

4

In step 3, File Type, you can select Save as JPEG, Save as PSD, or Save as TIFF. You can choose to select only one of these, or you can select more than one file type. In addition, you can specify the quality and select sRGB color space for JPEG files and LZW compression for TIFF files.

If you want specific image dimensions, select the Resize to Fit option, and type the desired Width and Height in pixels.

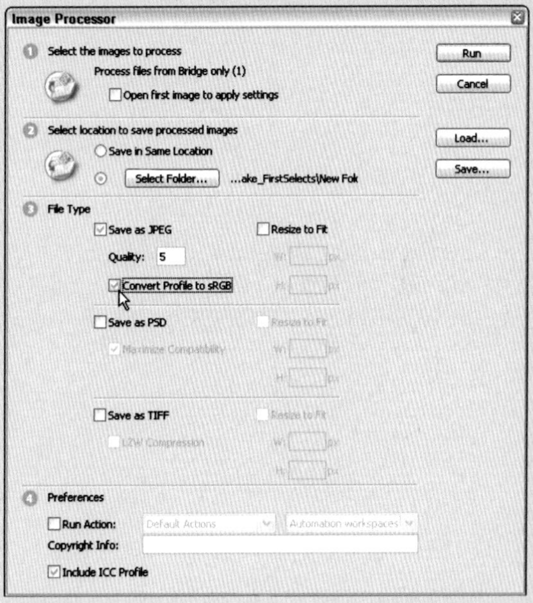

▶2.21

5

In step 4, Preferences, select Run Action if you want to run a preset Photoshop CS2 action or a custom action that you've already recorded. To choose the action, click the drop-down arrow next to the action selection boxes, and choose the action you want.

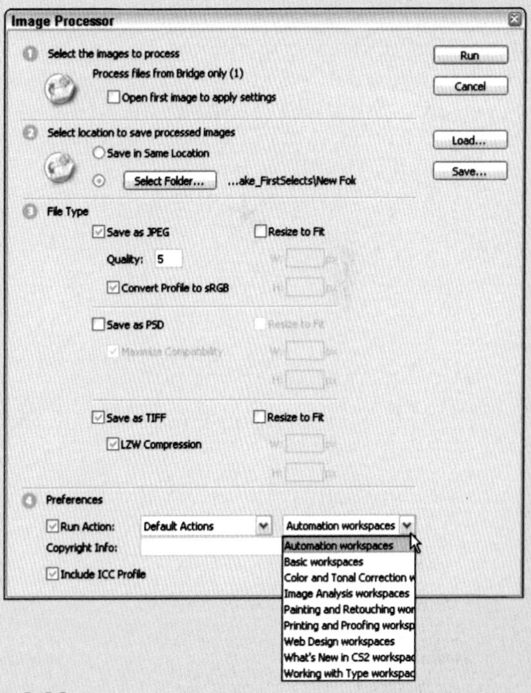

▶2.22

In the Copyright Info box, type the copyright information that you want.

Deselect the Include ICC Profile check box if you want. If you are creating PSD or JPEG files, leaving the Include ICC Profile checked is a good idea so that profile mismatches are identified in Photoshop. However, if you're using Image Processor to create JPEG files and you've specified sRGB in step 5, you can deselect this check box.

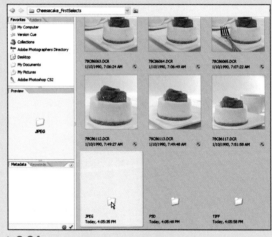

►2.23

6

Click Run. Photoshop displays progress messages as it opens and converts the files. Depending on the options you chose, Photoshop also creates separate folders for each file format you chose and places the images in separate folders. For example, if you chose to save all three formats, Photoshop creates folders named TIFF, PSD, and JPEG and puts the images in the appropriate folders.

►2.24

Tips for Creating RAW File Batch Actions

Although Bridge and Camera Raw offer excellent shortcuts for applying RAW image edits to multiple files, recording Photoshop actions or using the Tools ➤ Batch or Image Processor commands in Bridge can often make tasks, including editing RAW files, even quicker. There are, however, some gotcha's when recording actions that you need to keep in mind:

- The Camera Raw dialog box uses the image settings that are in effect when you create the action, including Space, Depth, Size, and Resolution. If an action includes opening a Camera Raw file, you may want to create separate actions for opening images that have different settings.

- If the action includes opening a file, select the Override Action "Open" Commands option to prevent the action from continuing to open the image you used to record the action. The action will use the settings without opening the specific file used to create the action.

- If you use the Batch command, also select the Suppress File Open Options Dialogs option to prevent Camera Raw from opening each image being processed.

- The same type of situation applies if you save files in a batch action. If you record a Save step, select the Override Action "Save As" Commands option to use the Save As instructions from the Batch command instead of the Save As instructions in the action. The action must then also contain a Save As command because the Batch command does not automatically save the source files. Images are saved using the name and destination folder specified in the Batch dialog box.

- If the color space that you use in Camera Raw differs from the space you use in Photoshop, be sure to select Suppress Color Profile Warnings, which will interrupt the action until you okay the warning dialog box.

Evaluate and Organize RAW Images

Chapter 03

In this chapter

Rate Images in Bridge

Contributor: Charlotte Lowrie ■ **Specialty:** Editorial and Stock
Primary Tool Used: Ratings

In a time-honored photography tradition, the photographer's first task after a shoot is to rate images. With images spread out on a light table, the photographer places one or more marks on the best images in the batch and groups them by the markings. The electronic equivalent in Bridge is marking selected images with one to five stars, which is explained in this technique. Just as on the light table, it pays to have an image-rating strategy that works for you in the long term.

1

In Bridge, choose Window ➤ Workspace ➤ Lightbox (or Filmstrip Focus). Your choice of workspace is purely personal. Viewing images in the Lightbox workspace allows you to compare similar shots side by side and is a good choice for making first pass selections.

Drag the Thumbnail slider to the right to increase the size of the thumbnail images in your your chosen workspace.

▶3.1

2

Select the image you want to rate, and then choose the star rating, from one to five stars, displayed under the image. On Windows XP, Bridge displays a message that ratings and labels are stored in XMP metadata; otherwise, they are stored in cache. Click OK in the message box. If you're using a Mac, you may not get this message.

> **Note**
>
> Ratings and labels are stored in XMP files or in cache. As a result, if you haven't set Camera Raw preferences (via the Edit menu) to store image settings in a sidecar XMP file, labels and ratings are lost if cache is purged.

You can use whatever meaning you want for the ratings. You may decide that five stars represent the first or best picks and that no stars indicate rejects—a system that gives you a total of six rating levels from 0 to 5. Or that one star represents the best picks. However, if more than one person rates images be sure that everyone understands and uses the same rating strategy.

To change a rating, or to promote or demote, choose the star level that you want to reassign to the image or click to the left of the stars to remove the rating entirely.

▶3.2

> **Tip**
>
> You can also combine ratings with labels, which is explained in the next technique in this chapter.

3

To display images by rating level, click the drop-down arrow next to Unfiltered and choose the option you want. Your options include showing all rated images, all unrated images, or images by specific ratings.

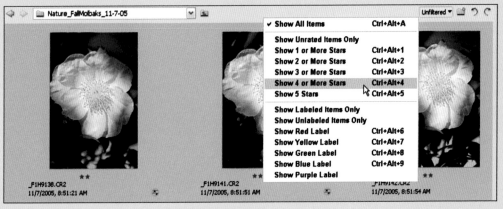

▶3.3

Color-Code Images in Bridge

Contributor: Bob Coates ■ **Specialty:** Wedding
Primary Tool Used: Labels

In addition to the one- to five-star rating available in Bridge, you can also color-code images. Unlike ratings, color coding provides no facility for promoting or demoting images, unless you assign a meaning to each color.

However, color coding can be useful for grouping images. For example, in a wedding shoot, you can use color coding to group images from pre-ceremony events, the ceremony, and the reception.

1

In Bridge, choose Window ➤ Workspace ➤ Lightbox. The choice of workspace is a personal one. The Lightbox workspace with a medium or small thumbnail size set using the Thumbnail size slider provides a handy view to group images.

Select the image or group of images that you want to label with a color.

> If you want to see groups of images together—for example, all the images from a wedding reception—just drag files in the Content pane so they are in the order you want.

▶3.4

2

Choose Label, and then choose the color you want to apply to the selected image from the menu. Bridge displays a message that ratings and labels are stored in XMP metadata; otherwise, they are stored in cache. Click OK in the message box. You can also right-click an image and choose the label you want from the menu.

Labels (just like ratings) are stored in XMP files or in cache. As a result, if you haven't set Camera Raw preferences (via the Edit menu) to store image settings in a sidecar XMP file, labels and ratings are lost if cache is purged.

To remove a label, select the image or images from which you want to remove the label. Choose Label ➤ No Label. Bridge removes the label from the image or images.

Tip ▶ If you want to make labels more helpful, you can change the name of the label. For example, you can change the Red label to "Ceremony." Choose Edit ➤ Preferences ➤ Labels (or on Macs, Bridge ➤ Preferences ➤ Labels), and then type a label name for each color. Click OK in the Preferences dialog box.

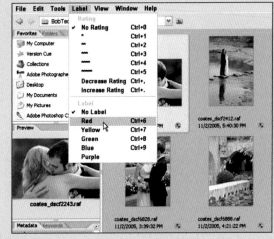

▶3.5

3

Once you have finished assigning labels to your images, you can sort the images by label. Click the drop-down arrow next to Unfiltered, and then choose the label option you want. You can choose to show all labeled images, all unlabeled images, or images by specific label color.

▶3.6

 Tip ▶ In addition to filtering the view in the Bridge content pane, you can refine the display by sorting files. Choose View ➤ Sort, and then choose the sort order you want.

Organize Images into Collections

Contributor: Charlotte Lowrie ■ **Specialty:** Editorial and Stock
Primary Tool Used: Find and Image Collection

Finding and organizing images becomes more challenging as image collections grow. Bridge makes it easy to find images and to save the search so that it can be run again. Then you save the search criteria with the resulting images as a collection for easy retrieval in the future.

1

To set up an image search, choose Edit ➤ Find. Bridge displays the Find dialog box with the current folder displayed in the Look in field.

In the Find dialog box, you can choose to Include All Subfolders and Find All. If you select the Include All Subfolders option, folders contained within the folder listed in the Look in field are included in the search. If you select the Find All Files option, the Criteria options are unavailable and Bridge displays all files in the specified folder.

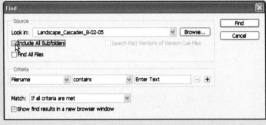

►3.7

2

If you have selected the Include All Subfolders option, options in the Criteria section are available. Click the drop-down arrow for the first field, and then choose a criterion. Choose a limiter in the second field, and enter the search text in the third field. In the third field, you can also use search terms such as AND or OR.

►3.8

3

To add another row of criteria, click + (the plus icon), and repeat the process described in step 2. You can add up to 12 more rows of criteria to the search. You can delete a set of criteria by clicking – (the minus icon) at the end of the criteria row.

►3.9

4

Click the Match field drop-down menu to choose If any criteria are met or If all criteria are met depending on the results you want.

►3.10

5

If you want the search results displayed in a separate Bridge window, leave the Show find results in a new browser window check box selected. This option is handy if you want to compare results from the search to the content displayed in the existing Bridge window.

Click Find to begin the search. Bridge searches the specified folder and subfolders, if selected, for images that meet the criteria and match specifications. If you chose to show the results in a new browser window, the results are displayed in a new window that shows the Find criteria and search folder name at the top of the window.

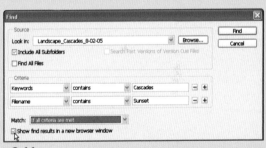

►3.11

6

Click the Save As Collection button at the top right of the window.

In the Save Collection dialog box, type a name for the Collection. Saved searches appear in the Favorites list in Bridge. To view saved searches, click Collections in the Favorites panel. If the saved Collection is not in the Favorites list, choose Edit ➤ Preferences ➤ General (or Bridge ➤ Preferences ➤ General on a Mac), , and then select the Collection in the Favorites Items section.

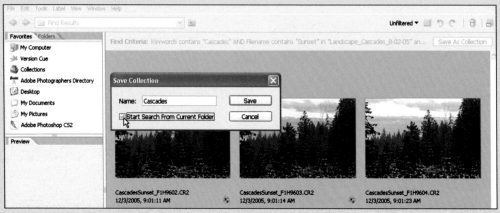

►3.12

You can select the Start Search From Current folder option to set the source folder as the one you've just used when making future searches. If you turn this option off, you have to reselect the folder each time you make a new search. If you know that you need to make additional searches in the same folder, select this option.

Click Save to save the collection.

Tip ►

You can access and modify previous searches or Collections in the Favorites panel in Bridge. Just select the search and click Edit Collection. Bridge displays the Find dialog box where you can modify the search criteria. Click Update to perform the search again.

Make Conversion Decisions Based on the Image Histogram

Contributor: Charlotte Lowrie ■ **Specialty:** Editorial and Stock
Primary Tool Used: Histogram

The histogram in Camera Raw is a barometer of the overall status of the image. It shows both the distribution of and the relative number of pixels at each tonal level. The Camera Raw histogram displays individual color channels plus areas where pixels from all three channels are present.

This technique shows you how to decipher the histogram and make image adjustments based on the histogram information.

▶3.13

1

Ensure that the color space you want is selected in Space in the Show Workflow Options section, and then evaluate the histogram. In this image, the histogram shows overall underexposure. On the left side of the histogram, the shadows are clipped, or shifting pixel values to pure white (255) or pure black (0) with no detail, in multiple channels. The gap between the pixels on the right and the end of the graph on the far right, or highlight side, indicate underexposure.

Here is what the indicators and colors used on the histogram mean:

- Spikes on the ends of the histogram indicate that some levels are clipped. No spikes means that the scene was within the range of the camera and no tones or colors are being clipped.

- White indicates pixels in all three channels, Red, Green, and Blue, are present. White spikes at the ends of the histogram indicate that highlights and shadows are being clipped. Color and/or multi-color spikes at either or both ends of the histogram indicate clipping in one or more channels.

- A fully or partially colored spike indicates color or tonal clipping. A red, green, or blue spike indicates gamut or tonal clipping in the respective channels.

  Camera Raw displays clipping in two channels as follows:

  - Cyan. Clipping in the Green and Blue channels.
  - Magenta. Clipping in the Red and Blue channels.
  - Yellow. Clipping in the Red and Green channels.

▶3.14

Note ▶ The RGB display above the histogram shows the values for the pixel under the cursor at a 5 × 5-pixel sampling from the preview image at zoom settings of 100 percent or smaller. At larger sizes, it indicates a 5 × 5-pixel sample from the actual image.

2

To get a better distribution of tones in an underexposed image such as this one, move the Exposure slider right until the pixels in the histogram reach the end of the graph. Here, a +0.05 exposure increase works. Sometimes increasing exposure so that the pixels move all the way to the right increases exposure too much. Leave a small gap depending on the rendering you want for the image.

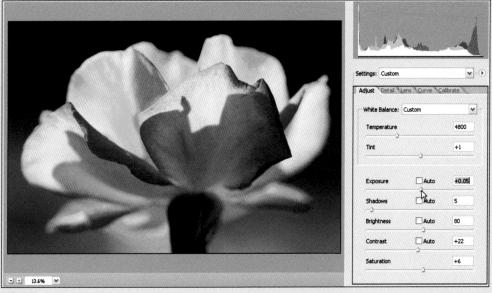

►3.15

3

To prevent shadow clipping in this type of image, move the Shadow slider left. In this case, a setting of 0 is used.

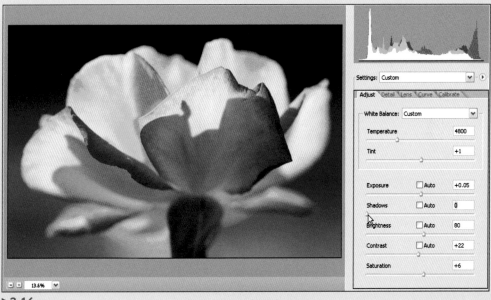

►3.16

4

Moving the Brightness slider to 48 provides a richer rendition of this image. Because the Brightness control adjusts midtones without moving the black or white points much you most often will move the slider to the right. For this image, however, a setting of 48 emphasizes the dramatic backlighting.

▶3.17

Adjusting Exposure, Shadows, and Brightness changes the distribution of tones on the histogram. But changes you make to Temperature also affect the histogram distribution of tones. If you know that the color temperature needs adjustment, adjusting color temperature first is a good idea.

Differences Among Color Spaces

Color spaces determine the color range possible within an image. Some color spaces, such as sRGB, offer a limited number of colors, whereas a color space such as ProPhoto RGB offers a large range of colors.

You can see the differences by changing color spaces in the Space option in the Show Workflow Options section in Camera Raw from Adobe RGB (1998) in the left image to ProPhoto RGB in the right image.

As you choose a color space with a larger range of colors, the image histogram will shift to show the wider or narrower range of colors. If you consistently get color clipping, try checking the color space selected and switching to a space with a larger range of colors.

Improve Even the Best Images in Camera Raw

Contributor: Bob Coates ■ **Specialty:** Wedding
Primary Tools Used: Image Adjust Tab and Vignetting

Detail images are extremely popular with brides. If brides spend money on something for the wedding, getting an artistic photo of it is worth it, as shown in this technique. These items include the bride's shoes, candles, table settings, and jewelry. But all images, no matter how good the initial capture, benefit from tweaks that give the image a professional edge. And using Camera Raw, you get the best working file from the RAW capture.

This technique shows you how Camera Raw adjustments add polish to an image that already has a lot going for it.

►3.18

1

Even with a well-exposed image such as this, it is important to look for opportunities to make tweaks to areas including exposure, white balance, contrast, and saturation. Image evaluation begins by checking the image's histogram in Camera Raw. To see the settings from your camera without Camera Raw's automatic adjustments, press Control/⌘+U on the Adjust tab. Then look at both ends of the histogram to see if pixels are crowded to the left or right side which indicates clipping.

The histogram for this image showed clipping in the shadows. Dragging the Shadows slider to 1 preserves shadow detail. To preview clipping, hold the Alt/Option key as you drag the Shadows slider. Camera Raw displays clipped areas as colors on a white background.

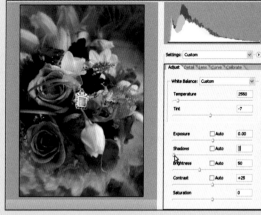

▶3.19

2

It is worthwhile even with a good exposure to see if it can be improved even slightly. In this case, a slight exposure increase provides an improvement. Drag the Exposure slider to the right to increase the overall brightness of the image, or to the left to decrease the brightness. In the example, with the exposure set at +0.20, the histogram shows some clipping of information in the highlights. However, for this image, some clipping is okay because part of the information being clipped is in the specular highlights on the metal frame.

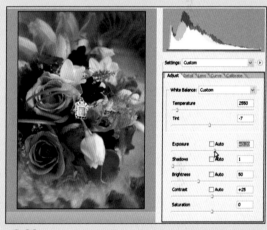

▶3.20

3

Check the image to see if the midtones need to be brought up. You can adjust the midtones by dragging the Brightness slider to the right to brighten the midtones or to the left to darken them. For this image, a Brightness of 81 provides pleasing midtones.

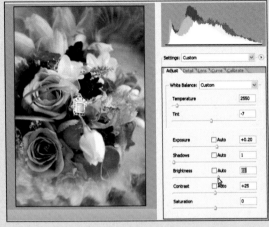

▶3.21

4

At this point, you need to decide to go warmer, leave the image as is, or go cooler. However, this is subjective and depends on the subject and the mood that you want to convey.

For this image, a slightly warmer feel is best. Drag the Temperature slider to the desired setting. Dragging the Temperature slider to the right adds warmth while dragging to the left decreases warmth. In this case, a Temperature of 2700 adds just a touch of warmth to the image.

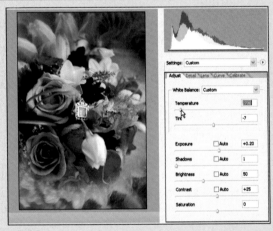

▶3.22

5

Evaluate the image to see if the contrast provides a nice snap. If the contrast is too low, the image will look dull and flat. If it is too high, dark areas are blocked and transitions between midtones and shadows are lost. You can zoom to 100% and experiment to see if more contrast improves the image. To increase contrast, drag the Contrast slider to the right.

For this image, a contrast setting of 32 gives the image nice snap. As you drag the Contrast slider, watch the histogram for clipping. If one or more color channels clip, a spike appears on the right side of the histogram and shows the color(s) of the channel(s) being clipped.

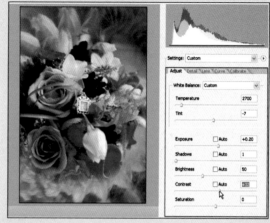
►3.23

6

Like contrast, adjusting the saturation level is subjective. But the need for saturation adjustment can also depend on your camera and the settings. Some cameras produce images that do not have colors that are as saturated as images from other cameras. And the need for saturation adjustment can vary depending on if you use different image settings that are available on some cameras. Generally, you'll make small to moderate Saturation adjustments in Camera Raw.

Watch the image as you drag the Saturation slider to the right to increase saturation. Adjusting Saturation too much produces color shifts that look unnatural and, at extreme increases, colors that look garish. Also watch the histogram for spikes that indicate clipping in the shadows. Adjusting Saturation to +12 works well in this image.

> **Tip**
>
> Be careful when adding saturation to your images. You can easily go too far, especially when work with skin tones. With inanimate objects like flowers, be on the lookout for color blooming where color appears to spill onto surrounding areas and increased noise.

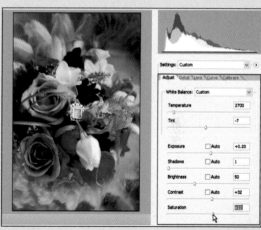
►3.24

7

Adding a vignette that darkens the edges of the image helps draw the eye to the subject, and can be a nice addition to some images as shown here. To add a vignette in Camera Raw, click the Lens tab. Drag the Amount slider to the left (negative side) to darken the corners or to the right (positive side) to lighten the corners. Then drag the Midpoint slider to the left to increase or to the right to decreases the effect. You can experiment with the settings to get the look you want. In this case, a setting of –76 for Amount and a setting of 48 for the Midpoint looks best. While this tool was originally designed to correct unwanted lens vignetting, it can be a creative tool that works well with images such as this.

> **Tip** ▶
>
> Most of the time, images are enhanced when you darken the corners and gradually move to lighter tones in the middle of the image. Vignetting helps direct the viewers' eyes to the area of the image you want them to concentrate on. Depending on the image, you can also try reverse vignetting and lighten the corners instead.

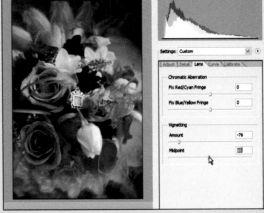

▶**3.25**

Beware of Tradeoffs in Image Quality

Contributor: Rob Sheppard ■ **Specialty:** Nature and Editorial
Primary Tool Used: Various image adjustments

A sunset's tonal range is often too much for any film or sensor to capture. Even with a graduated neutral-density filter, the foreground and sky often can't be properly exposed in one shot. I overcome this tonal range problem by shooting two exposures to combine a properly exposed sky from one shot with properly exposed foreground from another.

Why not try to do it all in one shot? Photographers sometimes compromise on exposure, hoping that Camera Raw will save the picture. In this example, the photo was exposed so the sky reproduces well, but the foreground is underexposed. This technique shows that Camera Raw can indeed "save" a single, badly exposed image—a scene that is beyond the dynamic range of the camera. But while you get a usable image, the result compromises overall image quality due to increased noise in the shadow areas and suboptimal tonality in the foliage. A better choice is outlined in the sidebar to get the best quality.

▶3.26

1

In Camera Raw, hold down the Alt/Option key and click the Exposure slider in the Adjust tab. Camera Raw displays the highlight threshold screen. The screen shows that this photo has good highlights in the sky and nothing is gained by increasing exposure.

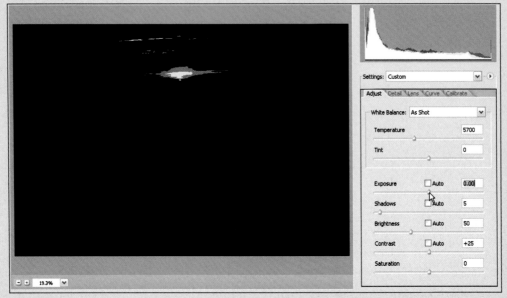

▶3.27

2

Hold down the Alt+Option key and drag the Shadows slider until some black is left in the image. Camera Raw displays the shadows threshold screen. Opening the dark areas much farther isn't possible because the blacks will be lost, meaning the image will not have its best contrast or color.

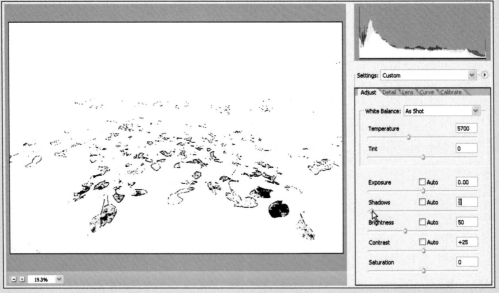

▶3.28

3

Click the Curve tab. Getting the right tonal curve can take a lot of time on an exposure like this one. It is certainly very subjective, too. Here I've increased the brightness of the water and plants in the foreground, while working to keep both the darkest and lightest areas from getting overly bright. This is the reason for the multiple points on the curve. The bottom point anchors the darkest areas, the second point up lifts some of the dark colors, and the third point lifts even more. The top point brings the curve back to the center line so the brightest areas don't get washed out.

▶3.29

4

Click the Adjust tab. In a shot that needs some color, drag the Saturation slider to the right to increase saturation as shown here.

As you can see, you can get a usable image from a single exposure but the tradeoffs reduce the overall image quality. A better approach is to take two images, each exposed for a specific area of the scene as outlined in the sidebar at the end of this technique.

▶3.30

The Value of a Properly Exposed Image

In this technique, a properly shot image is one that uses two exposures—one that captures the sky well and one that renders the foreground accurately.

In this example, both images are processed in Camera Raw specifically to get the most out of the areas that the exposure was made for. I processed the sky shot for the sky and the foreground shot for the foreground. I created the final shot by combining the good sky and the good foreground shots into one. This type of compositing technique is detailed in Chapter 6, Double-Process Files to Increase Dynamic Range. Compared to the single shot of the same scene, the combined image has excellent sky tonality and color, as well as better overall tonalities in the darker part of the photo.

The dark foreground areas point out how important exposure is to getting the best image possible. Yes, processing in Camera Raw made a useable image from the single exposure based on the sky. And the sky could then be intensified to make something similar to the composited shot. The sky photo could also have been double-processed in Camera Raw—once for the sky, and once for the foreground—and then composited for a nice-looking image. So using Camera Raw can "save" a poorly exposed foreground after all (though with more work and some tonal challenges).

But you can dig deeper into images such as this one by looking at cropped detail areas of the image to reveal some interesting things that affect quality use of digital images. Looking at enlargements of the single image in this technique as an example, you can see the huge differences in noise.

Compare the four cropped details of the plants and water in the foreground in both shots.

In the underexposed foreground, noise becomes the water surface whereas with proper exposure, you can see algae below the water surface, as well as different greens and tonalities. Sometimes noise introduces colors not present in the original scene; noise degrades the detail and appearance of the foreground leaves in this shot.

Can a badly exposed image be saved in Camera Raw? Perhaps. Certainly a useable image can often be developed. But if the image is exposed well in the first place, you can achieve the final results more easily and with far better color, tonality, and lower noise, all values that affect the final print quality of the image.

Section 2

Image Processing Techniques

Raw Conversion Strategies

Chapter 04

In this chapter

Guide to Basic RAW Image Conversion

Contributor: Macduff Everton ■ **Specialty:** Travel and Editorial
Primary Tool Used: Adobe Camera Raw

The goal of RAW image conversion is to bring out the best in an image while ensuring that the image pixel integrity remains high. Camera Raw adjustments should produce the best image possible for the intended client or for output to a commercial or inkjet printer. To improve the final image quality, Brantlea Scruggs, Picture Arts creative technical advisor, shared conversion techniques that I've incorporated into my workflow.

This technique demonstrates some of those adjustments.

▶4.1

1

In Bridge, select the image you want to convert, and then choose File ➤ Open in Camera Raw. In Camera Raw, select the Show Workflow Options check box, click the Space drop-down menu, and choose the color space you want. The more colors a color space supports, the more data you will have to work with as you make adjustments.

X-Ref

There are details for choosing a color space later in this chapter, but you can also check out Chapter 5.

►4.2

2

Click the Depth drop-down menu and choose 16 Bits/Channel.

Bit depth determines the number of tones that are available to describe how light or dark a pixel is, or the pixel's tone. At 8-bit depth, a total of 256 tones are available to describe a pixel ranging from white (255) to black (0) with intervening shades of gray. But at the 16-bit setting, a total of 65,536 possible tonal values are available to describe a pixel.

►4.3

3

In the Resolution field, type the resolution you want. The resolution depends on your workflow and the intended output. A setting of 300 pixels/inch is appropriate for images to be printed on commercial printing presses and for stock use. But if your workflow and output involves printing images on an inkjet printer, then you can set the Resolution to 240 pixels/inch.

▶4.4

4

If you want to resize the image by downsampling or upsampling the image, click the Size drop-down menu and choose the size you want.

Note

Making an image smaller than its original size is called *downsampling*. Conversely, making an image larger than its original size is called *upsampling*. Resampling is explained later in this chapter.

▶4.5

5

To turn automatic adjustments on and off, click the right-pointing triangle next to Settings and choose Use Auto Adjustments from the menu, or press Ctrl/⌘+U.

Auto Adjustments represents Camera Raw's best guess at what image adjustments are needed after analyzing the image data. Most photographers prefer to work with Auto Adjustments turned off to get a truer representation of the image off the sensor and because they prefer to make adjustments themselves.

►4.6

6

If necessary, drag the Temperature slider to tweak the color temperature of the image. Drag the slider to the left to make the image cooler (bluer), or to the right to make the image colors warmer (yellow). In this image, a Temperature setting of 3100 cools the scene slightly. If a tint remains in the image, you can drag the Tint slider to the left to add green or to the right to add magenta.

You can also set white balance by clicking the White Balance drop-down menu and selecting one of the preset White Balance settings. The As Shot option resets white balance to the camera's setting; Auto provides Camera Raw's interpretation based on its analysis of image data.

Tip ▶

To balance colors to neutral, you can use the White Balance tool. On the toolbar, select the White Balance tool, and click a white or neutral gray area in the image. If you use a white area, be sure the area has detail and is not a specular highlight.

▶4.7

7

Evaluate the histogram for clipping, which is shown as spikes on either end of the histogram. In this image, the specular highlights in the lights cause clipping, but adjusting the Exposure control can help avoid clipping in other areas where you want to preserve detail. Hold down the Alt/Option key as you drag the Exposure slider. Camera Raw displays areas that will be clipped against a black background. Drag the slider to the left until no or few color areas are visible.

For this image, an Exposure adjustment of −1.65 avoids most clipping, but it also darkens the image considerably. You can, of course, disregard specular highlights as you make this adjustment, especially if you later find that adjusting Brightness doesn't brighten the image enough.

X-Ref ▶ For more details on reading the histogram, see Chapter 3.

In addition, watch the histogram as you make adjustments.

▶4.8

8

Hold down the Alt/Option key as you drag the Shadows slider. Camera Raw displays areas that will be clipped as colored areas against a white background. Drag the slider to the left until no or few color areas are visible.

For this image, and for virtually all of my images, a setting of 0 helps ensures that shadow areas will be as open to show shadow detail as possible. Setting Shadows as low as 1 or 2 can block up to obliterate shadow detail.

▶4.9

9

Drag the Brightness slider to increase or decrease the image brightness. In this case, a setting of 104 brings up the brightness to compensate for the negative Exposure setting. The Brightness control brightens the midtones without changing the black or white points set in previous steps.

However, excessive brightness adjustments can cause clipping. Be sure to watch the histogram as you make adjustments. In some cases, you can make tradeoffs between the Exposure and Brightness to maintain a healthy histogram.

▶4.10

10

Drag the Contrast slider to the right to increase contrast or to the left to decrease contrast. For this image, a setting of roughly 45 is typical for my work.

Adjustments that you make to contrast and brightness work like setting a classic S curve in Photoshop. The default contrast setting is +25. Increasing the contrast lightens tones above midtones and darkens tones below midtones—all without affecting the brightest highlight and darkest shadow.

▶4.11

11

Click the Zoom level drop-down menu under the preview image, and then choose 100% (or press Z, and click until the zoom level is 100%). Press the Spacebar to access the Hand tool and then move to a shadow area in the image. Click the Detail tab, and then drag the Color Noise Reduction slider to the left to reduce the amount of color noise reduction or to the right to increase the amount.

The Color Noise Reduction setting helps reduce unwanted color artifacts that are seen as flecks of unwanted color, especially in shadow areas of the image. But the default setting may be higher than necessary to control chroma noise. The goal is to use as little color noise reduction as possible while still minimizing unwanted flecks of color, especially in shadow areas. For this image, a setting of 17 is appropriate.

The adjustments you make for your image will vary from those given here, but the process is the same regardless. Once you have the basic image adjustments made, you can open the image in Photoshop or save it and come back to finish edits in Photoshop later.

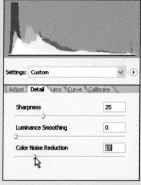

▶4.12

 Tip

When adjusting for color noise, always zoom to at least 100 percent. Drag the Color Noise Reduction slider to 0, and then gradually drag it to the right until the chroma noise fades.

Resample Images

Contributor: Bob Coates ■ **Specialty:** Weddings
Primary Tool Used: Size

Deciding whether and when to resize your images in Camera Raw or using another method depends on output quality and how you like to work with your files. Resizing an image to a smaller size in Camera Raw can, for example, speed up your workflow provided that the smaller image suits the final use.

This technique shows you how to increase and decrease the size of images based on how you want to use them.

►4.13

1

In Bridge, select the image you want to resample, and then choose File ➤ Open in Camera Raw. In Camera Raw, click the Show Workflow Options check box if the options aren't already displayed. Camera Raw displays the Workflow Options including image size.

The Size option initially displays the camera's native resolution. Depending on your camera's resolution, several choices are available in the Size box, all shown in pixels with a + or − sign after the numbers, or with no + or − sign which indicates the image's native resolution.

To make the image smaller than the camera's native resolution, click the Size drop-down menu, and then choose a size with a − sign after the resolution, such as 1424 by 2128 (3.0 MP) − as shown.

You might want to downsample images that you are only going to print to a very small size or images that you will use only on the Web. Downsampling saves disk space due to the smaller file sizes.

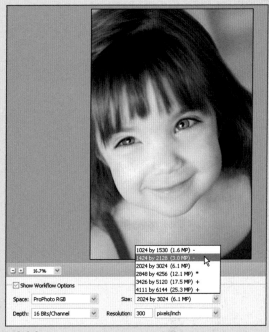

▶4.14

2

To make your image larger than the camera's resolution, click the Size drop-down menu and choose a resolution that is larger than the camera's native resolution, as indicated by a + sign after the resolution, such as 3426 by 5120 (17.5 MP) + as shown in the image.

Creating larger files allows you to make larger prints. When you upsample images, the larger files may slow down retouching and production time. You can experiment to see which sizes work best for your situation.

> **Note**
>
> Opinions differ as to whether upsampling is the best way to create larger images. The decision is somewhat dependent on the image, but some images enlarge best using this technique. For alternate methods, see the accompanying sidebar at the end of this technique.

Be aware that Camera Raw remembers the last settings you used to process an image. This feature can be a problem if you forget to check settings, and then you process a batch of 1.6MB images when you really wanted 17MB images. Always check the Workflow Options before you begin processing images.

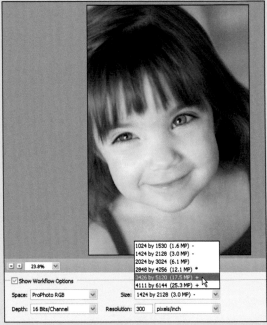

▶4.15

3

Continue the conversion by making the adjustments you want to the image. If you resized the image for a specific use, you may want to save the resized images in a new subfolder or folder. For example, if you downsampled an image for Web use, you can create a new folder designated for only the image you processed for the Web.

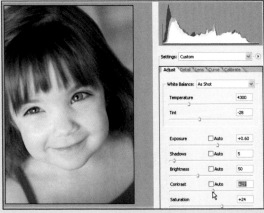

▶4.16

Other Resizing Options

You can create larger files for making larger prints by using Photoshop CS2's Image Size dialog box and an action that increases the size of the image in 10 percent increments.

To create the action, open an image. At the top right of the Actions palette, click the right-pointing triangle and choose New Action from the menu. Type a descriptive name for your action, and click Record.

Choose Image ➤ Image Size or press Alt/Option+Ctrl/⌘+I to open the Image Size dialog box. In the Document Size section, click the Width drop-down menu, and then choose percent. Change both the width and height to 110. Click OK.

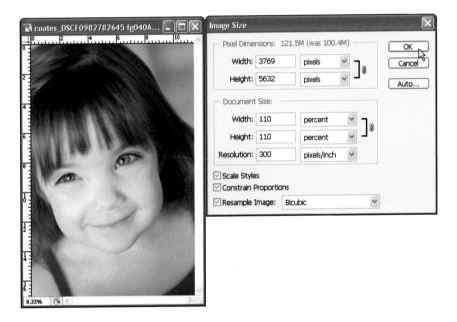

Click the Stop playing/recording button at the bottom of the Actions palette.

When you want to upsize an image, play the action one or more times until you have the size of image you need. This method allows Photoshop to make the image larger in small increments. Incremental increases are best because Photoshop has to do very little guessing as to the colors of the nearest pixels as it adds pixels to increase image size. When you try to resample an image to a larger size by jumping right to the size you want, Photoshop has to guess at too many of the pixels, and the results are not as good.

Also with this method, retouching and processing images is faster because you're working with a smaller file. Then you can upsample the image just before printing. Some types of images work better with one of the other techniques.

Synchronize Edits Among Multiple Images

Contributor: Charlotte Lowrie ■ **Specialty:** Editorial and Stock
Primary Tool Used: Synchronize

Back in the day, the only way to work with RAW images was one image at a time. The process was tedious, repetitive, and time consuming, especially for large numbers of images that were shot under the same lighting conditions, and replicating the same processing across different images could be difficult. But thanks to Camera Raw you now have multiple ways to get consistent results across a series of RAW images—and get the results quickly.

Regardless of which method you use, processing 2, 10, 50, or more RAW images at a time has never been faster or easier.

►4.17

1

In Adobe Bridge, hold down the Ctrl/⌘ key as you click each image in the series that you want to process, and then choose File ➤ Open in Camera Raw.

Camera Raw opens in Filmstrip mode and displays the first image in the preview area. Remaining images appear in the film strip on the left side of the window. If you open more images than can be displayed in the visible area of the filmstrip, you can move forward or back through the open images using the navigation arrow located under the preview image. However, using the navigation control changes the currently selected picture. If you want to keep the current image selected, just drag the scroll bar along the filmstrip to display other images.

Likely candidates for synchronized adjustments are images shot under controlled lighting such as in a studio or outdoors under where the lighting conditions remain relatively stable, such as the series of still life images seen here.

Once you open all the images for synchronized processing, you need to make your basic image adjustments.

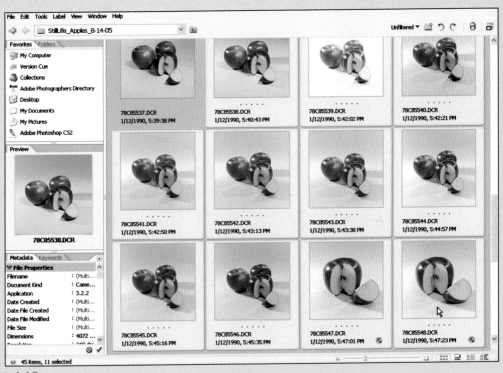

▶4.18

Note

If you're concerned that opening multiple images will degrade computer performance, no discernable performance slowdown occurs with 25, 50, or more images open on fairly recent computer systems.

2

In the Adjust tab, drag the Temperature slider left for a cooler (more blue) temperature or right for a warmer (more yellow) temperature. This image was taken under studio light, so I set the Temperature to 5550. Drag the Tint slider left for more green or right for more red. No adjustment to Tint was needed for this image.

▶4.19

3

Drag the Exposure slider right to increase the exposure or left to decrease it. To preview clipping, hold down the Alt/Option key as you move the Exposure slider. Here the best setting was -1.00.

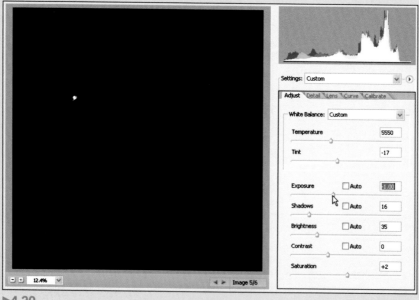

▶4.20

4

Drag the Shadows slider left or right to set the black point. Preview clipping by holding down the Alt/Option key as you drag the Shadows slider. A setting of 14 works well for this image, and because all the images were taken under the same lighting, the setting will work for all the images when they are synchronized.

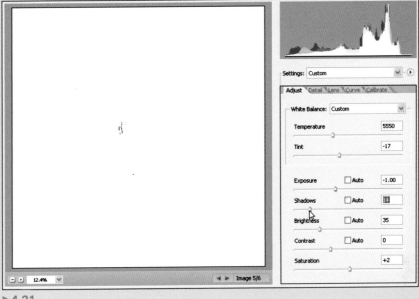

▶4.21

5

Drag the Brightness slider to adjust the image midtones. For this image, a setting of 65 works nicely. This adjustment does not affect the white point set with the Exposure adjustment or the black point set with the Shadows adjustment.

▶4.22

6

Drag the Contrast slider left to decrease contrast or right to increase contrast. For this image, a +7 setting is appropriate. And again, because all the images were taken in similar lighting, this setting can be applied across the board during synchronization.

You can also adjust sharpening, correct lens aberrations or vignetting, tweak the tonal curve, and adjust shadow tint using the other controls offered. These options are found on the Detail, Lens, Curve, and Calibrate tabs, respectively.

With basic adjustments made, you can apply all or part of the adjustments to all or some of the open images.

▶4.23

7

To apply adjustments to all open images, click the Select All button in the upper left corner of the screen. To apply the adjustments to specific images, hold down the Ctrl/⌘ key as you click images in the film strip.

Make sure that the image you've adjusted in the previous steps is still selected; otherwise, you'll get results that you neither expected nor wanted. The currently selected image appears in the filmstrip with a darker border.

When you select additional images, either by clicking Select All or by Ctrl/⌘+clicking, Camera Raw activates the Synchronize button.

▶4.24

8

Click the Synchronize button. Camera Raw displays the Synchronize dialog box where you can choose to apply all the adjustments you made or deselect individual options that you don't want to apply.

Click the Synchronize drop-down menu to display additional options, including the option to create a Custom Subset. The Custom Subset option takes a work-backward approach by clearing all selected settings so you can choose the adjustments to include in the subset.

Click OK when you finish choosing options.

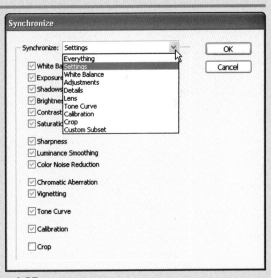

▶4.25

Click one of the following buttons:

- Save [number of images] to save the selected images, or hold down Alt/Option to change the button to Save without opening the Save Options dialog box.

- Cancel to discard changes, or hold down Alt/Option to change the button to Reset.

- Open [number of images] to open the images in Photoshop.

- Done to apply the adjustments so that the images appear adjusted the next time you open the files in Camera Raw.

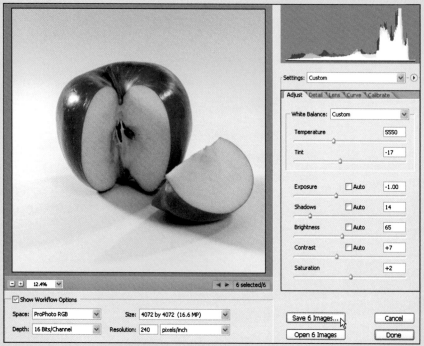

►4.26

SB Sidebar

Why Use Synchronization?

Camera Raw offers several ways to apply image adjustments from one file to multiple files. The advantage of using the Synchronization technique is that all the images that are likely candidates for similar processing are open in a single place with reasonably large previews.

Another benefit is that after you synchronize the image corrections, you can quickly run through the synchronized images to see whether any need individual tweaks. If they do, you can make the tweaks before saving or closing the images.

Process Multiple Images Quickly

Contributor: David H. Wells ■ **Specialty:** Photojournalism and Editorial
Primary Tool Used: Copy/Paste Camera Raw Settings in Bridge

Software programs are notorious for offering multiple ways to do the same, or essentially the same, task. Bridge and Camera Raw are not exceptions. Just as you can open and synchronize image adjustments to multiple images, you can also copy and paste the settings from one processed image to other files in Bridge, all without explicitly opening them in Camera Raw.

Depending on the images and your workflow, this technique may serve you well for applying everything from broad-brush adjustments to more detail-level adjustments to multiple files.

▶4.27

1

In Adobe Bridge, select an image from a series of images that need similar adjustments. Choose File ➤ Open in Camera Raw, or press Ctrl/⌘+R. Camera Raw opens and displays the image.

Make the image adjustments that you want in Camera Raw. The best practice is to limit the adjustments to those that apply to the entire series.

For example, if all the images need a slight white balance adjustment, you might limit the image adjustments to adjusting Temperature and Tint. The more the images have in common in terms of needing the same adjustments, the more adjustments you can make to the file in Camera Raw and be confident that the adjustments will be appropriate for other images.

▶4.28

Click Done. Camera Raw saves the adjustments you made to the file. If you reopen the image in Camera Raw, the settings are just as you left them so you can make further adjustments to the image.

In Adobe Bridge, right-click the image you adjusted in the previous step and choose Copy Camera Raw Settings from the menu that appears.

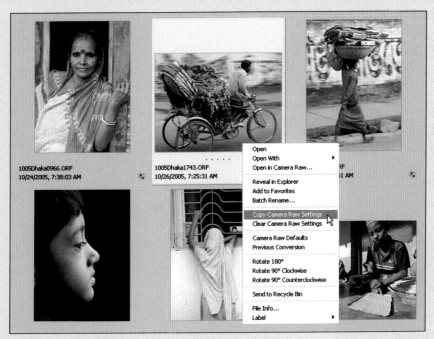

▶4.29

3

Hold down the Ctrl/⌘ key as you click the other images that you want to apply the settings to. To select consecutive images, click the first image, and then hold down the Shift key as you click the last image in the series. Right-click (Ctrl-click on Mac) the selected image(s) and choose Paste Camera Raw Settings from the menu that appears. Bridge displays the Paste Camera Raw Settings dialog box.

▶4.30

4

Select or clear the settings you want and click OK. You can't undo the settings after you paste them, so be sure that the selected images will benefit from them. You can, of course, open the images in Camera Raw and make changes. The basic corrections made to the first image on the Adjust tab in Camera Raw, and then shown as the Custom subset on the menu here, are applied to selected images that were taken in similar lighting. This makes quick work of image adjustments.

> **Note**
> You can also open the Paste Camera Raw Settings dialog box by choosing Edit ➤ Apply Camera Raw Settings. Select or clear the settings you want to apply, and then click OK.

Paste Camera Raw Settings

Subset: Custom Subset

☑ White Balance
☑ Exposure
☑ Shadows
☑ Brightness
☑ Contrast
☑ Saturation

☐ Sharpness
☐ Luminance Smoothing
☐ Color Noise Reduction

☐ Chromatic Aberration
☐ Vignetting

☐ Tone Curve

☐ Calibration

☑ Crop

OK / Cancel

▶4.31

> **Tip**
> The keyboard shortcut for copying Camera Raw Settings is Ctrl/⌘+Alt/Option+C. The shortcut for pasting settings to other images is Ctrl/⌘+Alt/Option+V.

Optimize Workflow

> **SB Sidebar**

The power of automated processing lies in making short work of the conversion process. Any photographers who have shot RAW images for more than a week know that unless they find efficient ways to process RAW images, they will spend more time in front of the computer than they do behind the lens—a turn of events that is unlikely to increase profits.

Even though this book provides some of the mainstream ways to make workflow efficient, looking for ways to reduce the need for corrections during the shooting phase also pays. Setting and saving custom white balances for frequently used shooting venues, such as the studio, a stadium, or an office environment, is one example.

Another option is to create a camera-specific profile that you can save as the default and apply in Camera Raw. By doing so, many of the adjustments are made automatically when images open in Camera Raw.

Whatever automation you find, combine, or create that trims processing time, the better your workflow will be.

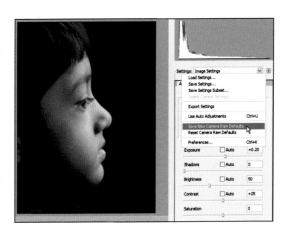

Recover Highlight Detail

Contributor: Charlotte Lowrie ■ **Specialty:** Editorial and Stock
Primary Tool Used: Highlight Recovery Using the Exposure Control

One of the ways that digital photography differs from traditional photography is that in digital photography a disproportionate amount of image detail is contained in the first f-stop of brightness. Specifically, fully half of the image data is contained in the first f-stop. In a six stop dynamic range, 4,096 levels are devoted to the brightest f-stop with progressively fewer levels being recorded for each of the successive f-stop. At the darkest f-stop, only 64 levels are recorded. As a result, most digital photographers know that "exposing to the right" of the histogram is the best way to take advantage of the full capability of the sensor. They also know that programs like Camera Raw can recover detail in overexposed highlights. But how much detail can be recovered, and how do you do it?

This technique shows you how to recover highlights in a slightly overexposed image.

▶4.32

1

In Bridge, select an image with overexposed highlights, and then choose File ➤ Open in Camera Raw. Camera Raw opens and displays the selected image.

Check the image histogram to evaluate the channels in which highlight clipping is occurring. A spike, or vertical line, on either end of the histogram indicates clipping. In this image, the thin spike on the right shows overexposure.

The color of the spike shows which channels are being clipped. A white spike means that all three channels are being clipped. Even in this case, Camera Raw tries to recover highlight detail and keep the area white, instead of turning it gray as some conversion programs do.

A spike of a single color means that color channel is being clipped. If information from one or two other channels exists, Camera Raw will do its best to extrapolate and fill in missing detail for the clipped channel.

Even though Camera Raw provides excellent highlight detail recovery, expecting Camera Raw or any conversion program to recover highlight detail where all three channels are blown out or have no detail is unrealistic. Be realistic when choosing an image for this technique.

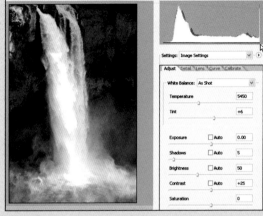

►4.33

2

In the Show Workflow Options section, click the Space drop-down menu, and then choose ProPhoto RGB. Whether or not your working color space is ProPhoto, Adobe RGB, sRGB, or another color space, ProPhoto RGB offers the widest range of colors. Often, switching to this color space resolves the clipping that appears in smaller color gamuts.

Note

Choosing ProPhoto RGB during the conversion phase does not lock you into using ProPhoto in later phases of production. You can always convert the image to your usual working space when you open the image in Photoshop.

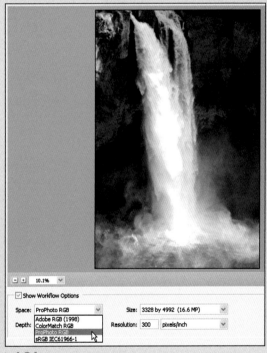

►4.34

3

Hold down the Alt/Option key and drag the Exposure slider to the left. By reducing Exposure, Camera Raw can recover detail in the highlights in this image as shown by the very small area of white remaining on the display. In this image an Exposure setting of −1.55 brings some detail back to the brightest areas. By placing the Color Sampler Tool over the brightest areas, the RGB reading shown above the Histogram shows that the areas now measure 247 in all three channels—an improvement over 255.

To see the pixel values, move the mouse pointer over a highlight area, and then look at the R: G: B: display in the upper right of the Camera Raw dialog box.

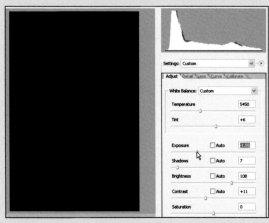

▶4.35

Note ▶ Make any significant changes to exposure before adjusting the white balance because the Exposure adjustment can affect color.

4

Hold down the Alt/Option key and drag the Shadows slider until few if any colored areas remain. In this case, a setting of 7 works well.

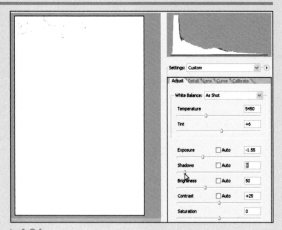

▶4.36

5

Drag the Brightness slider to the right until the brightness is pleasing. This adjustment helps to counteract the darkening caused by setting a negative Exposure adjustment. Then drag the Contrast slider to adjust the contrast. Using a 108 Brightness setting and a +5 Contrast adjustment finishes off the main adjustments for this image.

You can go on to make other adjustments to the image using the other tabs in Camera Raw, or open the image in Photoshop for final editing. The steps provided in this technique should be helpful anytime you have an image in which you need to recover highlight detail within one or one-and-a-half f-stops.

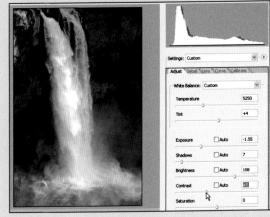

▶4.37

SB Sidebar

More About Highlight Recovery

The amount of highlight recovery that you can achieve depends on your camera. Some cameras offer more latitude than others. Getting a good working knowledge of your camera's latitude, and then shooting within it, is a good idea. Just take a series of images, each overexposed by 1/4 or 1/2 stop successively. Then use the steps in this technique to see how much detail you can recover at different levels of overexposure.

Highlight detail recovery is impressive, but in high-contrast scenes, the dynamic range often exceeds the image sensor's ability to record it. You'll know when this happens because the image histogram will show spikes on both ends of the histogram. In other words, the darks were darker and the highlights were brighter than the image sensor could record and hold detail in.

Certainly adjustments in Camera Raw can improve the image, but most photographers prefer to take multiple images exposed for the extremes in the scene and composite the images in Photoshop. The composite results in an image with a greater dynamic range than the camera can capture in a single image. Chapter 3 includes more information on this approach.

Correct a Listing Horizon

Contributor: Rob Sheppard ■ **Specialty:** Nature and Editorial
Primary Tool Used: Straighten tool

Much landscape photography deals with horizons where sky joins land or water or land and water come together. In the heat of the photography, it is very easy to end up with a horizon that is not horizontal.

In the pair of images here, you can see the scene listing to the left in the left image, and the corrected horizon in the next image. It also shows something uncommon in nature photographs—man's influence. This photo presents a now-rare saltwater marsh in California surrounded by man's development. Can such natural areas be protected and preserved? It is a very real question that photography can pose for all of us.

▶4.38

1

Open the image that needs straightening in Camera Raw, and then select the Straighten tool from the toolbar. Drag a line that follows the horizon.

> **Note**
>
> Camera Raw offers better straightening options than Photoshop. Although both have similar tools, the implementation in Camera Raw is more functional.

▶4.39

2

Release the mouse button, and Camera Raw instantly gives you a cropped photo overlay for the image that is aligned properly for the horizon.

The cool thing about this process is not just the automatic horizon correction, but also the suggested crop to make it work. The correction is only applied when you open the file in Photoshop, although it is saved in the XMP sidecar file.

X-Ref

For more information on XMP sidecar files, see Appendix B.

▶4.40

3

Check the horizon. Here is a trick to use to be sure the horizon is now horizontal, which means it is parallel to the top or bottom of the photo: Drag the bottom or top edge of the crop box until it is close to the horizon. Now you can quickly see how closely the horizon matches a pure horizontal. You can then either use the Straighten tool again, or just move the cursor outside the crop box until it turns into a curved arrow and click and drag the box to rotate it.

▶4.41

4

Drag the bottom line back into place, and then make any cropping adjustments that you feel work better than the crop that Camera Raw gave you. Camera Raw will not let you move the crop box beyond the boundaries of the image, so if you find you can't move the crop edge where you want, you probably have one corner of the box already hitting the edge. Move one side in to compensate, and you can make the change.

▶4.42

SB Sidebar

The Straight Photo

People generally like their nature photography to show nature "as it is" or at least unaltered from its original elements. Viewers expect horizons to be horizontal and without a lean one way or another. In today's photographic world, a slanted horizon looks odd at the least and makes the viewer think the photographer is sloppy at the worst. Luckily, correcting a listing horizon is very easy to do.

You can also correct leaning verticals using the same technique (instead matching the Straighten tool to the vertical), but you must be cautious. One problem with verticals is that they can look like they are leaning just because they were photographed with a wide-angle lens looking up and not because the camera was leaning left or right. This is a wide-angle perspective effect, and verticals on both sides of the photo will lean in, making any correction impossible in Camera Raw because it can only correct all verticals tilted in one direction from a misaligned camera angle. To correct the wide-angle perspective lean, you need to use the Lens Correction filter in Photoshop (choose Filter ➤ Distort ➤ Lens Correction).

This is not to say that a creative approach to a scene might not look great with a crooked horizon. In the movies, a crooked horizon is called a Dutch angle and was made famous for its effect in the classic movie, *The Third Man*, with Orson Welles. It can be an effective way to make a dramatic, attention-getting photo. A strongly angled image can create compositions that communicate new messages to your viewers, perhaps making the subject more compelling and remarkable. However, if you are going to deliberately make a horizon crooked, you need to really do it. A slightly slanted horizon just looks like a mistake. A strongly skewed line looks dramatic and like you meant to do it.

Crop Multiple Images Simultaneously

Contributor: Charlotte Lowrie ▪ **Specialty:** Editorial and Stock
Primary Tool Used: Crop tool

Cropping is often thought of as being a task that should be done one image at a time. But Camera Raw can speed up the process of cropping by allowing you to apply a basic crop to multiple images. Once the general crop is made, you can tweak the crop to individual images where necessary.

Anything that saves time in the workflow is worth exploring, and multiple image cropping is a technique worth trying.

▶4.43

1

In Adobe Bridge, choose the images that you want to have the same crop, and then choose File ➤ Open in Camera Raw. Camera Raw opens and displays the images.

Simultaneous cropping works best with images that are made using the same camera orientation and at approximately the same camera-to-subject distance. But because you can tweak the crops individually, opening some images that would not at first glance appear to be good candidates for simultaneous cropping is also okay.

▶4.44

2

Select the image on which you want to make the basic crop. Camera Raw displays the selected image with a darker border. Select the Crop tool from the toolbar. The Crop tool is initially set to Normal. If you click and hold the triangle on the bottom right of the Crop tool icon, you can choose from common aspect ratios, or you can set your own ratio by choosing Custom.

►4.45

If you choose Custom, the Custom Crop dialog box appears. Click the Crop drop-down menu and choose Ratio, Pixels, Inches, or cm. Type the ratio or measurement you want. Click OK.

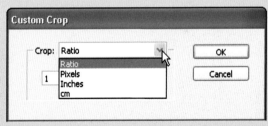

►4.46

3

Click and drag the Crop tool across the image to set the crop. Camera Raw displays the cropped area as a screen. The image in the filmstrip is also shown cropped.

Camera Raw changes the Size control to Crop Size in the Show Workflow Options section.

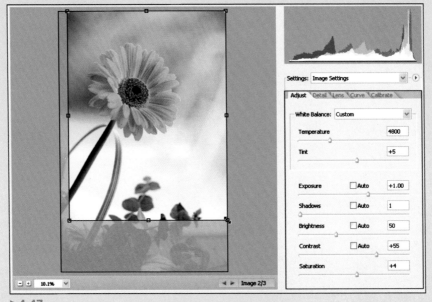

►4.47

4

Click Select All. Or, if you want to crop only some of the open images, hold down the Ctrl/⌘ key and click each image you want to apply the crop to. Click Synchronize. The Synchronize dialog box appears.

Click the Synchronize drop-down menu and choose Crop. Click OK.

►4.48

If you need to adjust the crop on an individual image, select only the image and select the Crop tool from the toolbar. Then drag a crop handle to enlarge or reduce the crop size. You can also move the cursor inside the crop area and drag to move the entire crop area.

To skew the crop, move the cursor outside a corner handle. The cursor changes to an arch. Then drag to skew the crop.

The crop you make is applied to the image when you save it or click Done in Camera Raw.

▶4.49

Process High Dynamic Range Images

Contributor: Katrin Eismann ■ **Specialty:** Artist, Author, and Educator
Primary Tool Used: Merge to HDR

High Dynamic Range (HDR) Imaging is a way to capture high-contrast scenes and maintain detail in both shadows and highlights. HDR imaging involves shooting and combining a series of at least three, but for better results five to seven, bracketed images. The resulting 32-bit HDR image provides approximately 4 billion "stepless" shades of gray (compared to 65,536 with a 16-bit image). HDR lets you capture the full dynamic range of a naturally lit scene in much the same way that the human eye sees the scene.

If you have never shot HDR images, you should first read this technique's accompanying sidebar. Then you can use the following steps to process HDR images.

▶4.50

1

In Bridge, select the images in the series that you want to merge to HDR. Choose Label ➤ *color* to select one of the standard colors offered that you want to use for the label. When Bridge displays a message alerting you that labels are stored in XMP metadata, click OK.

Using a color label for each HDR series makes finding the images in different series easier.

►4.51

2

Ensuring that no automatic adjustments are made to the images is essential. Select all the images in a series, and then choose File ➤ Open in Camera Raw or press Ctrl/⌘+R. Camera Raw displays the images in Filmstrip mode. Click Select All. Click the right-pointing triangle next to Settings and make sure that the Use Auto Adjustments option is not checked. Click Done. Camera Raw closes and returns you to Bridge.

When Auto Adjustments are turned off, you can see the differences in the bracketed images in Bridge.

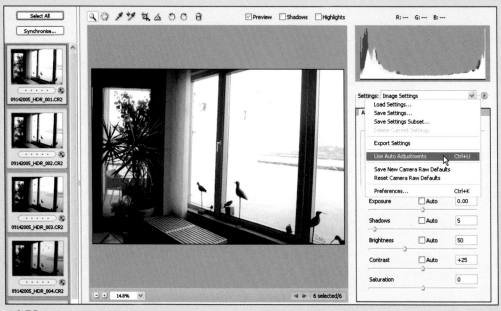

►4.52

3

In Bridge, select all the images in the series. Choose Tools ➤ Photoshop ➤ Merge to HDR. Photoshop launches if it's not already active, and it brings the images into the initial HDR interface (the Merge to HDR dialog box), which shows images that are referenced for the HDR image with their exposure values displayed on the left.

You can click the check box under the images on the left to remove a referenced image. Photoshop recalculates the HDR image. For example, if you don't need the image bracketed at two stops under, you can uncheck it, and see whether you like the results. If you don't like the new preview, just click the check box again to include the image. If you uncheck one of the referenced images, it is ignored in the calculation.

Drag the slider under the histogram on the upper right to adjust the white point. For this image, moving the slider just inside of where the histogram begins works well. Click OK in the Merge to HDR dialog box. Photoshop merges the series and displays the HDR image; in this case, the image is a 94MB file.

▶4.53

4

The image looks murky, but that's fine for now. If you check the menus in Photoshop, many commands are unavailable. However, you can use the commands that are available to effectively improve the image.

To color correct the image, choose Image ➤ Adjustments ➤ Channel Mixer. The Channel Mixer dialog box appears. For this image, pumping up the Red slightly to 102 gives the image a little extra warmth. Click OK.

▶4.54

5

Choose Image ➤ Adjustments ➤ Exposure to open the Exposure dialog box. The Exposure controls were created specifically for HDR images, although photographers often use them on non-HDR images.

Drag the Exposure slider to adjust the highlights in the image. If you slide it to the left, the image gets lighter and vice versa. You'll be amazed at the change a slight adjustment can make. In this image, the Exposure is set to 1.00.

▶4.55

6

Drag the Offset slider to set the shadows. In this image, moving the slider too far to the left blocks up the shadows completely. Moving it to the right, even a +0.0150 change opens up the shadows. Keeping the shadows open is important. After all, it is one of the objectives of HDR imaging.

▶4.56

7

Drag the Gamma slider to set midtones. If the image has too much contrast, drag the slider to the left. Keep in mind that you are working on four billion shades of gray, so slight moves make a big difference. For this image a setting of 1.06 works well.

▶4.57

8

Click one of the eyedroppers in the lower right to set the black, gray, and white points in the image. These eyedroppers work in the same way that the eyedroppers work in Photoshop's Levels and Curves dialog box. However, setting the gray point in this image also changed the Exposure, Offset, and Gamma settings slightly. You can go back and reset the settings if this happens. Click OK in the Exposure dialog box.

The image doesn't look that great yet. In fact, it looks like someone is burning the bacon in the kitchen. But by tweaking the HDR image as shown in these steps, you bring out the best of the image.

The next step is to convert it to 16-bit where you have more control in Photoshop to make additional corrections.

> ▶ Tip
>
> As you work, check the adjustments by using the Undo command. Press Ctrl/⌘+Z to see the image without the adjustments. If everything looks good, press Ctrl/⌘+Z again to change it back to use the adjustments.

►4.58

9

Choose Image ➤ Mode ➤ 16-bit/Channel. Photoshop displays the HDR Conversion dialog box. From the Method drop-down menu, choose Local Adaptation.

Here is a look at the options and reasoning for rejecting or using them:

- **Exposure and Gamma.** You already set the Exposure and Gamma in the preceding steps, so this option isn't what you want.

- **Highlight Compression.** This option compresses luminance values to fall within the range of 8- or 16-bit image files. But it doesn't make sense to use it because the point of HDR is to have the broad luminance range.

- **Equalize Histogram.** This option compresses the dynamic range of the HDR image — something you don't want either.

- **Local Adaptation.** This option calculates the amount of correction necessary for local brightness regions throughout the image and adjusts the tonality. The results are initially unattractive, but this option lets you adjust the image curve, which is why it is the most useful conversion method for photographers.

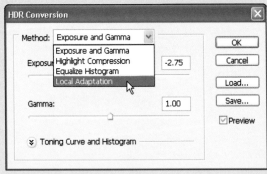

►4.59

10

Click the upward-pointing double arrow next to Toning Curve and Histogram. Photoshop displays the toning curve and histogram. Drag the shadow point on the bottom left of the histogram to where the pixels begin on the left side of the histogram. At the top right of the histogram, drag the white point to where the pixels begin on the right side of the histogram.

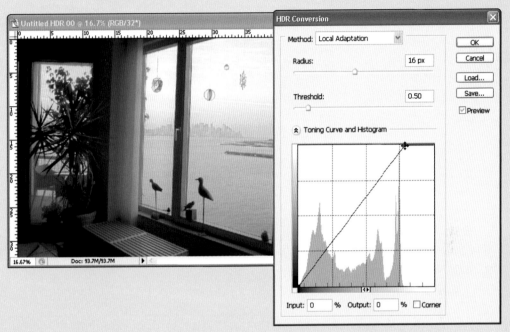

▶4.60

11

Click to set curve points on the histogram and create a slight S curve as shown in the figure. Click OK in the HDR Conversion dialog box. Photoshop converts the image and shows the progress.

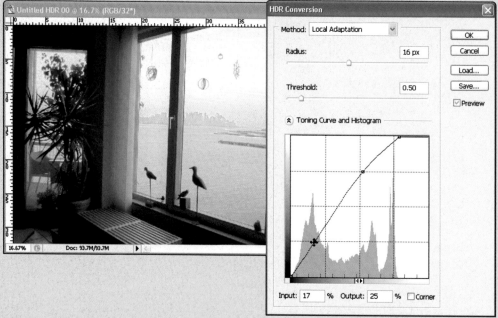

▶4.61

12

In Photoshop, you can make the adjustments you would normally make on an image. In this case, I straightened the building lines, made local adjustments to contrast, added a warming filter, and, before printing, sharpened the image.

▶4.62

Shooting HDR Images

Shooting HDR is ideal for scenes with a very broad tonal range—the type of extreme tonal range where most cameras, film or digital, would either sacrifice shadow or highlight information. With HDR images, you can keep detail in both shadows and highlights.

In fact, after I started shooting HDR and seeing what the possibilities were, it changed the way I looked at the world photographically. Until HDR, I would look at a scene and think, "why bother taking it," because I knew that the camera couldn't fully capture it. But with HDR, if I have a tripod with me, I know I can get the shot.

When you shoot images for HDR, you capture a full stop of information in every tonal range by making multiple exposures.

Here are the fundamentals of shooting HDR:

- **Use a good tripod.** You cannot shoot HDR handheld.
- **Work when the wind is still.** If the wind is moving the subject, such as tree branches or grasses, you'll get color artifacts.
- **Set the camera to RAW capture mode.**
- **Set the camera to Manual mode, or set it to full-stop auto bracketing using shutter speed to bracket exposures.** You *should not* manually change the aperture to bracket. When you change the aperture, the depth of field changes and as objects become sharper, they become ever so slightly smaller, changing the size relationship between exposures; thus the images will not merge correctly.
- **Meter the scene for the average exposure.** Then adjust the shutter speed to bracket two to three f-stops in both directions from the average exposure—for example, three stops above and three stops below average exposure for a total of seven shots. You can shoot the bracketed shots in either direction; moving up by full f-stops from the middle exposure and then moving down by full f-stops, or vice versa.

Stopping down five to seven stops enables you to capture the light source. In a way, HDR images appear odd and disconcerting because most people aren't used to seeing the actual light source, such as the sun, in the scene.

Use Smart Objects to Maintain Flexibility

Contributor: Katrin Eismann ■ **Specialty:** Artist, Author, and Educator
Primary Tool Used: Smart Objects

For photographers, Smart Objects are helpful for processing a RAW file when you need multiple versions of a single file for production or creative needs. Using Smart Objects, you can use multiple versions of a file and maintain the flexibility of Camera Raw controls. In this technique you will learn to process one image twice: once for the top part of the image, and a second time for the darker lower part of the image.

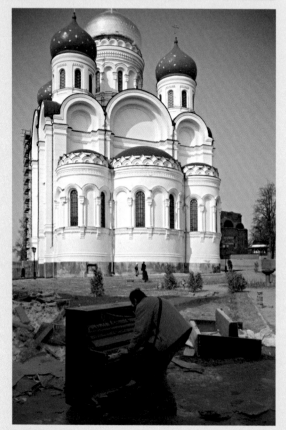

▶4.63

1

Open any image in Camera Raw. In the Show Workflow Options section, click the Size drop-down menu and note the smallest file size that your camera will produce. You will set up a Photoshop document at this size later in this technique. Also, ensure that the Depth is set to 16 Bits/Channel and that the Resolution is set to 240 pixels/inch. Click Cancel.

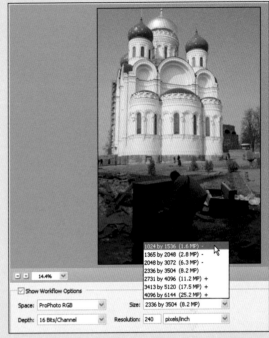

▶4.64

2

In Photoshop, choose File ➤ New. The New dialog box appears. Click the Width drop-down menu and choose pixels. In the Width box, enter the smallest width that your camera will produce, and in the Height box, enter the smallest height that your camera will produce. In this case, 1024 x 1536 is the smallest size for the Canon EOS 20D camera. Set the Resolution to 240 pixels/inch and the bit depth to 16. Click OK.

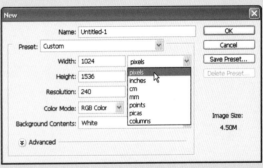

▶4.65

3

Choose File ➤ Place, and then navigate to the Camera Raw file that you want to process. Select the document, and then click Place. The selected file opens in Camera Raw.

In this example, I wanted to process the image first for the highlights while ignoring what happens in the darker areas of the photo.

In Camera Raw, Auto Adjustments work well for the top half of this image, so no adjustments are made. Your image may require adjustments, and you may prefer to work with Auto Adjustments turned off. Click Open in the Camera Raw dialog box. The image opens in Photoshop with an X over it.

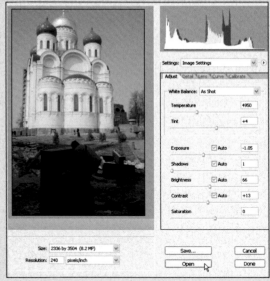

▶4.66

4

Click the Commit Transform checkmark in the Options bar to place the file, or press Enter/Return. In the Layers palette, the file looks like a regular image, but the thumbnail has an icon in the corner that signifies that it is a Smart Object.

Evaluate the image and decide what adjustments it needs. If you decide that it needs adjustments, and if any of the adjustments can be made in Camera Raw, that's where you should make them.

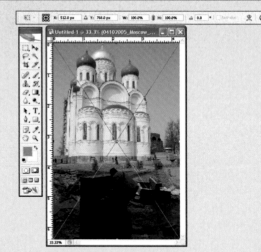

▶4.67

5

Double-click the Smart Object icon on the thumbnail image in the Layers palette. The image opens in Camera Raw.

Now you can make other adjustments to the image in Camera Raw. For this image, the tone curve is adjusted. To adjust the curve, click the Curve tab. Click the Tone Curve drop-down menu, and then choose Strong Contrast. Click Done in the Camera Raw dialog box.

As you can see, getting back to the RAW file information in Photoshop at any time is possible with Smart Objects.

For this image, the next step is to process the bottom of the image because it is too dark and too blue.

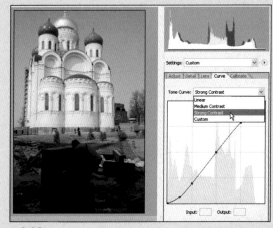

▶4.68

6

Choose Layer ➤ Smart Objects ➤ New Smart Object via Copy. Photoshop creates a new Smart Object that appears in the Layers palette.

Double-click the Smart Object icon on the thumbnail image in the new layer. The image opens in Camera Raw. This time, adjustments will enhance the bottom half of the image.

> **Note**
>
> It is very important to make the new Smart Object copy via the menu command. Do **not** duplicate the Smart Object by dragging it to the New Layer icon at the bottom of the layers palette.

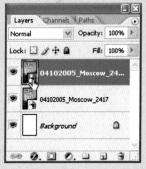

▶4.69

7

In Camera Raw, you can make adjustments for the other half of the image as necessary. In this case, the dark tones in the bottom of the image need to be opened up. Click the Curve tab, and then adjust the curve to open up the dark tones. Here, I didn't worry about what's happening to the top half of the image.

You can also go back to the Adjust tab and use the gray eyedropper to neutralize the shadows and make any other adjustments you want. Click Done in the Camera Raw dialog box. The image is updated in Photoshop.

You now have two files sitting on top of each other in Photoshop where you can make further adjustments to transition adjustments between the two versions.

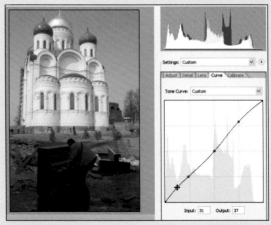

►4.70

8

If you have an image similar to this where the foreground is darker and there is a bright sky, you may want to add a Gradient layer mask. Here, I added a black-to-white gradient on a layer mask to transition from the good church on the top file to the good shadows file below. Click the Add layer mask icon at the bottom of the Layers palette. Select the Gradient tool in the Tools palette and click on the black-to-white gradient on the Options bar. Drag the Gradient tool on the layer mask to add the transition. For this image, the gradient begins under the church window and extends to the top of the man's shoulder. The gradient reveals the well-adjusted church in the first file with a gradual transition via the gradient mask to the well-adjusted pianist at the bottom of the image.

Of course, the Camera Raw commands are still available in case you want to make more adjustments. All you have to do is double-click the Smart Object icon for either of the images and it opens in Camera Raw again. For this image, a vignette around the church and more contrast on the pianist would enhance the image, and both can be done in Camera Raw by double-clicking the Smart Object icon of the layer with the upper part of the image and making the changes.

▶4.71

9

In the early steps of this technique, you set the small file dimensions. Now you can upsize the image to a larger size. Choose Image ➤ Image Size. In the Image Size dialog box, type the dimensions you want in the Width and Height boxes. For the Canon EOS 20D, the full resolution size is 3504 × 2336. Click OK.

Regardless of the size you set, the original RAW data will be accessed. Yet working with the smaller file size throughout these steps sped up the workflow and made experimenting during image processing easier.

When saving the image, make sure to choose a file format that supports layers, such as PSD or TIFF. And, verify that the Layers option is selected.

▶4.72

More Ideas for Using Smart Objects

By using Smart Objects, you can reprocess a file multiple times to get the rendering you want. In this example, the file was processed in Camera Raw once using Tungsten light to create the blues, and once more to add more saturation to the top of the image. Then the light was masked out in Photoshop.

Although you can't paint or use filters with Smart Objects in Photoshop, you can make a lot of adjustments by using Smart Objects. For example, you can use blending modes to add contrast. Just bring in a Smart Object and set the blending mode to Hard Light to bring up the contrast just a little. In short, you can do a lot. You just have to take the time to try out different options.

In addition to using Smart Objects with RAW files, Smart Objects are especially useful when you're working with

- A high-quality film scan, which upon converting to a Smart Object you can safely downsize, and continue working much more quickly on the smaller file, while maintaining the original image quality, even when you resize the image up again.

- Illustrator and Photoshop files and want to bring Illustrator files into Photoshop and maintain Illustrator editing capabilities.

- Graphical treatments where you need to substitute one element for another element and have all the element's attributes applied.

- For compositing work in which image elements will be transformed and resized many times. By converting an image or layer to a Smart Object, you can resize as needed as many times as you like, all without degrading the image information.

Perfecting Exposure

Contributor: Kevin Ames ■ **Specialty:** Fashion
Primary Tool Used: Color Sampler and Exposure

I continue to marvel at how much easier, better, and more fun digital capture makes photography. After a film shoot, photographers often used to test a clip from each roll of film. Based on these tests, the rest of the roll was chemically pushed to get more exposure or pulled for less exposure by the lab, often for another 50 percent of the processing price. The process took extra money and time, and waiting to see whether the film "came out" could be nerve wracking.

Fortunately those days are past. Now, tweaking exposures is a simple matter in Camera Raw. This technique assumes that you have a gray scale or similar card and use it in the first of a series of images that you want to correct.

▶4.73

1

In Bridge, select the image you want to open, and then press Ctrl/⌘+R to open it in Camera Raw. Camera Raw opens and displays the image.

In Camera Raw, look at the Exposure, Shadows, Brightness, and Contrast sliders. The Auto Adjustment settings are probably turned on. You can turn them off so you can see the way the file was shot originally.

►4.74

Note

This technique demonstrates exposure correction with an image that includes a GretagMacbeth ColorChecker Gray Scale or similar card. GretagMacbeth ColorChecker Gray Scale cards are available at www.gretagmacbeth.com/index.htm?. Choose the region you're in, and then click Products & Services, Color Checker Charts, and then click ColorChecker Gray Scale. You can't find a better tool to have in your kit.

2

Click the right-pointing triangle next to Settings, and then choose Use Auto Adjustments from the Settings menu to turn them off (or press Ctrl/⌘+U).

Once Auto Adjustments are off, you can make the change permanent by choosing Save New Camera Raw Defaults from the same menu.

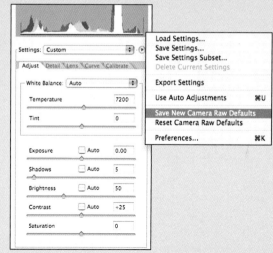

▶4.75

3

Select the Color Sampler tool or press S. Click the white area of the chart, and then click the black area. Color Samplers labeled #1 and #2 appear above the preview.

In this example, the photograph looks warm because of the late afternoon sun. Making the image neutral makes the model's skin more natural in color and deepens the blue of the sky.

▶4.76

4

Select the White Balance tool or press I. Click the white patch. The numbers for Sampler 1 now read R=245, G=245, B=245. The colors are neutral, or have the same value for Red, Green, and Blue, and the image is very slightly under-exposed. Now that the color is neutral, it's time to tweak the exposure.

▶4.77

5

Hold down the Alt/Option key and drag the Exposure slider to the right. The preview goes black. Keep dragging while watching sampler #1. In this image, as it reaches 253 you'll see some red appear around the chart. Keep dragging the slider to the right, increasing the exposure until the white patch is white (the numbers are R=255, G=255, B=255). At the same time, the color red appears in the model's cheeks and legs indicating that the red channel is clipping.

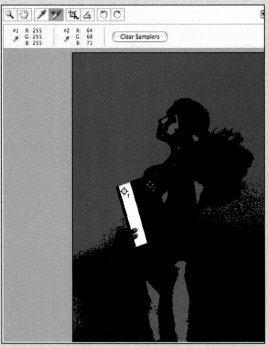

▶4.78

6

In this image's case, I dragged the slider back to the left until the channels read 253. Having some clipping in a channel is okay.

Human beings love contrast. We just love deep, rich, black shadows. Making the preview in Camera Raw sport rich blacks is truly tempting. The problem really shows up on any prints made with these high-contrast settings. The reason increasing shadow density in Camera Raw is not a good thing is that when the file goes to the printer, the shadows usually get darker. No detail at all would appear in the model's suit. The next step helps you to resist this temptation.

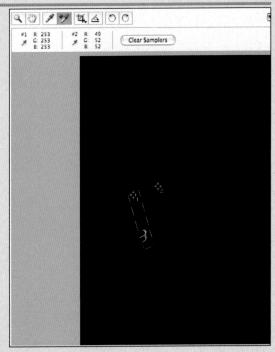

▶4.79

Exposure Adjustment by the Numbers

Exposure in digital photography is best done by the numbers. Camera Raw's tools display the RGB numbers or values above the histogram. Or you can choose the Color Sampler tool and place samplers on the ColorChecker Gray Scale card.

The #1 sampler is on the white patch and shows that the light is orange with R=255, G=242, B=224. Any time there is more red, less green, and a lot less blue, the light has an orange cast. The #2 sampler is on the black, representing the shadows and the color of the model's swimsuit. Those readings are R=51, G=44, B=27, once again an orange colorcast. The arrows show the reading for each in the Camera Raw dialog box. What do these numbers mean? Zero is black, and 255 is white. The key to good exposure is to have the highlights that you

want to hold detail to read no higher than 249. The darkest that a shadow can be and still have any detail in the shadows is 25. Generally, a good practice is to leave the Shadows setting in Camera Raw alone.

Hold down the Alt/Option key and drag the Shadows slider to the right. The preview is white. If you look at the previous image, you can see that the color sampler #2 reads in the high 40s and low 50s. As the slider moves right, the colors that appear in the display show where the channels are at a 0 value—total black. The temptation is great to continue making the shadows darker. But if the shadows are too dark to begin with, the print will have large black areas.

You can move the Shadow slider to the left until the whole preview pane is white. Remember that you can always use Levels in Photoshop to make the shadows darker if your print looks flat. But no controls exist that will do a good job of getting detail back that has been blocked up in Camera Raw. In this image, you can see detail in the model's suit. See the belt? Fashion clients really want to see the details they worked so hard to put in their designs.

Release the Alt/Option key. Click Done in Camera Raw to apply and save the changes.

▶4.80

Tip You can go back to Bridge and select all the RAW files in the series. Choose Edit ➤ Apply Camera Raw Settings ➤ Previous Conversion. Bridge applies the white balance and exposure tweaks from the most recently edited file to the rest of the RAW files.

Get the Best Quality RAW Conversion

Contributor: Eddie Tapp ▪ **Specialty:** Still Life and Portraits
Primary Tool Used: Adobe Camera Raw

Everyone has his or her own take on RAW image conversion. But there is no right and no wrong way to convert RAW files. In other words, the right take is what works for you and your workflow. If you have a good understanding of the image chrominance and luminance data, and if you keep the pixel integrity as high as possible, then you're in good shape. If not, you'll lose out somewhere, usually on the output opportunity by printing a smaller rather than a larger image.

This technique provides the basics for keeping high pixel integrity and a healthy histogram when converting RAW images.

▶4.81

1

In Camera Raw, set the Workflow Options. From the Space drop-down menu, choose ProPhoto RGB. Even if your working color space in Photoshop and for printing is Adobe RGB, setting ProPhoto RGB in Camera Raw yields all the data that files can have.

Of course, the difference between color spaces isn't visible on a typical computer monitor because monitors display a smaller range of colors—on the order of the sRGB gamut. But using ProPhoto RGB, you get a much smoother transition when you make color and tonal adjustments because more color data is available.

And while the ProPhoto RGB color gamut is beyond the capability of output devices, maintaining as much data in the file as possible while you're working is important. You can convert the color space for specific output devices or display after you complete the final edits in Photoshop.

►4.82

From the Depth drop-down menu, choose 16 Bits/Channel. The high bit-depth, like a wide color gamut, ensures that the files are as data rich as possible and will stand up well to adjustments in Camera Raw as well as later in Photoshop.

Type 240 pixels/inch for Resolution if your workflow includes inkjet output devices. If your images are intended for commercial printing or stock submission, you can type 300 pixels/inch.

The adjustments in this step set up Camera Raw to provide the greatest amount of data in the RAW file. The greater the amount of data, the more latitude you have in making color and tonal adjustments to the image, and the better the conversion.

2

Press Ctrl/⌘+U to turn off Auto Adjustments, and then study the histogram at the top right of the Camera Raw dialog box. For this image, the histogram shows underexposure with some clipping in the shadow areas. But given the highlights on the model, a few adjustments can correct the shadow areas without clipping highlights.

For a quick check for tonal clipping, you can turn on the Shadows and Highlights previews, although the next steps provide a more accurate way to view clipping in shadows and highlights.

▶4.83

3

Drag the Temperature slider to adjust the white balance. For this image, a warmer temperature emphasizes dramatic colors of the sky. Adjusting the Tint to a warmer setting completes the white balance adjustments. The changes are reflected in the histogram.

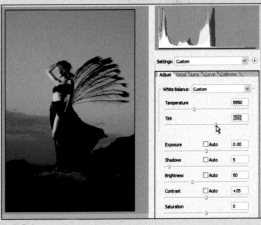

▶4.84

4

Hold down the Alt/Option key as you drag the Exposure slider. Camera Raw shows any highlight clipping as white or color areas against a black background. This image needs no Exposure adjustment.

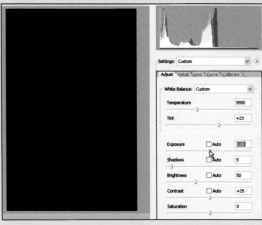

▶4.85

5

Hold down the Alt/Option key as you drag the Shadows slider. In this image, dragging the slider to the far left minimizes shadow clipping and redistributes the tonal range in the image.

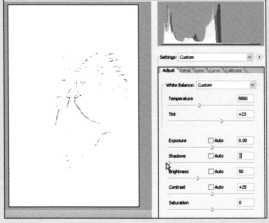

▶4.86

6

Drag the Brightness slider to generate the midtone brightness regions. Drag the Contrast slider to create a stronger or weaker contrast. This image needs no adjustments for Brightness or Contrast.

As you make these adjustments in Camera Raw, you are still working with original pixel data. However, Photoshop adjustments made using the Image ➤ Adjustments ➤ Brightness and Contrast commands are destructive edits, and pixels that are discarded from these edits cannot be retrieved. In Camera Raw conversion, the most important goal is to maintain a healthy histogram.

▶4.87

7

Drag the Saturation slider to the right to increase saturation or to the left to decrease it.

There is no right way or wrong way to do any of the adjustments aside from the mandate to maintain as much pixel integrity as possible during the conversion.

Note

You may like increased saturation as shown in the adjustments made to this image. I sometimes like my images to be more saturated than when I photographed them, and in those cases, I love the Saturation control in Camera Raw.

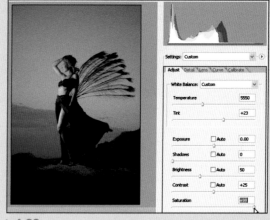

▶4.88

8

Click the Lens tab, and drag the Amount slider in the Vignetting section to the setting you want. Then drag the Midpoint to set the amount of vignetting. For this image an amount of –42 and a midpoint of 7 created a soft vignette.

▶4.89

Get Precise Tonal Control with Curves

Contributor: John Paul Caponigro   ■   **Specialty:** Fine Art
Primary Tool Used: Curves tab

To set midtone contrast, you can use a tool that gives you precise control over it—the curve. Like the histogram, a curve graphs the tones within an image, and it plots change. What differentiates the curve interface from the histogram is that in addition to the three points of control—the black point, midtone, and white point—the curve allows you to place many more points that allow you to control the tonal structure of an image.

With the curve you can place and move additional points, modifying contrast without clipping. The curve is ideal for fine-tuning midtone contrast.

▶4.90

1

In Camera Raw, set the Exposure and Shadows on the Adjust tab. Click the Curve tab to refine midtone contrast. In this image, the goal of creating a custom curve is to accentuate contrast between shadows and highlights across the snow-covered cliff face. As the highlights want to be very full in this image, no true white point has been set. Breaking the rules is fine. What matters is that you do so for a reason.

The Curves panel in Camera Raw includes a histogram in its interface. While useful for monitoring potential problems such as clipping, gapping, and spiking, use the appearance of the image rather than the histogram to evaluate the corrections you make.

The curve displays black at the bottom left and white at the top right. Like the histogram, a curve graphs the tones within an image on an XY axis where every point has an input (starting) and output (final) value. Although moving the black and white points on the curve often increases contrast, you typically need to stop before an optimum midtone contrast is achieved to avoid clipping shadow or highlight detail.

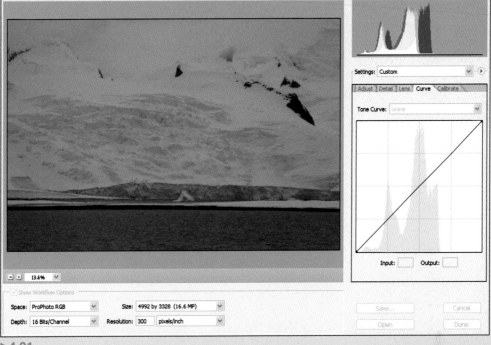

▶4.91

To place a point, click on the graph as shown in the figure. To remove a point, highlight it and drag it out of the window or press the Delete key. Pressing Ctrl/⌘+Tab activates the next highest point on the curve; you can use this shortcut to move to a specific point without causing the point to move.

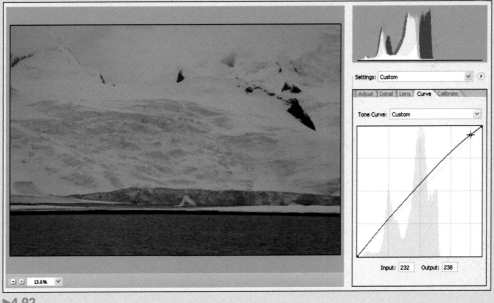

▶4.92

3

If you hold the Ctrl/⌘ key and move the cursor into the image, a hollow circle appears on the curve indicating where the tone that you are sampling lies on it. If you click while holding the Ctrl/⌘ key, a point is placed on the curve. This method allows you to precisely target the tones in a specific area of the image. In this image, midtone contrast was dramatically accentuated—specifically, in the region between the two points sampled from shadows and highlights across the cliff face.

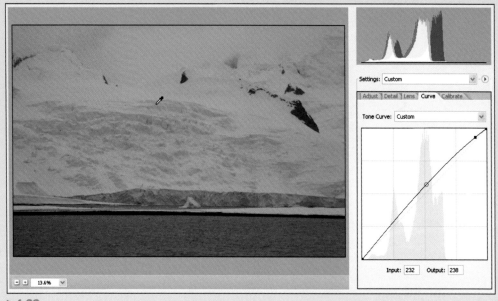

▶4.93

4

When you adjust the curve of an image, you can increase the contrast by brightening the highlights and darkening the shadows. To move a point on the curve, you can drag the point:

- Up to lighten
- Down to darken
- Left to increase the contrast below and decrease contrast above in a curve with multiple points

> ▶ **Note** If you want to undo the last move you made, press Ctrl/⌘+Z. Ctrl/⌘+Alt/Option+Z cycles back through the History states allowing multiple levels of Undo.

- Right to increase contrast above and decrease contrast below in a curve with multiple points

You can use the arrow keys to move points in fine increments. You can also move a point by entering in a new value in the Output field.

If you want to start over, select a curve from the Tone Curve drop-down menu:

- Linear, a straight line with no change
- Medium Contrast, which targets shadows a bit more than highlights
- Strong Contrast, which is a slightly more aggressive setting of Medium Contrast

I recommend that instead of using a default curve, you build a custom curve designed specifically for an individual image.

►4.94

Tip

►

Here's a strategy for using the curve. Because the eye is drawn to contrast, decide where you want to direct the viewer's attention. Next, determine what tones comprise that area. Then, add contrast in that portion of the curve. Finally, add additional points to compensate for any adverse effects above and below that region.

SB Sidebar

Working with Curves

As you work with the curve, you'll notice that moving one point affects all other points of a curve. If you don't want this to happen, avoid this problem in one of two ways: Place a point on a portion of the curve you don't want to move before you move another point; or, after you move a point, return to an area you don't want to move, place a point there, and return it to its original position (or near its original position). This method is called locking down a portion of the curve.

The curve is an extremely powerful and precise tool. Here are a few guidelines to help you make the most of it:

- Sliding the black point to the right or the white point to the left may cause clipping.
- Raising the black point makes black gray.
- Lowering the white point makes white gray.
- If a portion of a curve becomes flat all the values in that range of the tonal structure become the same tone. Your image will lose separation and saturation.
- If a point to the left gets raised above a point to the right the image will solarize, or reverse some of the tones.
- Too many points make for an unruly curve. Try to use as few points as possible and keep curves liquid smooth for a continuous tone look and feel.

Perfecting Image Color and Detail

Chapter 05

In this chapter

Basic Color Correction

Contributor: Eddie Tapp ■ **Specialty:** Still Life and Portraits
Primary Tool Used: Temperature and Tint

One of the best ways to control color during a shoot is to set a custom white balance in the camera. Almost all digital SLR cameras allow you to set a custom white balance. Check the manual for details on how to set it. Setting a custom white balance using the ExpoDisc white-balance filter or a white or gray card establishes the white balance as the source in the camera. After you've centered the chrominance and luminance data in the camera, your workflow is much easier and more consistent than it is when you don't use a custom white balance.

This technique demonstrates basic color correction on images shot using a custom white balance.

▶5.1

1

In Bridge, select the series of images shot using a custom white balance. Choose File ➤ Open in Camera Raw. Camera Raw opens in Filmstrip view with the first image selected. Turn off Auto Adjustments by clicking the right-pointing triangle next to Settings and choosing Use Auto Adjustments, or by pressing Ctrl⌘+U.

X-Ref For more details on using the Synchronize tool, see Chapter 4.

Generally the images shot using a custom white balance are right where you want them to be in terms of color. But if they are off, they will all be equally off and you can correct them at the same time using the Synchronize tool in Camera Raw.

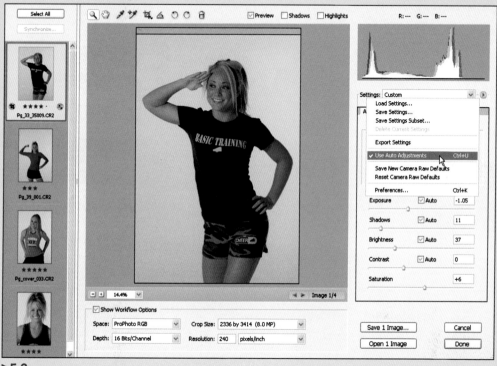

▶5.2

2

In the Show Workflow Options section, choose ProPhoto RGB from the Space drop-down menu. ProPhoto RGB yields all the data the file can possible have, and the wider color gamut makes for much better transitions as you make adjustments than smaller color spaces.

Although no current output device accepts the ProPhoto RGB color gamut, maintaining as much data in the file as possible while you're working on it gives you more leeway in making adjustments. Before printing to an inkjet printer or sending the image to a lab, you can convert the image in Photoshop to Adobe RGB.

▶5.3

3

From the Depth drop-down menu, choose 16 Bits/Channel. In the Resolution field, type **240** and select pixels/inch if you print to an inkjet printer or type **300** and select pixels/inch if the images are destined for commercial printing.

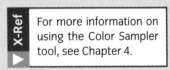

▶5.4

4

If the image color is off, drag the Temperature slider to the left for a cooler (more blue) temperature or to the right for a warmer (more yellow) temperature. For this image, I didn't pay much attention to what the temperature slider indicated; rather, I moved the slider until I liked the results. Usually, changing the tint isn't necessary, although you can adjust it slightly if needed.

X-Ref For more information on using the Color Sampler tool, see Chapter 4.

For critical work, you can use the Color Sampler tool to determine whether color casts are in the image and then neutralize them.

Every image that you shoot is different and adjusting the Temperature can improve the color, or you can use it to give a different feel to the image. A photo's color temperature doesn't have to be perfect all the time. You may want the image to be warmer or cooler depending on your intended use for the image.

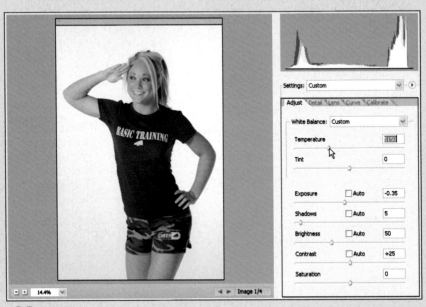

▶5.5

5

Adjust the highlight and shadow regions of the image using the Exposure and Shadows controls. For this image, the Exposure is set to –0.20 change and the Shadows control is set to 0 from the default of 5.

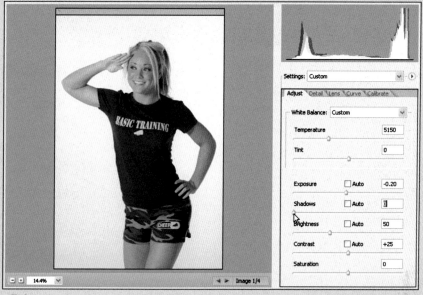

►5.6

6

Drag the Brightness slider to increase the midtone brightness. Then drag the Contrast slider to the right to create stronger contrast or to the left to create weaker contrast. In this image, the Brightness setting is left at 50 and the Contrast is fine at +25.

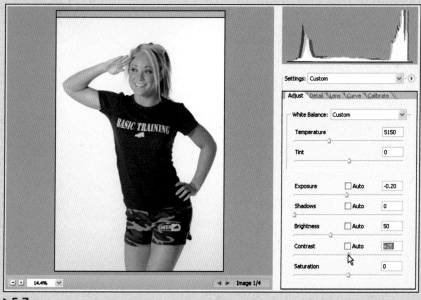

►5.7

7

Drag the Saturation slider to the right to increase saturation or to the left to decrease it. Most images can use a small amount of saturation, such as +5, which is used here.

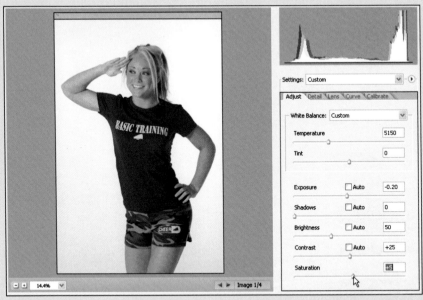

▶5.8

8

With the color and tonal adjustments complete, click Select All. Camera Raw selects all the open images displayed in the filmstrip. Because multiple images with multiple settings are selected, the Adjust panel settings are temporarily blank.

If you want to select only some of the images, press Ctrl/⌘ as you click to select each image.

►5.9

9

Click Synchronize. Camera Raw displays the Synchronize dialog box. Select or deselect options until only those that you want to apply to the images are checked, and then click OK. Camera Raw applies the selected settings to the selected images.

You can check each image to see whether localized adjustments are needed, and if additional adjustments are needed, you can make them now. For example, the last image in the filmstrip shown here required a slight decrease in the Exposure setting to –0.50; making the tweak after the settings are synchronized is easy enough.

Save the adjusted images using one of the available options in the lower right-hand corner of the screen. If you do not like the changes that have been applied, click Cancel or press and hold Alt/Option to change the button to Reset.

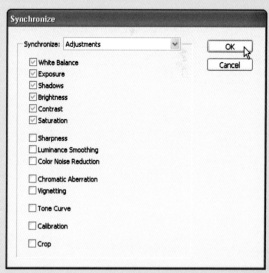

►5.10

Shoot Tethered

Contributor: Kevin Ames ■ **Specialty:** Fashion
Primary Tool Used: Temperature

In the earlier days of digital photography, photographers would "go ape," so to speak, shooting images and checking the results on the camera's LCD. When they loved what they saw, they jumped up and down shouting, "Oh! Oh!" The dance became known as "chimping." But the hottest and coolest way to get maximum feedback on your images is to shoot *tethered*—shooting your images directly into your computer, which is what this technique shows you how to do.

The beauty of tethered shooting is that you have a lot more storage, and you see the photographs as they pop up in Bridge. Plus you can fine-tune the exposure and white balance in Camera Raw.

▶5.11

1

Create a capture folder on your computer's desktop. Set up the capture software according to the manufacturer's instructions. Browse in the capture software to the capture folder and select it.

Note that software written by the camera manufacturers often allows you to set the shutter speed, ISO, and aperture of the camera from the computer such as the example shown in this figure. Some even allow you to control the camera's shutter release from the computer as well.

►5.12

2

In Photoshop, click the Go to Bridge icon on the Options bar. In Bridge, select the same capture folder you created in the previous step from the Folders pane in Bridge. Click the Thumbnails View icon at the bottom of the Bridge window or choose View ➤ As Thumbnails.

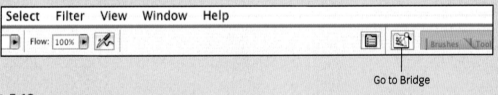

Go to Bridge

►5.13

3

Start by shooting a reference, such as the GretagMacbeth ColorChecker Gray Scale card (www.gretagmacbeth.com). The image thumbnail appears in Bridge. Click the thumbnail, and then press Ctrl/⌘+R to open the file in Camera Raw. In Camera Raw, choose the 100% zoom level to check the focus by viewing the actual pixels.

Adjust the Temperature, Exposure, Brightness, Contrast, and Saturation to your liking.

▶5.14

4

To make these adjustments the default setting for the rest of the shoot, click the right-pointing arrow next to the Settings menu, and then choose Save New Camera Raw Defaults.

Now all the settings will be applied to your photographs as they are captured—saving you a huge amount of time. When you save the new defaults, the settings will be applied to future images. If you don't want to apply them to future shoots, choose Reset Camera Raw Defaults from the Settings menu after you finish the shoot.

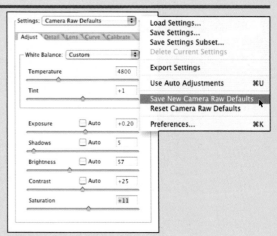

▶5.15

> **Tip** ▶ By default, Bridge displays the lowest image file number first, as numbered by the camera, and then populates the screen with the higher numbers. Scroll down to view the latest image. To display the most recent image first, choose View ➤ Sort and clear the Ascending Order box. Bridge now displays the most recent photograph in the upper-left hand corner of the preview pane.

Shooting Tethered

SB Sidebar

In the studio, I always shoot tethered. The computer is on a rolling cart with a large monitor so I can check images as I shoot. Art directors and clients love seeing the images appear as they are shot. They know when the shoot is over that they have exactly the image they want.

Tethering works with a laptop on location, too (see image). Shooting landscapes or building exteriors is an exercise in patience waiting for the light to get "just right." The feedback on the laptop ensures that the photograph is exposed properly with the right white balance. And if the capture software allows you to control the camera, then the laptop also becomes a remote release.

Below is the final shot of the Idaho State Capitol Building I made recently. Tethered shooting takes the worry out of any photographic project.

Now you know tethering can be done, how cool (and hot) it really is, and how to set up Bridge and Camera Raw to take advantage of it. So dig into the box your dSLR came in and find the disc of tethering software, load it onto the computer, and get into the world of maximum photographic feedback.

Add Some Punch to RAW Images

Contributor: Bob Coates ■ **Specialty:** Wedding
Primary Tool Used: Smart Objects

Within every image there exist multiple interpretations. Often the interpretations reflect the style biases of the photographer and/or the prevailing trends of the photographic specialty and its clients. In wedding photography and portraiture, stylistic interpretations can set photographers apart from the competition. Interpretations may be applied with a light or heavy hand—it's up to the photographer.

In this technique, you see how increasing the image contrast and color helps emphasize the idyllic venue while using a mask provides gentle lightening to set off the couple within the scene.

▶5.16

1

Open the image that you want to work on in Camera Raw. In the Show Workflow Options section, note the file size. Be sure that the Depth is set to 16 Bits/Channel and that the Resolution is set to 240 or 300 pixels/inch. Click Cancel.

►5.17

2

In Photoshop, choose File ➤ New to open the New dialog box. In the Width box, type the width in pixels that you noted in Step 1. From the Width drop-down menu choose pixels. In the Height box, type the height. For this image the file's size is set to 2024 × 3024 pixels, the Resolution is set to 300 pixels/inch, and the bit depth to 16. Click OK.

►5.18

3

Choose File ➤ Place to open the Place dialog box, and then navigate to the Camera Raw file that you want to process. Select the document, and then click Place. The selected file opens in Camera Raw.

This image needs to have more contrast, but retain the initial processing of the couple's clothing and skin tones.

►5.19

4

In Camera Raw, make the adjustments you want for the base interpretation of the image. Click Open in the Camera Raw dialog box. Photoshop displays the image with an X over it.

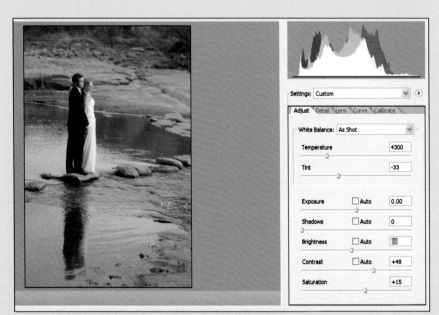

►5.20

5

Click the check mark icon in the Options bar to place the file, or press Enter/Return. In the Layers palette, the file looks like a regular image, but it has an icon in the corner that signifies that it is a Smart Object. A Smart Object in Photoshop serves as a container in which another file, in this case, a RAW file, is embedded. The embedded file is still editable in Camera Raw, providing flexibility to revisit the RAW file to make changes later.

For this image, the next step is to punch up the contrast in the scene to make it more dramatic.

►5.21

6

Choose Layer ➤ Smart Objects ➤ New Smart Object via Copy. Photoshop creates a new Smart Object as shown in the Layers palette.

Double-click the Smart Object icon in the new layer. The image opens in Camera Raw.

►5.22

7

For this image, adjustments include decreasing the Exposure slightly, and increasing the Shadows, Brightness, Contrast, and Saturation settings to add punch to the landscape areas. Click Done once you've made all your adjustments.

Of course, the settings also changed the clothing and skin tones, but a mask can restore the original settings as shown in a later step.

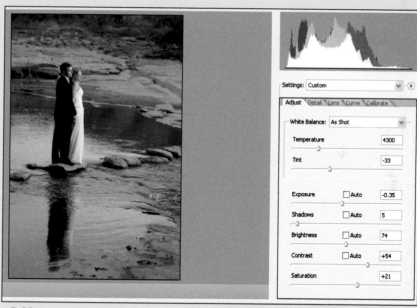

►5.23

153

8

Click the Add Layer Mask icon at the bottom of the Layers palette.

►5.24

9

Choose the Gradient tool in the Toolbox, and then click the black-to-white gradient in the Options bar.

►5.25

Click the diamond gradient on the Options bar. Click and drag in the image to set the mask. In this image the mask is large enough to mask the couple and a small area surrounding them.

The effect reveals the original processing in the first image for the couples' skin tones and clothes and provides a transition between the two.

On the Options bar, you can click the right-pointing arrow next to Opacity and drag the slider to adjust the strength of the transition. In this case a 68 percent Opacity setting softens the effect.

As long as you save the image in a format that supports layers, you can return to both files and make adjustments in Camera Raw. Alternatively, you can save a copy of the image, flatten the layers, and make further adjustments using Photoshop tools.

▶5.26

Balance Color Without Losing Ambiance

Contributor: Bob Coates ■ **Specialty:** Wedding
Primary Tool Used: Temperature

In many scenes, the color of ambient light lends a special mood to images that you want to maintain. In this image, slight adjustments to the color Temperature and Tint in Camera Raw preserved and improved on the warmth of the light. I double-processed the image shown here, once for the exposure on the subject, and a second time to bring back detail in the window and curtain. After merging the two images, I added noise in Photoshop to enhance the timeless quality of the image.

This image and technique is a great example of how Camera Raw can save an underexposed image.

►5.27

1

Open the image you want to process in Camera Raw. Turn off Auto Adjustments by clicking the right-pointing triangle to the right of Settings and choosing Use Auto Adjustments, or by pressing Ctrl/⌘+U.

►5.28

2

In this example, the image is underexposed in order to hold some detail in the window and curtain area. To correct the exposure in an image like this one, drag the Exposure slider right. A setting of +0.75 for this image exposes the subject nicely. The increased exposure blows out the detail in the

X-Ref For more on double-processing RAW images, see Chapter 6.

curtains to the subject's left, but you can add detail by processing the file a second time for these highlights, and then merging the second version with this version in Photoshop.

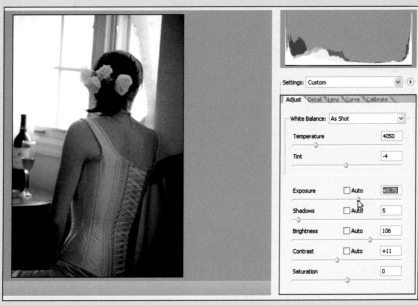
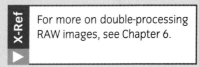

►5.29

3

The natural light in this image has inviting warmth that enhances the subject. But the as-shot color balance could be warmed slightly more. Dragging the Temperature slider to the right increases the color temperature. In this case, I adjusted the Temperature from 4050 to 4350.

►5.30

4

A slight green tint remains. To correct the tint, drag the Tint slider to the right to add magenta or to the left to add green. I increased the Tint in this image from −4 to +22.

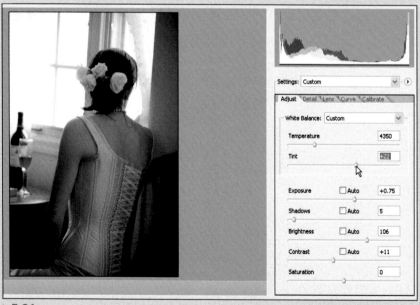

►5.31

5

Click the Lens tab. In the Vignetting section, drag the Amount slider to the left to create a soft vignette, and then drag the Midpoint slider to set the size of the vignette. For this image, an Amount setting of −56 and a Midpoint setting of 37 work well.

►5.32

6

Click Save. In the Save Options dialog box, type a name for the file and set the format to what you want. Because you will process this image again to regain highlight details, type a name that includes a short description of the processing to help distinguish it from the second processed file.

For example, you might name this file BrideWaitingBase and the second processed file as BrideWaitingHighlights. This helps you identify the files when you select the files to combine them in Photoshop later. When merging the two images together drag one image on top of the other while holding the Shift key to ensure perfect registration. Then add a mask to hide and reveal pieces of the image.

►5.33

X-Ref

For more information on compositing images, see Chapter 6.

More on Color Temperature

You can adjust the Temperature setting in Camera Raw to correct an image to the color temperature of the scene, or you can use it to create a radical reinterpretation of the scene. In practice, you can consider adjusting the overall scene color as a creative tool to either slightly or significantly modify the image.

For example, in this slightly tinted rendering, I adjusted the Temperature and Tint to 6050 and +15, respectively, and lowered the Saturation to –55. Of course, you can make further adjustments in Photoshop.

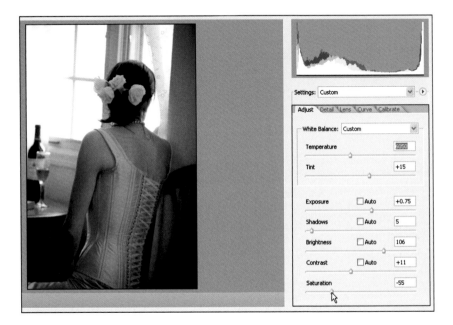

Camera Raw provides another set of tools that photographers can use to creatively enhance and stylize images.

Tame Color Noise and Preserve Detail

Contributor: Charlotte Lowrie ■ **Specialty:** Editorial and Stock
Primary Tool Used: Luminance Smoothing and Color Noise Reduction

In digital photography, two kinds of noise exist: Chroma, or color noise, that appears as unattractive color flecks and striations particularly in shadow areas of an image; and luminance, or grayscale noise, that resembles traditional film grain and appears in continuous tone areas such as the sky. Both types of noise degrade image quality. And noise can become obnoxious when images are sharpened for printing.

In this technique, you use both Luminance Smoothing for grayscale noise and Color Noise Reduction to counter chroma noise.

►5.34

1

Open the image that you want to process in Camera Raw. Adjust the controls on the Adjust tab the way you want them. In this image the adjustments include a Shadows setting of 0. Although this setting opens up the shadows and minimizes clipping, it also exposes noise that almost certainly lurks in the shadow areas.

Tip

To avoid losing detail and softening images, use a light hand with Luminance Smoothing and Color Noise Reduction controls for the best results.

In addition, I chose a Saturation setting of +7. Although this adjustment is moderate, increases in saturation exacerbate noise.

▶5.35

2

Click the Detail tab. To determine what noise reduction setting is correct, begin by dragging the Color Noise Reduction slider to 0. Select the Zoom tool and zoom to 100 or 200 percent. Select the Hand tool and move to a shadow area of the image.

Note

For this image, I increased the Exposure from the first illustration to better show the noise.

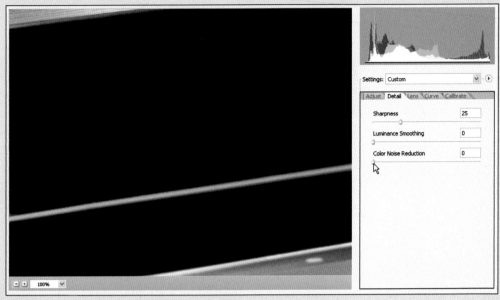

▶5.36

Drag the Color Noise Reduction slider to the right while watching the effect on the noise. Move the slider in small increments and release the mouse button after each move so that Camera Raw can update the preview. For this image, a setting of 5 is an acceptable reduction in chroma noise.

To check the difference, select the Preview option at the top of the image pane. Turn the Preview on and off to compare the before and after adjustments. Also move to other areas of the image to see what effect the setting has elsewhere.

The default Color Noise Reduction setting in Camera Raw is 25, a setting that you may find is consistently more than you need. The downside of accepting the default setting is the potential loss of fine detail in color areas. Evaluating images individually and using the lowest setting you can to mask color noise is best.

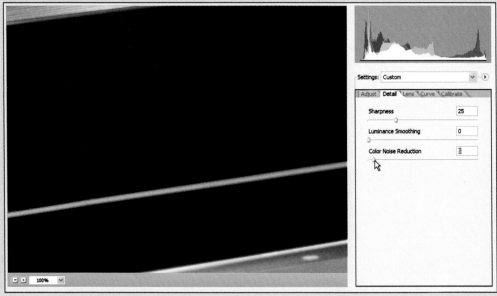

▶5.37

4

Luminance Smoothing is the adjustment that deserves judicious use and an especially light hand because it, more than Color Noise Reduction, can overly soften the image.

To illustrate how Luminance Smoothing softens detail, the left image has a Luminance Smoothing set to 0. Compare it to the second figure, which has a Luminance Smoothing setting of only 5—edge detail begins to blur and the image begins to soften overall.

▶5.38

5

Alternately, you can use exposure and tonal controls to help mask some color noise, thereby allowing you to set even lower Luminance Smoothing and Color Noise Reduction settings. Click the Curve tab. From the Tone Curve drop-down menu, select Linear.

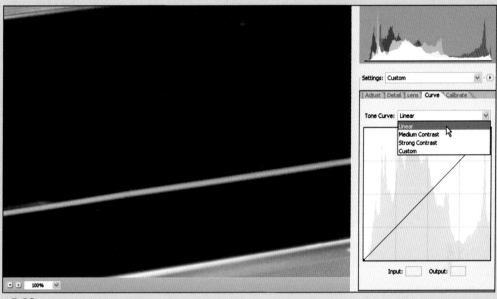

▶5.39

6

Click the line to set a highlight point, and then click the lower quadrant to set two shadow points. The deeper shadow adjustment helps mask some of the color noise.

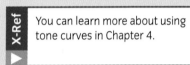

You can learn more about using tone curves in Chapter 4.

Now is a good time to zoom out and evaluate the entire image. You may need to set additional points on the curve to brighten or subdue other areas of the image.

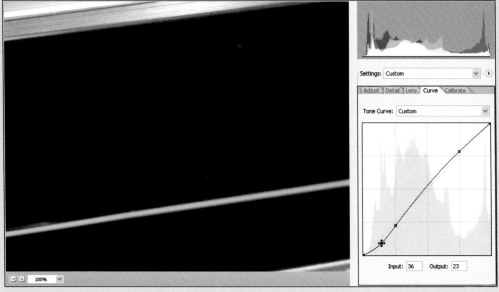

►5.40

7

Click the Detail tab. Drag the Color Noise Reduction slider until the color noise is effectively masked. By using the curve, a setting of 3, rather than the previous 5, provides adequate noise reduction. In addition, a lower Luminance Smoothing setting (in this case, 5) smoothes out the continuous tones nicely with much less impact on the overall crispness of the image.

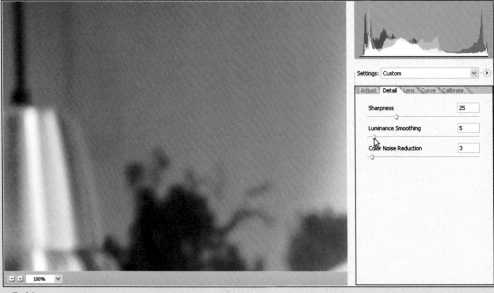

►5.41

Tame Noise in the Camera

The best way to reduce noise is in the camera—by avoiding situations that inevitably increase noise in digital images. Here are a few tips on taming noise as you shoot:

- **Avoid underexposure.** Although underexposed images may look richer on the camera's LCD, they are inevitably a headache to process. During processing, the relatively few tones devoted to shadows in the digital capture will be stretched to redistribute the tonal range during processing—a process that only emphasizes noise lurking in shadow areas.

- **Keep the exposure time short.** Long exposures also tend to increase the incidence of noise in digital images. In some cases, making the trade-off between ISO and shutter speed may be difficult, but doing a series of test shots to determine which delivers the highest quality image—one at a higher ISO, or one at a slower shutter speed—is worth it.

- **Determine your tolerance for noise and your camera's maximum ISO setting that reaches it.** Digital SLR cameras are not all created equal, and some handle noise with more aplomb than others. Take test images at different ISO settings in various venues. Then study the images at high magnification in Camera Raw to see what your personal tolerance is for noise and at what ISO setting your camera reaches it. Then do your best to shoot within your tolerance limit.

In addition to using the control in Camera Raw, you should definitely check out the noise reduction features in Photoshop CS2 (choose Filter ➤ Noise ➤ Reduce Noise). Photoshop CS2 offers controls to Preserve Details and Sharpen Details.

You can also consider other noise reduction programs, including Noise Ninja from PictureCode (www.picturecode.com) and Nik Sharpener Pro from Nik Software, Inc. (www.niksoftware.com).

Correct Lens Aberration

Contributor: Rob Sheppard ▪ **Specialty:** Nature and Editorial
Primary Tool Used: Chromatic Aberration

I have a full-frame fisheye lens that gives me wonderful effects with my advanced compact digital camera. These little cameras offer all the controls of a digital SLR (including RAW files) in a very portable package, along with the outstanding live and rotating LCD. Such an LCD offers photographic possibilities that a digital SLR can't match.

But one problem is that this lens attaches over the original camera's non-removable zoom lens. It is not made by the camera manufacturer and has very definite optical aberrations, especially along the edges. Camera Raw includes superb chromatic aberration tools for fixing such optical problems.

▶5.42

1

Not all photos need lens correction adjustments. Once you open a photo for editing in Camera Raw, the only way to tell what your photo needs is to greatly enlarge it and check the outer parts of the image. If the edge at contrasting tonalities shows colors that don't belong there, then some lens correction can help. Such edges should be clean, without the added colors shown in this image. Once you find a photo with these kinds of contrasting tonalities, you know that it needs lens correction adjustments to look its best.

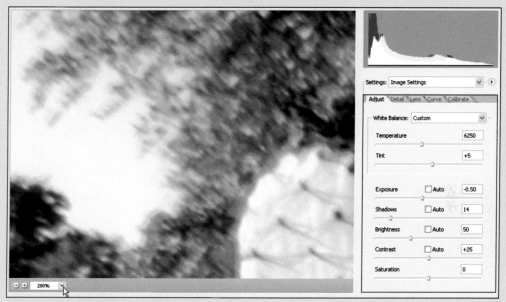

▶5.43

SB Sidebar

Optical Defects

Chromatic aberration is a color defect due to colors not focusing consistently at the focal plane of the camera (the position of the sensor or film). What happens is that most colors focus properly, but some wavelengths in the color spectrum go through the lens differently, and end up focusing on some phantom point in front of or behind the sensor. This faulty focusing shows up as color fringing along contrasted elements of the photo, most noticeably in the outside edges of the composition.

Photoshop CS2 also has lens aberration correction in Filters. However, making corrections in Camera Raw lets you adjust the photo at a point where it has less-processed data, including having color information closer to the data actually captured by the sensor. This means that potentially you can correct color aberrations more accurately than when correcting a file that is already a completed, full-color image (as is anything that goes into Photoshop).

2

Click the Lens tab and notice the two color correction sliders: Fix Red/Cyan Fringe and Fix Blue/Yellow Fringe. Not all fringe colors will be as obvious as in this example, but you have nothing to lose by just trying the sliders and seeing whether fringe colors improve. In this image, the red fringe is very strong, with some blue fringe as well. Setting the Fix Red/Cyan Fringe slider to its left maximum has a big effect. The Fix Blue/Yellow Slider in this case actually weakens the contrast in the image if set all the way to its maximum, though some adjustment helps.

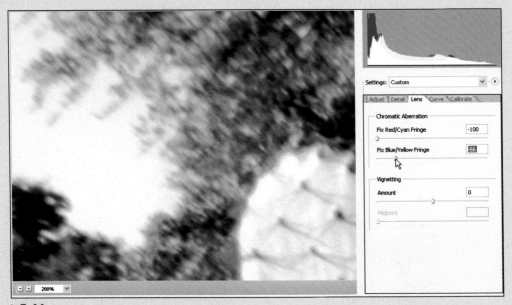

▶5.44

3

Move the photo around to see edges in other parts of the photo by holding the space bar down to turn the cursor into a hand, and then clicking and dragging the preview around. Depending on the photo, you may need to tweak the Fix Red/Cyan Fringe and Fix Blue/Yellow Fringe sliders so that the picture has the right correction for the whole image. Sometimes a specific area's own colors and contrasts can influence your overall adjustments.

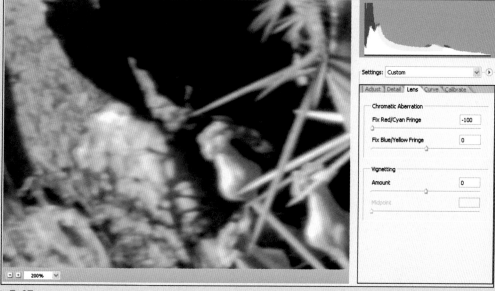

►5.45

4

If you find that the corners are a little dark when the preview returns to full image size, this could be caused by optical vignetting. The Lens tab has a Vignetting section just for this problem. Try moving the Amount slider to the right to reduce the corner darkness. For most photos, leave the Midpoint at 50 (the middle of the photo).

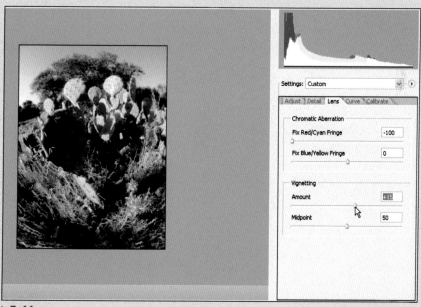

►5.46

Sharpen Images or Not

Contributors: John Paul Caponigro and Charlotte Lowrie ■ **Specialty:** Editorial and Stock
Primary Tool Used: Sharpness setting

For many subjects, nothing is quite as satisfying as a sharp image. But your out-of-camera images may be less than perfectly sharp. In addition to the in-camera sharpening options, you can also sharpen images in Camera Raw—either the preview image only, or both the preview and the converted image. But should you sharpen now or wait, as many photographers do, to sharpen in Photoshop after images are sized for their specific use?

The benefits to sharpening in Camera Raw are negligible except for saving time in the workflow. However, as this technique demonstrates, sharpening the preview may offer a better look at the image contrast you ultimately get in Photoshop.

▶5.47

1

Open the image you want to convert and sharpen in Camera Raw. Click the Detail tab.

Camera Raw's default adjustment is 25. You can select and deselect the Preview option to see the difference with

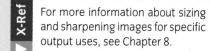

X-Ref For more information about sizing and sharpening images for specific output uses, see Chapter 8.

and without the sharpening. But in general, you should decide whether you want sharpening applied to only the preview image or to the converted image. You can set the option you want in the Camera Raw Preferences dialog box.

The advantage of sharpening the converted image in Camera Raw is that you can get an acceptably good image for display to clients quickly. But you also run the risk of introducing oversharpening later in the process if you resize the image and resharpen it in Photoshop during the last phase of the workflow.

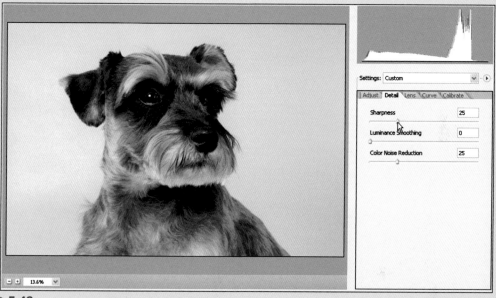

▶5.48

Click the right-pointing triangle next to Settings, and then select Preferences from the drop-down menu that appears.

You can access Camera Raw Preferences in Camera Raw and in Bridge. Regardless of how you access Preferences, be sure that you've set the options the way you want.

In the Camera Raw Preferences dialog box, select the Apply sharpening to drop-down menu, and then select the option you want. If you choose All images, Camera Raw sharpens the preview image and the converted image. If you choose Preview images only, then the converted image will not be sharpened, but the sharper preview does give you a general idea of how the image will ultimately appear after sharpening in Photoshop.

►5.49

Photoshop's Sharpening Tools

There are significant differences between Camera Raw's sharpening setting which provides only limited control and the sharpening tools in Photoshop. In Camera Raw, the sharpening control offers control over the strength of the sharpening only. As with most adjustments, the more control you have, the better the results. Sharpening depends not only on the image characteristics such as shadow noise, but also on the output — so having more control — in Photoshop — is the better choice in most cases.

By contrast, Photoshop offers a variety of options for sharpening, including Smart Sharpen and the familiar Unsharp Mask. Both tools allow you to control the Amount and Radius, and Unsharp Mask allows you to set the Threshold. Smart Sharpen gives you control over shadow sharpening, which is particularly important if discernable noise is in the shadow areas that you don't want to emphasize with sharpening.

3

Click OK. Camera Raw uses the setting you choose on the current and future images. In addition, Camera Raw adds a notation (Preview Only) next to the Sharpness control on the Detail tab to remind you of your choice.

Drag the Sharpness slider to the right to increase the sharpness or to the left to decrease it.

You can also turn the Preview on and off to check the differences as you make adjustments. In some cases, you'll notice a slight difference in image contrast.

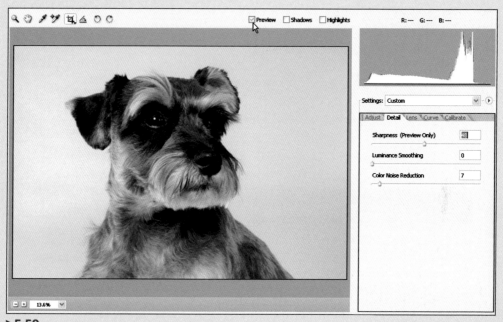

▶5.50

4

Now is a good time to zoom in on shadow areas and check for noise, especially if you chose to sharpen the final image. Click the Zoom tool and enlarge the image to 100 percent. Click the Hand tool, or press H, and move to a shadow area to evaluate color noise. You can reduce the noise using the Color Noise Reduction and Luminance Smoothing sliders, which was explained earlier in this chapter.

Also be sure to preview the effect of sharpening at different levels on noise in the image if you're setting sharpness for the converted image.

►5.51

Sharpening: The Last Step

The last step in the workflow is sharpening images, and doing it after all other corrections are complete in Camera Raw and Photoshop is best. Among other things, sharpening increases the contrast of pixels around the edges of objects to increase the image definition. This process gives the impression of sharpness. Because tasks such as changing image contrast, or cloning or healing areas of the image can affect object edges you should complete them before you sharpen the image.

Equally important, you should complete the final image sizing as well. If you sharpen an image at full size, and then make a copy of it to use at a much smaller size, the image will likely be oversharpened with light-colored haloes along high-contrast edges. In short, it will have an unnaturally sharp look.

Although the general approach is to sharpen the entire image, sometimes only local sharpening is best. For example, John Paul Caponigro prefers to apply local sharpening in Photoshop, and sometimes he doesn't sharpen images at all.

In people shots, overall sharpening emphasizes pores and skin imperfections. The approach for portraits is to sharpen eyes, hair, lips, and clothing. Selective sharpening at different levels is also often the best tactic.

Correct Shadow Tints

Contributor: Charlotte Lowrie ■ **Specialty:** Editorial and Stock
Primary Tool Used: Calibrate tab

Regardless of how close to neutral you get the overall image, a color tint may remain in the shadow areas. The Calibrate tab in Camera Raw can be a big help in correcting the shadow tint to neutral. The calibration adjustments may necessitate further interplay with the Adjust tab controls to get the right balance.

This technique shows one approach to correcting a shadow tint. But be sure to read the sidebar to learn how to use the Calibrate controls, among other controls, to create a custom camera profile.

▶5.52

1

Open the image you want to process in Camera Raw. On the Adjust tab, make the White Balance adjustments you want. Press Ctrl/⌘+U to turn off Auto Adjustments. For this image, a Temperature adjustment to 4250 and a slight Tint change to +20 works well.

Now is a good time to check the shadow tint. Select the Color Sampler tool and move the mouse pointer into the shadow areas that you are concerned about. In this example, the shadow under the petal is key in getting a neutral overall color. Many factors can affect shadow tint, including reflections from nearby objects, the overall light, and the camera profile.

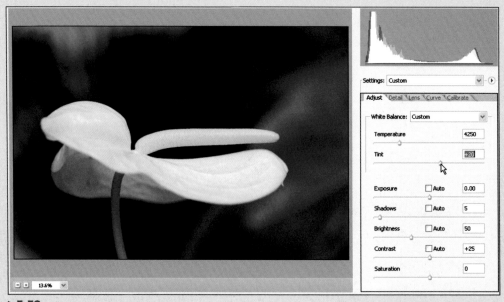

▶5.53

2

Complete basic adjustments to Exposure, Shadows, Brightness, Contrast, and Saturation. To preview clipping of highlights and shadows, hold down the Ctrl/Option key as you drag the Exposure and Shadows sliders. This image received slight adjustments.

►5.54

3

Click the Curve tab and make adjustments as necessary. In this image, using the curve darkens the shadows slightly to increase the contrast between the background and the blossom.

X-Ref ► Chapter 4 covers more about sizing and sharpening images.

►5.55

4

Click the Calibrate tab. Select the Color Sampler tool and click in a primary shadow area. Click the Color Sampler tool and move to a shadow area of the image. The color values display above the Histogram. The shadow under the petal is marked showing a slightly higher green tint in the shadows than I like.

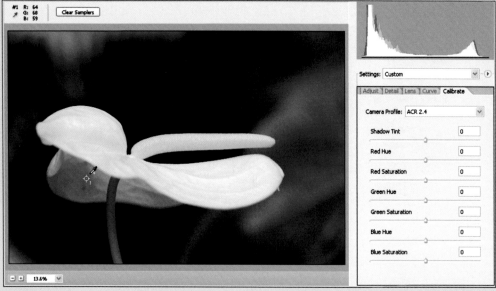

▶5.56

5

Drag the Shadow Tint slider right to increase magenta or left to increase green in the shadows. Watch the RGB sampler values above the preview image. Here, a +22 setting brings Red and Green within one level of each other. Using additional settings can bring the shadows closer to neutral.

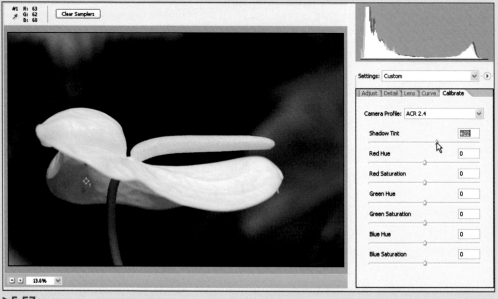

▶5.57

The Red, Green, and Blue Hue and Saturation sliders increase or decrease the other two colors. In short, the Red sliders affect colors except red. Positive and negative changes increase or decrease the colors. Here's a summary:

- **Red affects blue and green.** Positive Red *Hue* settings increase green and decrease blue. Negative settings decrease green and increase blue. Positive Red *Saturation* settings decrease green and blue equally, and negative settings increase green and blue equally.

- **Green affects red and blue.** Positive Green Hue settings increase red and decrease blue. Negative settings decrease red and increase blue. Positive Green Saturation settings decrease blue and red equally, and negative settings increase them equally.

- **Blue affects red and green.** Positive Blue Hue settings increase green and decrease red. Negative settings decrease green and increase red. Positive Blue Saturation settings decrease green and red equally, and negative settings increase them equally.

For example, drag the hue and saturation sliders until the Shadow Tint is neutral or so the values are within approximately one level of the others. Neutral means that the RGB values shown in the sampler area are the same for red, green, and blue, or they are very close.

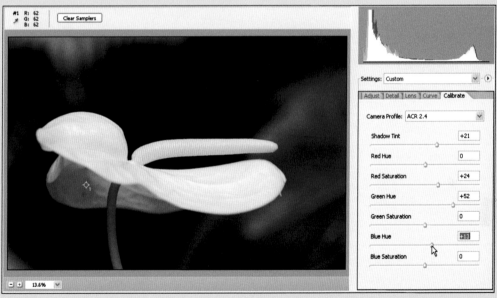

▶5.58

7

The result of your adjustments on the Calibrate tab may affect the initial adjustments on the Adjust tab. Click the Adjust tab and evaluate the image. For this image, the shadow adjustments clipped shadow areas, so I set the Shadows at 0 to minimize clipping. In addition, I reset the Tint to +15 and increased Saturation slightly.

Post-conversion adjustments to this image in Photoshop also included an increase in contrast, clean up, and a slight crop.

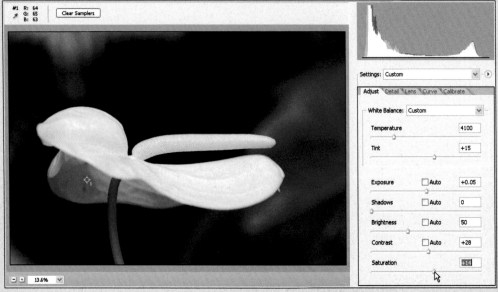

▶5.59

Creative Techniques for RAW Conversion

Chapter 06

In this chapter

Convert RAW Files to Black-and-White Images

Contributor: Seán Duggan ▪ **Specialty:** Fine Art
Primary Tools Used: Saturation slider and Calibration tab

Camera Raw offers a great deal of control for crafting black-and-white interpretations of color images. When used on a desaturated file, the white balance options and the color control sliders in the Calibrate tab allow you to modify the gray tones in a way that is very similar to the panchromatic response of black-and-white film when photographed through colored filters.

Like all Camera Raw settings, you can save different combinations of settings and easily apply them to other files, either in the Camera Raw dialog box, or through Bridge. This technique shows you how to convert a color image to black and white.

▶6.1

1

Open the file you want to convert to grayscale in Camera Raw. Although you are likely to see the most dramatic differences in black-and-white tones when using an image with bright and distinct colors like shown here, sometimes even subtle, muted color images can offer a surprising range of tonal possibilities.

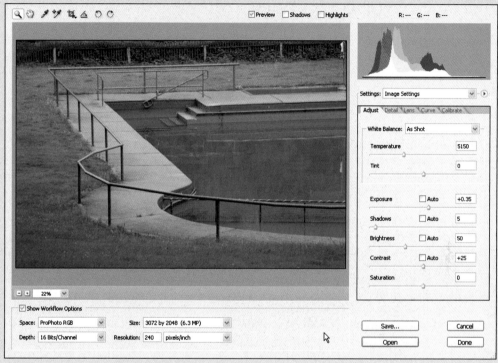

►6.2

2

In Camera Raw, press Control/⌘+U to turn off automatic adjustments, and then adjust the photo using the Exposure, Shadows, and Brightness sliders in the Adjust tab to get the color image looking good—even though you will eventually convert it to black and white. Although this step is optional, doing it is worthwhile because good color images make good black-and-white images.

The main goal that you want to achieve from these adjustments is to have the shadow and highlight points set appropriately for the image and to have good contrast. Because the final product will be black and white, don't be concerned about color casts or white balance issues.

Tip

To preserve bright highlights with detail, identify them by holding down the Alt/Option key and dragging the Exposure slider to the right until the highlight area appears—indicating the brightest point. Then click that spot using the Color Sampler tool. You can monitor this sample throughout the process to ensure that detail is maintained. Then re-adjust the Exposure slider so the image looks good.

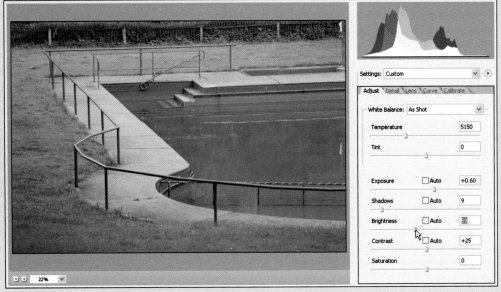

►6.3

3

On the Adjust tab, drag the Saturation slider all the way to the left to −100 to remove all color values from the image. Once you remove the color, get ready to fine-tune the grayscale tonal balance.

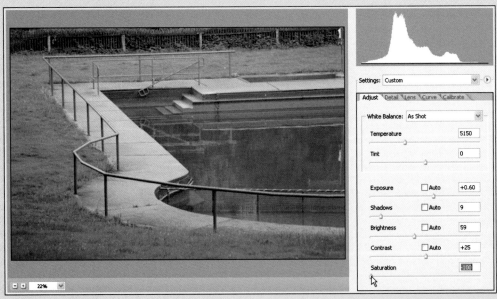

►6.4

4

Try adjusting the White Balance, Temperature, and Tint sliders. These controls usually do not offer too many possibilities, but they are worth exploring. The actual results that you get depend on the color balance in the image you're working on. As the old saying goes, your mileage may vary.

Moving the Temperature slider to the left brings down the overall key of the image and darkens it. Moving it to the right brightens the image. Now is also a time when a color sampler point on a bright highlight is useful—you can monitor it so that you don't blow the highlights out to 255, the brightest point at which there is no detail in any channel.

The White Balance adjustments do not do too much for the image in this example, so I restored the settings to As Shot. To restore settings, click the arrow next to White Balance, and then choose As Shot from the menu.

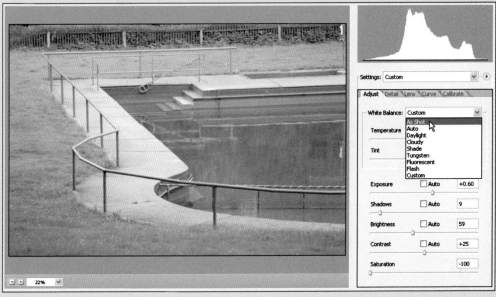

►6.5

5

Click the Calibrate tab. The Calibrate controls affect the image in a way similar to those in the Hue/Saturation dialog box in Photoshop, but they are more subtle. In a color image, the Shadow Tint slider shifts the tint of the shadow tones between green on the left (negative values) and magenta on the right (positive values). With a grayscale conversion, the effect of this slider is usually on the brightness and contrast of the image rather than significantly altering the relationships between the tones.

Moving the Shadow Tint slider all the way to the right (+100) gives this image a pleasing boost in density and contrast.

Tip

When working on an image with subtle details in the deep shadows, be cautious with your Shadow Tint adjustments because you can cause the shadow details to block up and become too dark.

▶6.6

6

Next are the Red, Green, and Blue Hue and Saturation sliders. Generally, my approach is to experiment with these sliders, but some images have certain colors that I know will be affected more by certain sliders. For most files, first check out how each pair of color sliders affects the image when moved to different ends of the scale. Look for basic tonal shifts and characteristics that you like, and then fine-tune them later.

In this image, moving the Red Hue slider all the way to the left darkened the steps and the red railing around the pool. Moving it all the way to the right lightened the railing and created much better contrast between the steps, walkway, pool, and surrounding lawn. Ultimately for this figure, I reset the Red sliders by clicking approximately in the middle of the slider track. You can also enter a 0 in the numeric field, but at this stage exact numeric values are not critical.

X-Ref

For more information on the effects of the Red, Green, and Blue Saturation sliders, see Chapter 5.

The Green sliders' adjustments also did not move me, so I reset the Green values to 0. In adjusting the Blue sliders for this image, things really began to look interesting. Moving both the Blue Hue and Blue Saturation sliders far to the left makes the pool interior look very light. This effect represents the most dramatic tonal change so far.

Moving the Blue Hue slider all the way to the right (+100) and the Blue Saturation slider to +30 makes the interior of the pool look very dark. I really liked the look of the dark water and how it influenced the feel of the entire image, and I decided to explore this look further.

►6.7

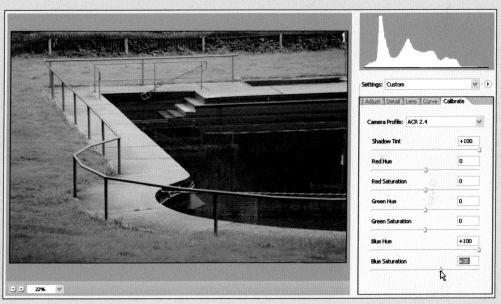

►6.8

7

Using these Blue settings as a base, it's time to experiment with the Red and Green sliders to see how they might alter the image. Working with these sliders reveals that adjustments are interrelated, so you may need to move back and forth adjusting the different controls. As you can see from the process here, once you find the color that really affects your image, you can go back and experiment with how the other two colors' adjustments affect the image.

In this image, the final grayscale conversion emphasizes the dark water and makes the pool look a little unsettling and mysterious. The settings I used combined the Shadow Tint and the Red and Blue Hue and Saturation sliders. I did not use the Green sliders at all.

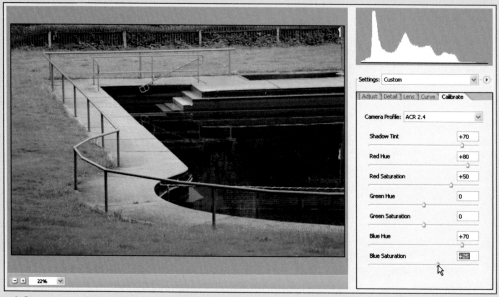

►6.9

X-Ref ► To access these settings and use them on other images, just save all or part of the settings. For details on saving settings, see Chapter 7. You can build up a library of settings and quickly apply them to one or more images in Camera Raw or Bridge.

8

As a final step, click the Curves tab and adjust the curve as necessary. For this image, I lift the curve just slightly for the highlights and lower it slightly for the shadows.

X-Ref ► For details on setting a tone curve, see Chapter 4.

The goal is to lighten the brighter parts such as the paved walkway around the pool and increase the contrast between it and the dark interior of the pool.

►6.10

A Faster Way to Apply Black-and-White Settings

Although using the Calibrate controls on a desaturated image gives you a lot of control in creating custom black-and-white interpretations of color images, this method is not fast and it sometimes requires a lot of adjusting back and forth between the different sliders until you get something you like.

Although this is not an issue for fine art photographers who generally don't mind spending time tweaking their images, it can be a major workflow logjam when you have to deal with a lot of images—such as converting hundreds of wedding shots into black and white. For those scenarios, consider creating and saving some very basic black-and-white settings that only involve the Saturation slider to remove color from the image and add a curve for images that need more or less contrast.

Settings for basic black and white, basic black and white (increase contrast), and basic black and white (reduce contrast) would be applicable to many images, and you could apply them to entire groups of images. Even though you might choose to further finesse images that you intend to make into large prints, these basic settings would be fine for the client proofing process.

Combine Black-and-White and Color

Contributor: Seán Duggan ■ **Specialty:** Fine Art
Primary Tool Used: Smart Objects

Combining color and black-and-white in the same image is a technique that has been around for almost as long as photography itself. For many years, photographers achieved this effect through the use of actual paints that they carefully applied to the photo paper. The advent of digital processes made this effect much easier to accomplish and enabled photographers to combine a color version of an image with a black-and-white one with great precision.

As shown in this technique, with Camera Raw and Photoshop CS2 you can use Smart Objects for maximum flexibility in interpreting your RAW files for a combined color and black-and-white effect.

►6.11

1

Select an image that you feel will work well with some elements treated as black and white while others retain the natural colors in the image. In this example, the photo is of an old wall taken in Germany. The technique is to process the same image twice—once in black and white and once in color—and then combine the results in Photoshop so that each version merges to make the final image.

For the most flexibility in interpreting the RAW file, both now and later in the process, you can place the RAW files as Smart Objects in Photoshop. This method allows you to double-

►6.12

click the Smart Objects in Photoshop, and then re-adjust the settings in Camera Raw. Although placing RAW files as Smart Objects is not necessary for every image, for some projects it can be very convenient and it is the method used in this technique.

2

To place a RAW file as a Smart Object in Photoshop, create an empty document of the correct size in Photoshop. This file serves as the destination for the Smart Objects created from the RAW file. Decide how large you want the file to be when you import it into Photoshop. You can generally use your camera's native pixel dimensions, which in this case is 3072 × 2048.

To find your camera's native pixel size, open a RAW image in Camera Raw and note the dimensions in the Size menu in the Show Workflow Options area. The pixel size without a plus or a minus sign is your camera's native size.

►6.13

3

In Photoshop, create a new file by pressing Ctrl/⌘+N. Set the pixel dimensions of the file to be the same as your camera's native size. For the Color Mode, choose RGB Color from the drop-down menu. Set the Resolution to what you normally process your RAW files. In this example, the Resolution is set to 240 pixels per inch because it creates excellent prints on inkjet printers. The Bit Depth can be whatever you choose to use. I use 16 bit for the most tonal-editing flexibility.

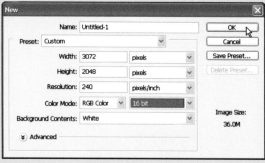

▶6.14

> **Tip**
> In Photoshop's New dialog box, you can click the Save Preset button and save this custom size as a choice that appears in the Preset menu of this dialog box.

4

In Bridge select the file you want to work with. Choose File ➤ Place ➤ In Photoshop. The Camera Raw dialog box opens. This step initiates the process that results in the RAW file being placed in Photoshop as a Smart Object. In Camera Raw, make adjustments so that the color image looks good. In this technique, I process the black-and-white version first, but getting a good black-and-white translation is easier if the overall brightness and contrast in the color image looks good from the beginning. In this case, darkening the image a bit using the Exposure slider on the Adjust tab results in richer tones.

Remember that any color casts in the image, for example whether it is warm or cool, don't matter because the result of this first image will be a black-and-white image.

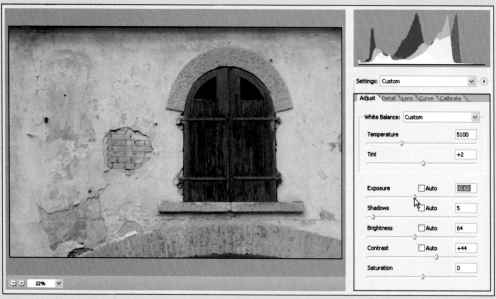

▶6.15

Tip ▶

To easily retrieve your initial adjustments to the color version of the image in the future, save them now before applying the black-and-white effect. Click the right-pointing triangle next to Settings and choose Save Settings. By default, Camera Raw saves the settings in a location that makes them show up on the Settings menu.

5

Convert the image to black and white by moving the Saturation slider on the Adjust tab to −100. Click the Calibrate tab, and then adjust the sliders until you arrive at a black-and-white interpretation that pleases you.

Double-check that the Size, Resolution, and Depth are set to the same as the empty target file in Photoshop that you created in Step 3.

Click Open to bring the image into Photoshop. The image appears in Photoshop with a bounding box around it and crisscross diagonal lines across it indicating that it is a Smart Object.

▶6.16

Tip ▶

When combining images, it doesn't matter whether you do the black-and-white or color version first. By doing the color version last, the image thumbnail and preview in Bridge is in color. By doing the black-and-white version last, the thumbnail is black and white, and you may want to reset it.

6

If you want, you can resize or transform the placed Smart Object now by dragging the control handles on the corners and in the center of each side. In this example, resizing isn't needed because the image is imported at the exact size as the target canvas. Click the Commit transform check mark on the Options bar, or press Enter/Return to place the image at the current size.

In the Layers palette, the layer has a Smart Object icon displayed on the bottom right on the thumbnail. Double-click the layer name and add a designation to indicate that it is the black-and-white version. In this case, I added "-BW". You may want to keep the original filename in the layer name in case you need to refer to the original file number.

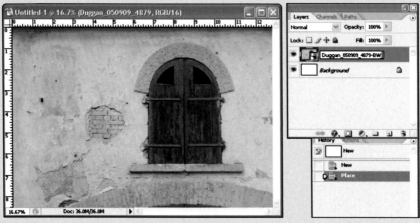

▶6.17

> **Note**
> Now is a good time to save the file in Photoshop (PSD) or TIFF format. You can add a designation to the filename. For example, I add "-M" to the original filename to denote that it is a Master file. The original filename is appended but never changed.

7

In Bridge, ensure that the original image is still selected. Bridge displays the black-and-white version now. Choose File ➤ Place ➤ In Photoshop. The image opens in Camera Raw.

If you saved the settings that you made to the color version of the image before converting it to black and white, click the triangle next to the Settings menu, and then choose Load Settings. Then navigate to where you saved the file.

If you did not save the settings, click the right-pointing triangle next to Settings, and then choose Camera Raw Defaults from the menu. Use the controls on the Adjust tab to make adjustments with an eye toward creating a good color version of the image. If necessary, you can also adjust the contrast in the Curves tab.

For this image, the exposure was very good to begin with, so the adjustments are relatively subtle ones to darken it a bit and increase the saturation.

When you finish your adjustments, click Open to import the image into Photoshop as a Smart Object. The color version of the file opens in Photoshop with a bounding box around it.

Click the checkmark on the toolbar or double-click in the image or press Enter/Return to place the file as a Smart Object at the current size. Double-click the layer name in the Layers palette if you want to modify the name. It's a good idea to name each layer to help you know what adjustments or version each layer represents.

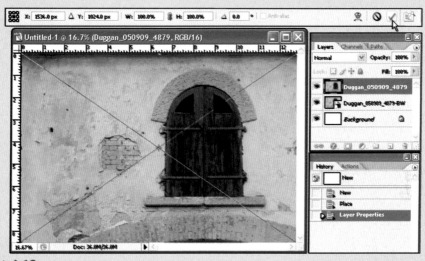

▶6.18

8

The next part of the process uses selections and layer masks in Photoshop to selectively hide and reveal portions of each layer to arrive at the final composite of the color and black-and-white image. The image you're working with and the complexity of the edges of the elements that you need to mask determine the exact techniques you need to use to create your selections or masks. The remaining steps in this technique are designed to work with this specific image, but you can use the steps as a starting point for working with your image.

I want most of this image to be black and white with only the wooden shutters, the lower arch of bricks, and the patch of bricks to the left of the window in color. To accomplish this, I used the Pen tool to create a path for the areas I wanted in color including the wooden shutters and the brick arch underneath the window. You could use other selection tools for this type of task, but I chose the Pen tool because of the precision that it offers.

▶6.19

9

After you make your selection, reveal it by making a layer mask out of it. In this example, after I created the path for my image, I held down Control/⌘ and clicked the thumbnail of the path in the Paths palette to load the path as a selection. Then I chose Layer ➤ Layer Mask ➤ Reveal Selection. This command creates a layer mask that reveals the areas on the color layer that had been selected and hides the rest, letting the black-and-white layer show through.

▶6.20

10

To expose an area in your image (in this example, the bricks to the left of the window), select the Brush tool (B) and open the Brush Picker on the Options bar to select a brush tip that is a good size to work on the area. I decide to use a 150-pixel, soft-edged brush. Press D to set the default colors of white in the foreground and black in the background. These colors are the default when a mask is active; when a regular layer is active the colors are in the opposite positions.

Before painting over the area, be sure that the layer mask is active and not the actual Smart Object layer. To do so, look for the border highlight around the layer mask thumbnail. Then, paint with white to reveal the colored areas; in this case, the bricks in the area where they are exposed.

►6.21

11

To complete your black-and-white and color image, you want to reveal all the areas of color you want to keep. But, you may not want to reveal them all at the same color strength. If this is case, you can add another layer mask at a different opacity to just those parts that don't need to be as strong.

In this image, I wanted to reveal the ledge under the window and the stone arch above it, but not at full strength. For the ledge, I modified the layer mask with a brush set to 50 percent opacity and painted it with white. For the arch above the window, I used the Pen tool to make a path, loaded it as a selection, and then chose Edit ➤ Fill. I then filled that part of the layer mask with white at 50 percent opacity.

Using a brush set to 10 percent opacity, I brushed in a little color in different areas on the wall. My goal was a mottled effect such as you might see in a color-wash painting technique. Finally, I zoomed in for a close view and painted in the color on the rusted shutter hinges at 100 percent opacity.

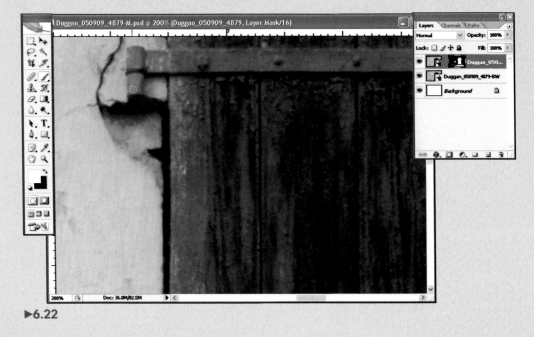

▶6.22

12

The last bit of mask customizing for this example was to draw a loose selection using the Lasso tool around the hard-edge parts of the mask—the shutters and the two arches. I choose Filter ➤ Blur ➤ Gaussian Blur to slightly soften the hard, precise edges left by the Pen tool. You may or may not need to make this type of adjustment depending on the image you are working on.

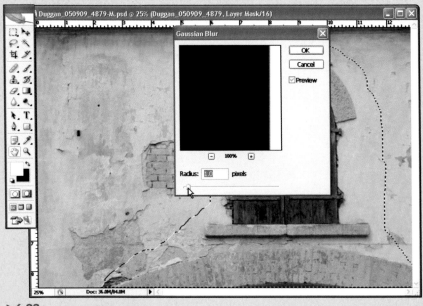

▶6.23

The black and white version you created may have looked fine on its own, but when combined with the color image, you may find additional adjustments help the final look of your combined images. In this example, I decided the black-and-white version needed more contrast, so I added more by double-clicking the Smart Object icon on the thumbnail and then modifying the tone curve in Camera Raw. Clicking Done updates the changes in the Smart Object in Photoshop.

Because the RAW data is embedded in the image as two Smart Objects, this working file is no longer tied to the location of the original camera file. What's very cool about using RAW files as Smart Objects is that you can easily edit the Camera Raw settings by double-clicking on the thumbnail of the Smart Object in Photoshop.

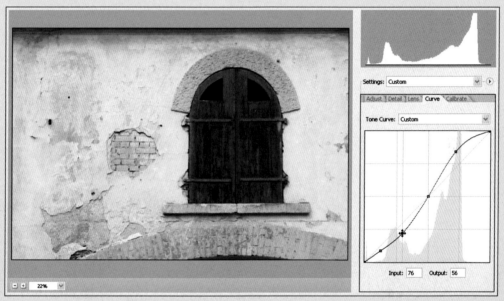

►6.24

Simulate a Sepia Look

Contributor: Charlotte Lowrie ■ **Specialty:** Editorial and Stock
Primary Tool Used: Temperature and Saturation

Sepia toning, a venerable photographic technique, never seems to lose its popularity with photographers and clients alike. Even though not every image works well in sepia, many portraits tend to lend themselves to this technique naturally. In digital photography, many interpretations exist of the sepia tones that range from red to orange and green tints. The choice of treatment is yours to make. My preference is toward a warm toning effect.

Camera Raw does most of the work in simulating a sepia tone, but you can do more post-conversion work in Photoshop to add finishing touches. This technique shows an easy method for creating a sepia-toned image in Camera Raw.

▶6.25

1

Open the image you want to convert to sepia tone in Camera Raw. Adjust the image using the Exposure, Shadows, Brightness, Contrast, and Saturation sliders on the Adjust tab. You can revisit adjustments later, but for now concentrate on getting a good rendering of the image.

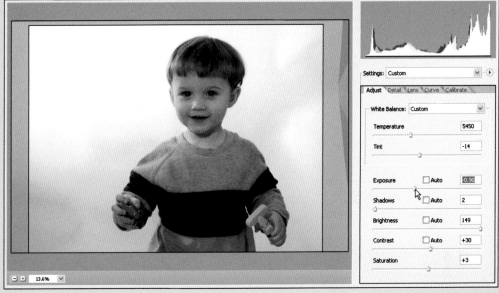

▶6.26

2

To set the basic tone, drag the Temperature slider right. This adjustment may seem radical, but drag the slider until you get the basic, underlying sepia tone. For this image a Temperature setting of 17000 works well. I also adjust the Contrast slider slightly to enhance the color effect. For your image, use whatever color bias looks good to your eye.

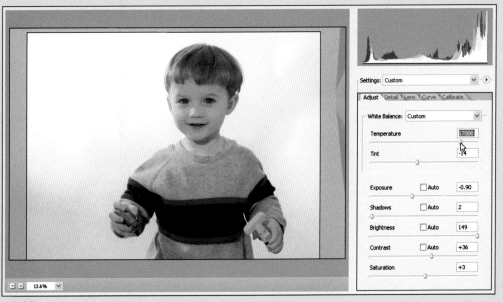

▶6.27

3

Drag the Tint slider right to add more magenta or left to add more green. In this image, moving the Tint slider to +2 from −14 adds more magenta.

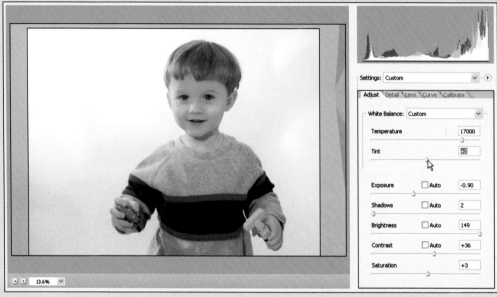

►6.28

4

Drag the Saturation slider left to decrease Saturation. The amount you use depends on the look you want to achieve. Leave some color in the image so that you can simulate sepia toning. Because the child is wearing a shirt with red stripes, choosing a red toning effect helps to blend the remaining saturation in the image with the sepia simulation.

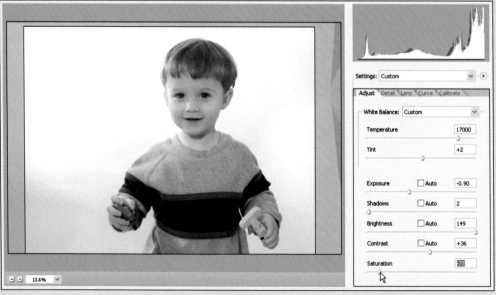

►6.29

5

Click the Calibrate tab. Drag the Shadow Tint slider to the right to increase the magenta tint or to the left to increase the blue/green tint. For this image, I use a Shadow Tint setting of +27.

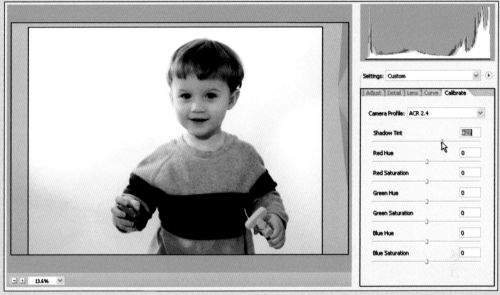

▶6.30

6

The Red, Green, and Blue Hue and Saturation sliders allow you to fine-tune the simulated toning effect. Because these controls give varying effects, the best approach is to experiment until you get the look that you like. Each move that you make affects the others, so spend some time finding a pleasing look. You can save the settings to use in the future.

> **X-Ref**
>
> For details on saving settings, see Chapter 7.

The settings I liked best for this for this image are:

- Red Hue -26
- Red Saturation -23
- Green Hue -27
- Green Saturation -44
- Blue Hue -29
- Blue Saturation -24

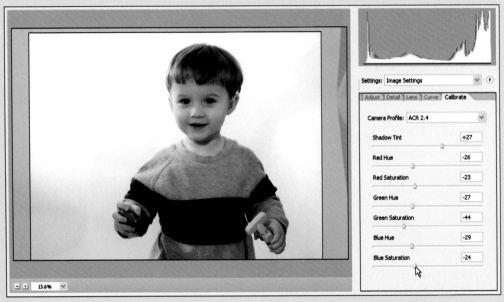

►6.31

7

As a final step, you can go back to the Adjust tab to tweak the settings. For this image, further reducing the Saturation, slightly increasing Contrast, and adjusting the Temperature and Exposure slightly fine-tunes the image.

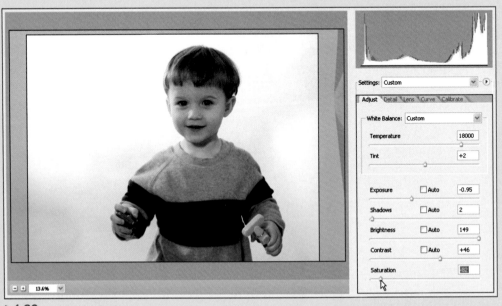

►6.32

Click the Save button, and then type a name for the image. Click Save in the Save Options dialog box. If you want to open the image in Photoshop for further touch-ups, click Open in the Camera Raw dialog box.

In Photoshop, you can add refinements such as a low-density photo filter by choosing Image ➤ Adjustments ➤ Photo Filter.

▶6.33

Use Color Temperature Creatively

Contributor: Ellen Anon ■ **Specialty:** Nature and Outdoors
Primary Tools Used: Temperature and Tint sliders

The potential creative applications available in Camera Raw are limited only by the photographer's imagination and time. Creative use of color temperature is one of the ways that you can transform an otherwise ho-hum sunset into an impressive image. The technique used in this image is a simple but effective way to liven up a photo. In this technique, your primary subject needs to be silhouetted for the technique to work well because it works mainly with the color of the sky.

However, you can use this technique as a jumping-off point for applying color temperature creatively in your photos.

▶6.34

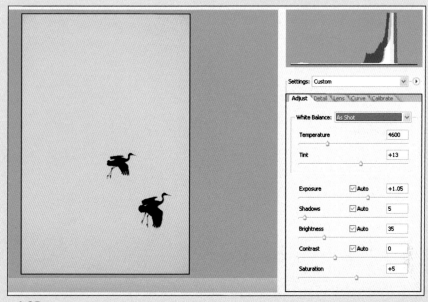

►6.35

1

Open the image that you want to convert in Camera Raw. This technique works well for images that need the extra drama that the color Temperature and Tint controls in Camera Raw can provide. In this image, I use the adjustments to add more pizzazz to the pale color of the sky.

2

Press Ctrl/⌘+U to turn off Auto Adjustments. Then adjust the Exposure, Shadows, Brightness, Contrast, and Saturation for the image using the controls on the Adjust tab in Camera Raw.

For this image, a slight increase in Exposure and adjustments to Brightness, Contrast, and Saturation complete the basic image adjustments.

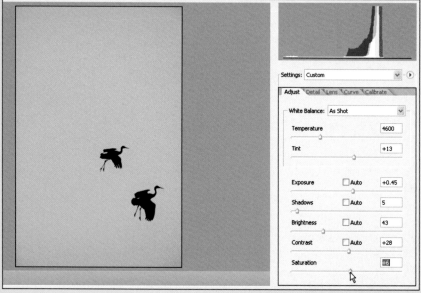

▶6.36

3

To change the color of the sky, drag the Temperature slider to the left to adjust to a cooler temperature or to the right to adjust to a warmer color temperature.

To change the color of the sky in this image, moving the Temperature slider to a cooler setting of 4150 changes the sky from a pale blue to a deeper blue.

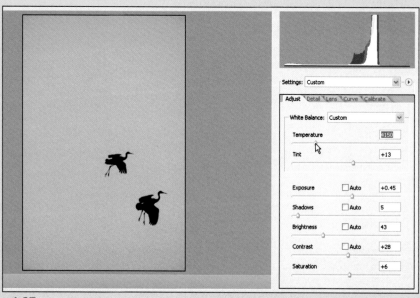

▶6.37

To add warmth to your sky, drag the Tint slider to the left to increase the green tint or to the right to increase the magenta tint. Setting the Tint for this image to +46 warms the sky by changing it from blue to shades of purple and pink.

Continue to adjust both the Tint and Temperature sliders to get the combination that works best in your image. For this image, moving the Temperature slider to the right also works well because it causes the image to take on subtle lavender and salmon hues.

You may want to readjust the Brightness, Contrast, and Saturation sliders after you've set the Temperature and Tint. Make any other adjustments you want in Camera Raw, and then save the file or click Done to save the adjustments you made.

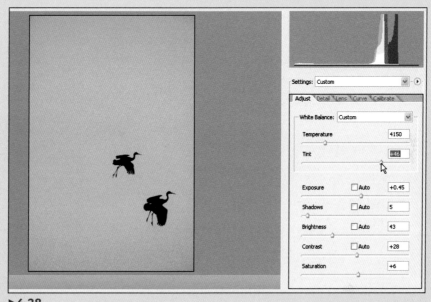

▶6.38

Creative White Balance

SB Sidebar

Certainly times occur when you want to get a white balance that accurately reflects the scene as you remember it. But photography throughout the entire workflow is a creative endeavor. Using white balance creatively is just one more tool you have to reinterpret your images for best effect. And in many cases, you can use the Temperature and Tint controls to simulate warming and cooling filters used on the camera.

When you use the Temperature and Tint controls in Camera Raw, think of them as moving across and up and down on a color wheel where magenta is at the top. The Temperature slider moves across the color wheel from blue on the left to yellow on the right. The Tint slider moves from bottom to top on the color wheel. A move to the left (or bottom of the color wheel) with the Tint slider increases green whereas a move to the right (or top of the color wheel) increases magenta.

Create a Faded Photo Effect

Contributor: Charlotte Lowrie ■ **Specialty:** Editorial and Stock
Primary Tools Used: Temperature, Saturation, and Calibration sliders

In times past, photo fading was done by time. Nowadays, creating a soft-faded look with Camera Raw is reasonably easy. Fading can be achieved with color images or with black-and-white images. Endless variations exist for the types of looks that you can achieve. The goal of fading is to enhance the subject and set the overall mood. You can use this technique for images of people, flowers, still life, and moody landscapes.

This technique demonstrates one approach to photo fading for a color photo, but, as with most of the creative techniques in this chapter, experimentation is the best way to achieve the rendering that's best for your image.

▶6.39

1

Open the image you want to tint in Camera Raw. Press Control/⌘+U to turn off Auto Adjustments. Then adjust the image's Exposure, Shadows, Brightness, Contrast, and Saturation using the sliders on the Adjust tab.

For this image, I decided that an Exposure setting of +1.55, a Brightness setting of 42, and a Contrast setting of +25 worked best.

▶6.40

2

To establish the basic tone, drag the Temperature slider to the left to adjust to a cooler temperature or to the right to adjust to a warmer color temperature. For this image, using a Temperature of 34000 warms the image but keeps the background fairly neutral.

Remember that the tinting process is a matter of making adjustments, evaluating the results, and then adjusting again to get the effect you want. You can always come back and tweak the Temperature again.

►6.41

3

Drag the Tint slider to the right to add more magenta, or to the left to add more green. In this image, I increase magenta from +22 to +36. The best gauge for adjustments are your personal preferences. If you're unsure how much or how far to go, find a faded family photo and keep it beside the screen as you work as a guide and as inspiration.

►6.42

4

Drag the Saturation slider to the left to decrease Saturation. Again, the amount of desaturation is a matter of personal taste. As with all other adjustments, you may want to come back to this adjustment later to try increasing or decreasing the Saturation. For this image, decreasing the Saturation to –65 works well.

▶6.43

5

Click the Calibrate tab. Drag the Shadow Tint slider to the right to increase the magenta tint, or to the left to increase the blue/green tint. I use a Shadow Tint of +39 for this image.

▶6.44

6

You can adjust the Red, Green, and Blue Hue and Saturation sliders to change the overall tinting. I made a good deal of back and forth adjustments to this image until settling on the settings shown in the figure.

▶6.45

7

Click the Curve tab. Click a preset point on the curve to adjust each tonal area. The top point affects highlights, the middle point affects midtones, and the bottom two points affect the shadows. Dragging a point higher lightens the tones and dragging a point lower darkens the tones. I made slight adjustments to the curve on this image.

The goal of tinting for this image is to convey a sense of soft emergence. The colors are deliberately faint, but not so faint that the outline of the rose is lost.

►6.46

8

You can go back to the Adjust tab to tweak the settings. This image needed a slight increase in the Saturation. Save your image. If you want to open the image in Photoshop for further touch-ups, click Open from Camera Raw.

Final production on this image in Photoshop included selective dodging and burning, bumping up contrast, touching up blemishes, applying a Nik Color Efx Pro Classical Soft Focus filter, and selective sharpening.

►6.47

Simulate a Film Look

Contributor: Charlotte Lowrie ■ **Specialty:** Editorial and Stock
Primary Tool Used: Calibrate tab

Any photographer who is familiar with film knows that each film has a distinctive look. Landscape photographers love the Fujichrome Velvia look with its bright saturated colors. Portrait photographers rely on film such as Kodak's Portra series or Fujicolor NPH for the excellent skin tones. Some of the newer cameras, including the Canon EOS 5D, offer film-like looks that you can choose as a setting in the camera. But you can also use Camera Raw to simulate familiar film looks that photographers know and love.

This technique shows you how to simulate the color-saturated Fujichrome Velvia look, but you can modify this technique to simulate other film looks.

▶6.48

1

Open the image you want to process in Camera Raw. Set the color Temperature by dragging the Temperature slider. For this image, which was taken close to sunset, setting the Temperature to 5300 works well.

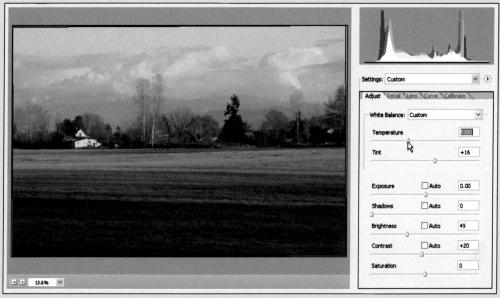

►6.49

Tip To set the white balance, you can also select the White Balance tool in the toolbar, and then click a white area that contains detail.

2

Drag the Tint slider right to add more magenta to the image or left to add more green to the image. In this image, adjusting the Tint setting from +16 to +9 works.

At a +16 setting, the white areas in the clouds showed a red tint. Reducing the Tint control setting produces a more neutral white in the clouds.

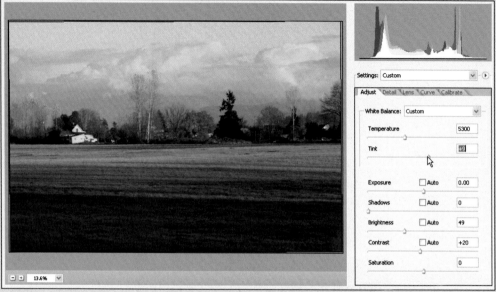

►6.50

3

Drag the sliders to set the Exposure, Shadows, Brightness, Contrast, and Saturation. For this image, a slight decrease in Exposure avoids the clipping of highlights on the house. I also made increases in Brightness, Contrast, Saturation, and Shadows.

Different cameras produce different contrast and saturation settings in RAW images, and thus require different settings in Camera Raw. The best guide to making adjustments for your camera is to watch the image as you make the adjustments. You can select the Preview check box above the preview image to see the before and after effects of the changes.

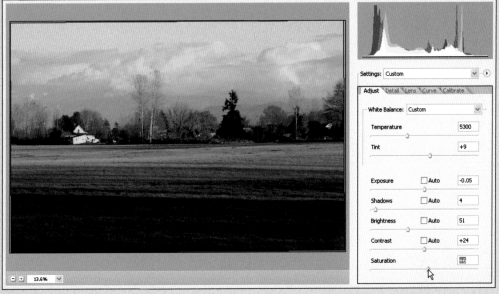

►6.51

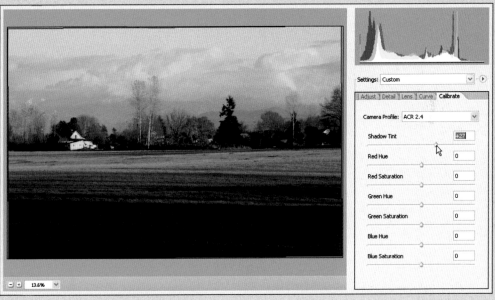

4

Click the Calibrate tab. Drag the Shadow Tint slider to the right to increase the magenta tint or to the left to increase the green tint. I use a Shadow Tint setting of +27 for this image.

►6.52

5

To increase the vibrancy of colors throughout the image, experiment with the Red, Green, and Blue Hue and Saturation sliders. You can see the settings I used in the figure. As a result of these changes, I decreased the Shadow Tint from +27 to +22 as well.

Use your judgment on how far to increase the saturation of the colors in the image. Everyone has a different take on how saturated the colors should appear, but, as always, the proof of the adjustment is in the print.

After saving the image and opening in Photoshop, additional adjustments included dodging and burning and cleaning up the image.

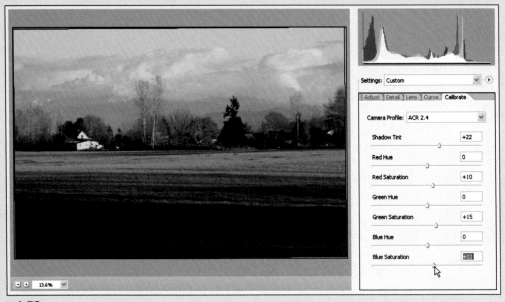

▶6.53

Double-Process Files to Increase Dynamic Range

Contributor: Rob Sheppard ■ **Specialty:** Nature and Editorial
Primary Tool Used: Camera Raw

The real world of nature doesn't always fit neatly onto a sensor. Very often, the tonal range of a scene stretches a sensor's capabilities, such as in this image, which shows a black bumblebee on white flowers in the sun.

You can try to optimize both the highlights and shadows for such photos in one Camera Raw processing. However, the processing that gives the best highlights isn't necessarily best for shadows and vice versa. An answer exists for this problem, though. Process the image twice—once to optimize highlights and again to get the most from shadows—then combine the two versions in Photoshop. This technique explains the basics of how to do this.

▶6.54

1

Open the image you want to process in Camera Raw. Process the image for the highlights by adjusting the settings on the Adjust tab in Camera Raw. As you make adjustments, the important thing is to watch the highlights and ignore the shadows. To preview highlight clipping, press the Control/⌘ key as you adjust the Exposure slider. Notice that the bee looks like a black pit of nothing at this point, but the flowers (called rangers buttons) look great. Click Open to open this file into Photoshop, and then save the file in Photoshop.

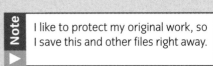

Note ▶ I like to protect my original work, so I save this and other files right away.

▶6.55

2

Process the image again, but this time for the shadows. By adjusting the settings on the Adjust tab in Camera Raw. This time, you want to concentrate adjustments to make the darkest parts of the photo look good. Press the Control/⌘ key as you adjust the Shadows slider. In a photo like this one where the critical dark areas are small, enlarge the photo so that they are more dominant in the preview. Ignore the highlights. When opening up dark areas, you may bring up noise too much—use the sliders in the Detail tab to reduce it. Click Open to open this file into Photoshop, and then save the file in Photoshop. It is important to make sure that you do not change resolution or file size between these two images while processing them.

▶6.56

3

In Photoshop, select the Move tool, click on one photo while holding down the Shift key and drag it onto the other. This action places the dragged photo in a layer exactly aligned over the other image. No absolute exists as to which image goes over the other. I like to put the one with the smallest good area over the other; in this case, the image processed for the bumblebee (shadows) goes on top.

▶6.57

4

Now you blend the two photos. Add a black layer mask (Alt/Option+click the Layer Mask icon), then paint in the detail from the top layer with white. In this case, the dark bee is painted in. At this point, you will often find you need to make additional overall adjustments in Photoshop, such as tweaking Curves or Levels, to optimize the new, blended image.

►6.58

Extended Tonal Range

This technique of combining highlight and shadow processed images also works well with a two-exposure technique. What you do is make one exposure specifically for the highlights, then another, separate exposure for the shadows. You then process the image that was exposed for the highlights so that the highlights look their best. Next, you process the shadow-exposed photo for the shadows. This method optimizes tonalities in both areas. Finally, you combine images in the same way you combine two images that were processed separately from the same exposure.

The advantage of a two-exposure technique is that you can capture a greater tonal range because you do not need to compromise exposure to fit all the tonalities into one image. The disadvantage is that you have to remember to take two exposures for a scene, plus you cannot use it for action. You would never be able to use such a technique with the bee and flowers photo shown in this technique.

You may discover an image that can even benefit from processing it three times—once for the shadows, once for the midtones, and once for the highlights. This situation happens when certain tones are compromised by the processing for the highlights or shadows. You can also capture extreme tonal ranges with three (or more) exposures. You then combine all of them using the same basic technique.

Photoshop CS2 includes a new tool, HDR, that allows you to automatically combine a range of exposures that cover a wide tonal range. It does work and some photographers like it a lot. I prefer working an image to optimize specific tonalities. HDR, to my taste, is too much of an overall, gee-whiz adjustment that tends to make things look a bit gray.

Add a Tint to an Image

Contributor: Charlotte Lowrie ■ **Specialty:** Editorial and Stock
Primary Tools Used: Temperature and Calibrate sliders

Tinting images for a unique look or to simulate a vintage film look can give an image an entirely new interpretation. The interpretation can range from predominantly warm gold and green tones to steely, cool blues. As with other creative interpretations, the approach you choose and the adjustments you make should enhance the subject and mood of the image.

This technique shows you how to apply a tint to an image; in this case, warm gold. You can use the steps in this technique as a starting point for creating your own tints.

▶6.59

1

Open the image that you want to tint in Camera Raw. Press Control/⌘+U to turn off Auto Adjustments. To set the color temperature, select the White Balance tool, and then click an area in the image that should be white or neutral gray. Here, I used the snow on top of Mount Rainer to set the Temperature.

▶6.60

2

Drag the Exposure, Shadows, Brightness, Contrast, and Saturation sliders until the image is to your liking. Hold down the Alt/Option key as you drag the Exposure and Shadows sliders to preview clipping. Areas that will be clipped display against a black background for Exposure and white background for Shadows. Drag the slider left until no or few color areas are visible.

▶6.61

3

Drag the Temperature slider right to add a warm yellow tint to the image or left to add a blue tint to the image. For this image, a setting of 14750 provides the base color bias for an overall gold tint.

The change in color temperature also necessitated decreasing the Exposure from the original setting. You may need to adjust other settings throughout the process to get the tint you want.

Drag the Tint slider right to increase the magenta tint or left to increase the green tint. In this image, the Tint setting is –25.

▶6.62

4

Click the Calibrate tab. Drag the Shadow Tint slider right to increase magenta in the image or left to increase green. For this image, a setting of +60 provides a good starting point. You can adjust this setting later in the process if necessary.

▶6.63

5

Drag the Red, Green, and Blue Hue and Saturation sliders to fine-tune the tint. I increased the settings for all of the Hue and Saturation except for Red and Blue Saturation. The changes show that the shadows are being clipped as indicated in the Histogram. To adjust the clipping decrease the Shadows setting on the Adjust tab.

X-Ref To learn more about the Histogram, see Chapter 4.

▶6.64

6

Click the Adjust tab and make any tweaks to settings to complete the look. The adjustments for this image include an increase in Tint; a decrease in Exposure, Shadows, and Saturation; and an increase in Brightness and Contrast. I wanted to keep the hint of blue in the sky but infuse a golden hue to the highlights with a hint of magenta in the midtones. The tint is purely a personal choice, so make adjustments that look good to your eye.

▶6.65

7

Click the Lens tab. In the Vignetting section, drag the Amount slider to the left to add a vignette. Then drag the Midpoint slider to blend the vignette. This image's vignette has an Amount setting of –34 and a Midpoint setting of 31. Save the image.

If you want to open the image in Photoshop for further touch-ups, click Open in the Camera Raw dialog box. Additional adjustments to this image in Photoshop included dodging and burning, slight adjustments to the tint, and cleaning up the image.

▶6.66

Add Photoshop Masks and Adjustments to RAW Images

Contributor: Seán Duggan ■ **Specialty:** Fine Art
Primary Tool Used: Photoshop Masks

The adjustments you make in Camera Raw are global in nature, meaning that they affect the entire image. The primary goal when processing RAW files is to do as much work as possible in Camera Raw because you have so much control for global adjustments and the changes are losslessly applied. But for some images, you have to make local adjustments that affect only a portion of the image. For those, you have to use adjustment layers and layer masks in Photoshop.

This technique shows you how to use a RAW image processed in Camera Raw (in this example, an image taken on a rainy day at the Lake of Constance in southern Germany) and then shows you how to add a few adjustment layers with layer masks in Photoshop to take the interpretation further.

▶6.67

1

Open the image you want to process in Camera Raw. Press Control/⌘+U to turn off Auto Adjustments. Make adjustments to create a good rendition of the image. The white balance was good, so the primary changes to this image were to lighten it by adjusting the Exposure and Brightness sliders and increasing the Saturation. Once you finish you initial adjustments, click Open.

The image opens in Photoshop. The process and methods you use to make adjustments and to create masks for your images will be governed by the images themselves and what you want to do with them. The methods shown in this technique are simply the ones that I chose to use with this image. You can use this technique to jumpstart ideas for processing your images.

▶ Note

At this point, you can save the image as a master file using either the PSD or TIFF file formats.

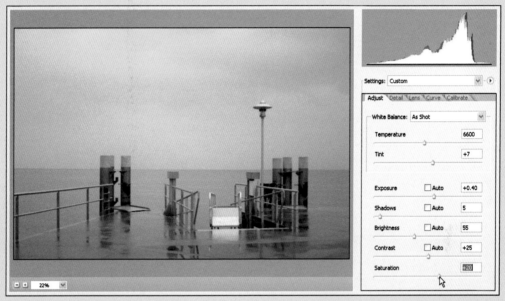

▶6.68

2

For this photograph, I wanted to darken the sky to give the sense of dark clouds and rain falling on the lake. It actually was raining as I took this photo, but I wanted to emphasize the stormy aspect of the day a bit more. To darken the sky, however, I need to create a mask so that the foreground elements of the dock do not get darkened as well. Many images already have the beginnings of a mask hiding in the image; the trick is to find and modify them to suit your needs.

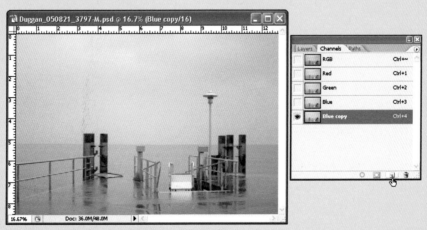

▶6.69

To find the hidden mask, select the Channels palette and search individual color channels to see whether anything is there that you can use. After clicking each color channel, I determined that the Blue channel had the most contrast between the sky and the dock. After you determine what channel to use for the mask, copy this channel by dragging it to the New Channel icon at the bottom of the Channels palette to create a mask channel.

3

A mask is made up of grayscale tones. When applied as a layer mask, white areas show adjustments to the layer and black areas do not show it. Gray areas will show adjustments partially. In this image, the copy of the Blue channel provided a good starting point for a mask; all that's required is to modify it.

To make modifications to the mask, choose Image ➤ Adjustments ➤ Levels, or press Ctrl/⌘+L to open the Levels dialog box. For this image, moving the sliders closer together creates a more pronounced contrast separation between the posts on the dock and the sky. Click OK in the Levels dialog box once you get the desired adjustment.

With your mask channel active in the Channels palette (in this case the Blue Copy channel), click the Eye icon at the top for the RGB composite-channel view. This view allows you to see the regular image and the mask channel at the same time. The black areas of the mask channel appear as a semi-transparent red overlay.

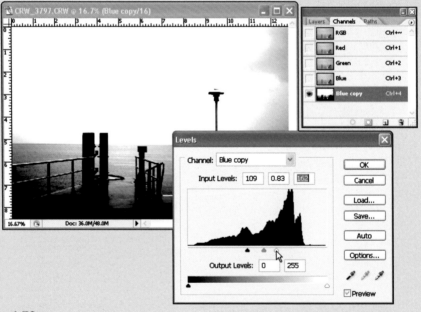

►6.70

> **Tip**
>
> When you use the Levels or Curves command to apply drastic contrast modifications to a mask, make sure that the *mask channel is the active element* and not the main image. The severity of these adjustments can wreak major havoc with the colors in an image!

4

Now, check the image for any areas where the mask needs to be adjusted. In this image, the only area where I need to manually alter the mask altered is the top part of the lamp post.

For this image, I used the Pen tool to create a path of the top section of the lamp.

▶6.71

5

Click the Paths palette. Then load the path as a selection by Ctrl/⌘+clicking on it. You then want to make sure that the mask channel is active, verify that black is the background color, and press Delete to fill the selection.

Choose Select ➤ Deselect and click RGB in the Channels palette to make the main image active and visible. Click the Eye icon for the mask to turn off the red overlay.

With a rough mask of the dock created, the next step for this example is to create an adjustment layer and layer mask to darken the clouds.

▶6.72

6

Depending on the image you're working on, you might want to make tonal adjustments to darken or lighten parts of the image. In this case, I added a Curves adjustment layer. For this image, I clicked in the clouds near the top of the image to see where these tonal values are located on the curve. You can Ctrl/⌘-click the image to place a control point on the curve for the tones you want to adjust. For this image, I pulled the point to significantly darken the entire image. Click OK in the Curves dialog box when you finish with your adjustments.

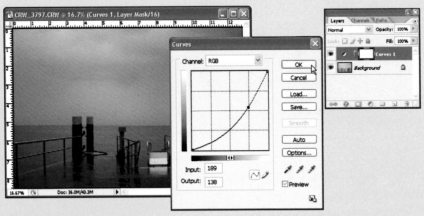

►6.73

7

If you want to create a gradual transition, you can use a Gradient. In this case, I selected the Gradient tool from the Tools palette and chose a gradient from the Gradient Picker on the Options bar. For this image, I selected the Black-to-White gradient. The gradient style is Linear, the Mode is Normal, and the Opacity is 100 percent.

►6.74

8

For this image, I positioned the cursor just above the tops of the posts. Then holding the Shift key, I dragged a line straight up to just about the level of the top of the lamp.

Using the Shift key constrains the line to a vertical when dragging up. The gradient is black where you start the line—hiding what this layer does—and the gradient is white where you release the mouse button—showing what this layer does. Everything in between is the gradient from black to white, which creates a gradual transition between the darkened clouds and the dock where no darkening is applied.

▶6.75

9

To integrate the mask of the dock, or the mask channel from earlier steps, into the gradient mask for the clouds, I chose the Blue Copy mask in the Channels palette to make it active. Then I inverted it by choosing Image ➤ Adjustments ➤ Invert.

I inverted the mask because I needed to add black to the gradient mask where the lamp pole intersects with areas that are being darkened. To do this, I inverted the mask so that those areas became white and are selected when the mask is loaded as a selection.

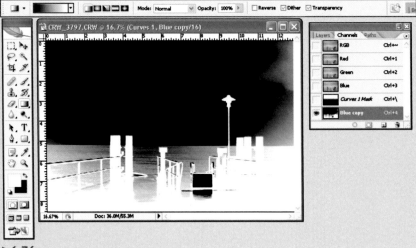

►6.76

10

Next, load the selection of your inverted (in this case, Blue Copy) mask by Ctrl/⌘+clicking its thumbnail. Click the layer mask for the Curves adjustment layer. With black set as the background color, press the Delete key to fill the selection with black. In this example, this prevents the lamp from being darkened by the clouds adjustment. Choose Select ➤ Deselect to remove the selection.

►6.77

11

Examine the image closely to see whether the edges of your selection need to be softened. Upon closer inspection of this image, I noticed the precise edges of the Pen tool looked too hard and cut out. To fix a problem like this one, use the Lasso tool to select this area. Choose Filter ➤ Blur ➤ Gaussian Blur. In this case, I applied a 1.0 pixel blur.

▶6.78

12

At this point, you may like the results of your image. But, if it still needs some enhancing, you can continue to make adjustments. For example, with this image, final adjustments included:

- Selecting and masking the lake area and adding a curve layer where I deepened the cyan/green lake color by pulling down the curve a bit on the Red channel.

- Adding a new Curves adjustment layer where I pulled down slightly on the RGB curve, and then added a bit more cyan by pulling down a bit on the red curve. Then I blurred the edges of the mask with a 1-pixel Gaussian Blur.

- On the Clouds adjustment layer, I used a large, soft-edged brush set to 10 percent opacity to brush in the appearance of falling rain over the lake.

False Colors and Special-Effects Processing

Contributor: Kevin Ames ■ **Specialty:** Glamour
Primary Tool Used: Calibrate tab

The power of Adobe Camera Raw runs much deeper than tweaking exposure and neutralizing colors. The high bit depth linear file lends itself to achieving extraordinary special effects. The possibilities include amazing black-and-white conversions, toning, and even false colors, as demonstrated in this technique.

In this photograph, I want the skin tones to go whiter than normal. This technique shows you how to make skin tones whiter and with more contrast to minimize skin flaws.

►6.79

1

Open the file you want to modify in Camera Raw. Drag the Saturation slider all the way to the left so that the setting is –100. This adjustment desaturates the image.

Note ▶ For more background on false colors, be sure to read the accompanying sidebar.

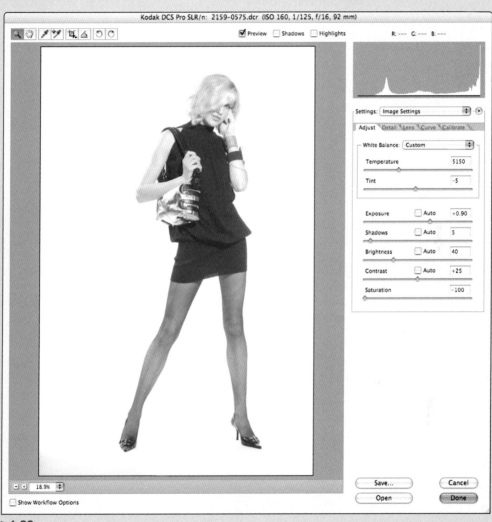

▶6.80

2

Click the Calibrate tab. Drag the Green Hue, Green Saturation, Blue Hue, and Blue Saturation sliders all the way to the left until they each read +100. These settings lighten the skin tones. To see the difference before and after the adjustments, click the Preview box, and then click it again.

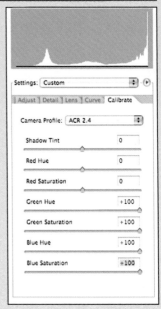

►6.81

3

Click the Adjust tab. Drag the Tint slider to the left. For this image, the initial setting is –98. Again, check the Preview box to see the difference. And, yes, the adjustment here is subtle. But you can fine-tune the conversion as necessary. For this image, I decide to increase the Brightness to 70.

However, this photograph looks flat. Further adjustments include dragging the Shadows slider to 11 and decreasing the exposure to +0.60. Finally, the Contrast is increased to +95.

What have these adjustments done to the color image? This is where the false colors come in.

►6.82

Drag the Saturation slider back to 0 to reveal the underlying color. In this image, the model is, well, really green. The settings forced the data in the Green channel to dominate the photograph. Making the Saturation −100 uses this Green channel information in black and white with the added benefit of being able to adjust the Shadows, Exposure, Brightness, and Contrast values to taste. By way of contrast, adjustments such as this are impossible to do in Channel Mixer in Photoshop alone.

▶6.83

X-Ref You can save your settings as a settings subset and use them on other files. For details on saving the settings, see Chapter 7.

5

This image is a progression of the effects of the steps in this technique. From left to right are the exposure and color-corrected version; the image at −100 Saturation (Step 1); the black-and-white model (Step 2); and the underlying greenness shown with the Saturation slider set to 0 (Step 4).

Play with combinations of the sliders in the Adjust tab in combination with those in the Calibrate tab. Remember that any changes you make to any of the sliders in Camera Raw are completely nondestructive. You can return to any setting at any time without degrading the file at all. And the output you create is 16 bit if you choose 16 Bits/Channel from the Depth menu in the Show Workflow Options section. This means that the editing options are unbelievable, all without sacrificing image quality.

▶6.84

More About Calibration Adjustments

SB Sidebar

In black-and-white photography, the color of the filter lightens that color and darkens the complement. A red filter darkens cyan and lightens red. A green filter lightens green while darkening magenta. A quick look at Photoshop's Info palette tells the tale. Digital photographs are comprised of three black-and-white channels—Red, Green, and Blue. Because the sliders on the Calibrate tab control the color of these channels, you can mix black-and-white values using the sliders.

The Calibrate tab has seven sliders, one for the shadow tint and two for each of the color channels—one for hue and one for saturation. The labels are for the most part self-explanatory. But there is a catch. These sliders don't adjust the color of their label. They control the other two. If this setup seems counterintuitive, remember this is photography. If it seems backwards, then it's probably right. Think back to the camera, for example. The big number (f/22) is for the smallest aperture whereas the smallest number (f/2.0) represents the widest aperture. Now, if that isn't backwards, I don't know what is.

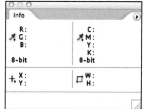

For more details on the Calibration controls, see Chapter 5.

Time-Saving Camera Raw Strategies

Chapter 07

In this chapter

Save and Apply Saved Camera Raw Settings

Contributor: Charlotte Lowrie ■ **Specialty:** Editorial and Stock
Primary Tool Used: Save Settings

One of the great advantages of using Camera Raw is its automation capabilities. You can save all or some of your image conversion settings for future use. Eventually, you can build a library of settings for everything from custom black-and-white image conversion to settings for images taken under specific lighting venues. After you save the settings, they are immediately accessible from the Settings menu in Camera Raw or from within Bridge. This technique demonstrates how you can save settings for one or more common shooting situations and reuse those settings for future shoots.

▶7.1

1

In Bridge, open the image you want to convert in Camera Raw. Choose an image taken under lighting conditions that you often shoot in, such as a studio or stadium where the lighting remains consistent. Or open an image that you want to convert to monochrome or sepia where the settings are likely to be useful for future conversions.

Apply the adjustments you want to the image. For this studio image, a Temperature of 5300 with a −2 Tint neutralizes the white areas and brings other colors in line. These are typical white balance settings for my studio setup, so saving these settings is a good choice for processing other studio shots. Because the lighting for food and other still life is often similar to the lighting in this image, saving Exposure, Shadows, Brightness, Contrast, and Saturation settings is possible as well.

Final adjustments to this image include tweaking the curve and setting the Shadow Tint to +4 on the Calibrate tab.

X-Ref For more information on setting up Camera Raw, see Appendix B.

▶7.2

2

Click the right-pointing triangle to the right of the Settings drop-down menu, and choose Save Settings. Camera Raw displays the Save Raw Conversion Settings dialog box. Type a name for the settings in the File name box, and then click Save.

Over the long term, choosing fairly specific names for settings pays off. The more descriptive and specific, the easier it is to distinguish between settings as your library of settings grows.

▶7.3

3

To apply the setting to a different image, open another image in Camera Raw. From the Settings drop-down menu, choose the setting that you saved in step 2. If you apply the settings to a similar image, few if any adjustments should be required. If you need to tweak the settings, you can make adjustments before you save the image.

▶7.4

Tip

You can also apply saved settings in Bridge. Just select the image or images to which you want to apply the settings. Right-click (Control+click on the Mac) the image or images, and then choose the saved setting name from the context menu. This method is great for quickly processing multiple images.

4

You can also save a subset of adjustments in cases where only some of the adjustments apply; for example, the color temperature or a custom curve. To save a subset of settings, open the image you want to convert and make the adjustments you want to the image.

Click the right-pointing triangle to the right of the Settings drop-down menu, and choose Save Settings Subset. Camera Raw displays the Save Settings Subset dialog box with All Settings as the default.

Adjustments to this image include straightening, tweaks to Temperature and Tint, and minor adjustments to Exposure, Shadows, Brightness, Contrast, and Saturation. In this case, the custom curve to increase contrast is the change I've made, and it is one that I should be able to use on future images.

►7.5

5

You can deselect any of the adjustments listed in the Save Settings Subset dialog box, or choose one of the options from the Subset drop-down menu. Using the latter method saves time and tedious clicking. In this case, saving the Tone Curve conveniently clears all the options except Tone Curve. Click Save in the Save Settings Subset dialog box when your selections are made.

►7.6

6

Click the right-pointing arrow to the right of the Settings drop-down menu again to open the Save Raw Conversion Settings dialog box. Type a name for the settings subset in the File name field, and then click Save.

Because this file is a subset, choose a name that clearly describes the setting that you're saving. Doing so makes identifying specific settings subsets in the future easier. This example shows "Strong Contrast Curve" as the name.

►7.7

Turn Off Auto Adjustments for Good

Throughout most of this book, photographers work with Camera Raw's Use Auto Adjustments turned off. Using the keyboard shortcut, Control/⌘+U, to turn off the automatic settings is easy enough, but if you want to avoid this step entirely, you can save the off setting as a default for images you open in Camera Raw.

To permanently turn off Use Auto Adjustments, click the right-pointing triangle to the right of the Settings drop-down menu, and uncheck the Use Auto Adjustments box. Then with automatic adjustments turned off, again click the right-pointing triangle, and choose Save New Camera Raw Defaults from the Camera Raw Menu.

If you decide that you want to return to the automatic adjustments, press Control/⌘+U to temporarily turn on automatic adjustments. If you are in Filmstrip mode in Camera Raw and you want to use automatic adjustments for all the images, click Select All, and then use the shortcut keys to turn on automatic adjustments.

Zoom and Check Focus Quickly

Contributor: Ellen Anon ■ **Specialty:** Nature and Outdoors
Primary Tool Used: Camera Raw Filmstrip Mode and Zoom Tool

The first task when selecting images to keep is to check focus. And if you've tediously gone through images one by one in Camera Raw magnifying them to 100 percent to check for critical sharpness, you know how slow the process can be. This technique shows you a faster way to check for tack-sharp focus in Camera Raw's Filmstrip mode.

▶7.8

1

In Bridge, select the images you want to check for critical sharpness. To select all images, choose Edit ➤ Select All. Choose File ➤ Open in Camera Raw. Alternatively, double-click one of the selected images; Camera Raw opens all the images in Filmstrip mode with the first image selected.

▶7.9

 Tip ▶ To select contiguous images, press the Shift key as you click the first and last image. To select noncontiguous images, press the Control/⌘ key as you click each image.

2

Click Select All in Camera Raw. Be sure to wait for the yellow exclamation mark icon to disappear. Until the icon disappears, the image will not appear sharp. Click the down arrow next to Select Zoom Level, and then click 100%. Press H to select the Hand tool, and then move to the area of critical focus.

►7.10

3

Select the next image in the filmstrip. When it opens in the preview area, it will already be at 100 percent magnification. Wait for the yellow exclamation icon to disappear. To move to a different area of the image, press the spacebar, and then click and drag to move to the desired part of the image to check focus. You can use the Previous and Next arrows at the bottom right under the image preview to move through the images, and you can press the spacebar and click and drag to move all of the images.

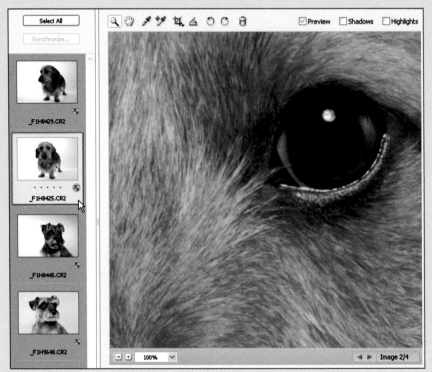

►7.11

4

To help you remember which images are best, you can add or delete stars for the image by clicking the star symbols below the thumbnails in the filmstrip. You can also click the Delete (trashcan) icon on the toolbar to mark for deletion any image that you discover is not sharp enough.

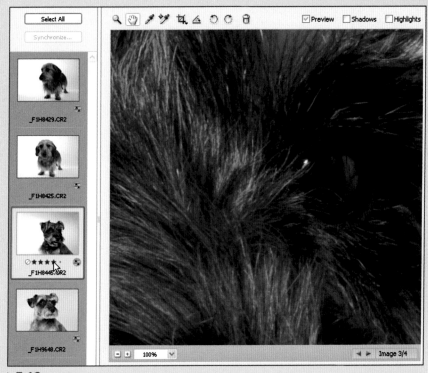

►7.12

Convert RAW Files to JPEG, TIFF, and PSD Painlessly

Contributor: Charlotte Lowrie ■ **Specialty:** Editorial and Stock
Primary Tool Used: Image Processor

The shortest distance between RAW files and JPEG, TIFF, or PSD versions of files is through Photoshop's Image Processor. Image Processor is a one-stop dialog box that makes quick work of getting JPEG files on your Web site for client viewing—and Image Processor automatically converts the files to 8-bit mode and sizes files to your specifications. In addition, you can use Image Processor to simultaneously save files in TIFF and PSD formats.

This technique illustrates getting selections on a Web site for client viewing and making a set of backup copies of the files in TIFF format.

►7.13

In Bridge, navigate to the folder that contains the images you want to save in one or more different file formats. Because Image Processor offers so many possibilities, you might choose to select a folder in which the images have already been processed in Camera Raw, as in this example, or you can run basic processing on the images based on a single processed image. Alternatively, you can use Image Processor for simple tasks such as embedding an ICC color profile or adding copyright metadata to the files.

As you gain familiarity with Image Processor, you can use it in multiple ways to save processing time. Part of the advantage of using Image Processor over Batch processing is that you do not have to create a Photoshop action beforehand. However, with Image Processor, you have the option of running an existing Photoshop action.

In the Bridge folder, you can select one, multiple, or all images in the folder for conversion. This example shows four images selected for processing.

Choose Tools ➤ Photoshop ➤ Image Processor. Photoshop launches, and the Image Processor dialog box opens.

▶7.14

> **Note**
>
> Image Processor runs in Photoshop, and you can use it on Photoshop PSD, JPEG, and RAW files. If you're working in Photoshop, you can access Image Processor by choosing File ➤ Scripts ➤ Image Processor.

2

If you want to process a group of images in Camera Raw based on settings applied to another processed image, select Open first Image to apply settings in section 1 of the dialog box. This option obviously works for a series of images taken under the same lighting and with the same exposure.

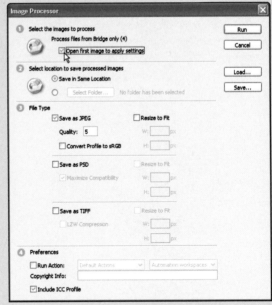

▶7.15

3

Depending on your workflow, you may want to save converted files in a new folder. However, Photoshop automatically creates and names separate folders within the destination folder for each file type—that is, JPEG, PSD, and/or TIFF. But if you want, you can create a new folder. In section 2, select the Select Folder option, and then click Select Folder. Photoshop displays the Browse For Folder dialog box.

Navigate to the folder you want, click the Make New Folder/New Folder button to create a new subfolder, and click OK.

> **Note**
> If you choose to save processed files in the same folder as the original files, Photoshop does not overwrite existing files with the processed files. Instead, each processed file is saved with a unique filename.

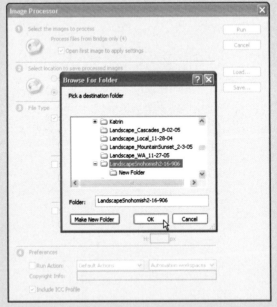

▶7.16

In section 3 of the Image Processor dialog box (File Type), you can select one or all of the formats: JPEG, PSD, and TIFF. Under each file type, you can choose additional options as follows:

- **Save as JPEG.** Saves files in JPEG format at a quality from 0 to 12 that you select. You can also choose Convert Profile to sRGB for Web use. If you choose this option, also ensure that the Include ICC Profile box is turned on in section 4 of the Image Processor dialog box. You can choose to Resize to Fit, and then specify the width and height in pixels.

- **Save as PSD.** Saves files in Photoshop file format. You can choose Resize to Fit and specify the pixel dimensions. When you choose this option, images are saved in a folder called PSD in the original folder. If you're working with layered images (unlikely if you're processing RAW files) you can choose Maximize Compatibility to save a composite version of the image so that it's compatible with applications that don't read layered images.

- **Save as TIFF.** Saves files in TIFF format in a folder called TIFF in the original folder. You can choose to use LZW Compression, a lossless compression that reduces file size. You can also choose Resize to Fit and specify pixel dimensions.

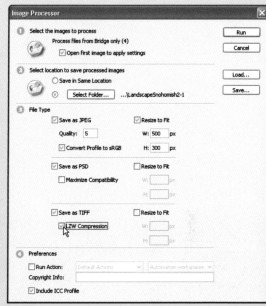

►7.17

5

In section 4 (Preferences) of the dialog box, you can opt to run an existing Photoshop action. Select Run Action, choose the action set from the Default Actions drop-down menu, and choose an action from the Automation Workspaces drop-down menu.

You can also type your copyright in the Copyright Info field. The text you type over-writes any existing copyright metadata in the original file. If you don't want to embed the color profile, click to clear the Include ICC Profile box.

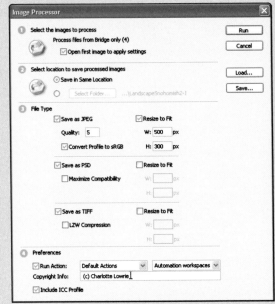

►7.18

6

You can save the settings you've made in the Image Processor dialog box for future use by clicking the Save button. Type a name for the Image Processor settings in the Pick a XML file to save dialog box, and then click Save.

The next time you want to run these specific Image Processor settings, you can choose the Load button in the Image Processor dialog box, and then select the settings.

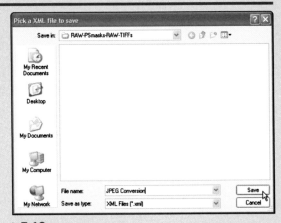

►7.19

7

In the Image Processor dialog box, click the Run button to process the images. Any processing tasks that require your intervention are displayed in sequence in Photoshop as the images are processed. When the processing is complete, you can view the saved files in the folders that Photoshop creates automatically in the destination folder.

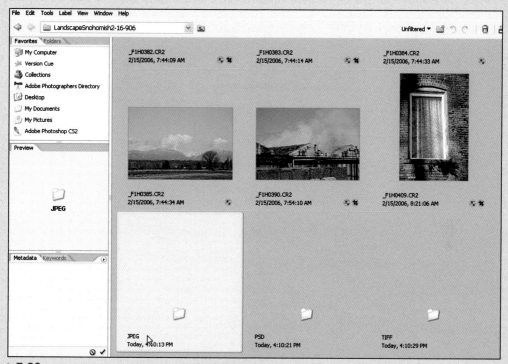

►7.20

Create a Web Site from RAW Images

Contributor: David H. Wells ■ **Specialty:** Photojournalism and Editorial
Primary Tool Used: Web Photo Gallery

Often after a shoot, you need to post low-resolution versions of the images for the client's review and selection. With Camera Raw and Photoshop CS2, you can quickly create a professional-looking Web site or add images to your existing Web site so that clients can view images. Of course, you need to have already contracted with an Internet Service Provider (ISP) to host the site and have a way to upload images, such as via an FTP program.

►7.21

1

Gather all the RAW files that you want to include on the Web site into one folder. For this example, I use a file of top images from India. You can also select the images that you want to make into a Web site by browsing a set of images in the Bridge and selecting the ones you want.

►7.22

Tip

Now is a good time to create a destination folder that you will use later in the process of creating the Web photo gallery. Be sure to create a destination folder that is outside the source folder to avoid getting an error message later.

If you haven't already adjusted the images, be sure to process them in Camera Raw by adjusting the image settings. The conversion process creates sidecar XMP files with the same name as the RAW files. The XMP files contain the instructions on how to correct the RAW images when you open and save them in another file format.

If you haven't added metadata information, append it now. At a minimum, the metadata should include your name, copyright notice, and your contact information in the metadata and IPTC areas of all image files.

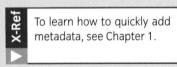

X-Ref
To learn how to quickly add metadata, see Chapter 1.

If you want to create a gallery from only selected files in the folder, select the files now. Also, the gallery will display images in the same order that they appear in Bridge. If you want to change the order, drag the images into the sequence you want.

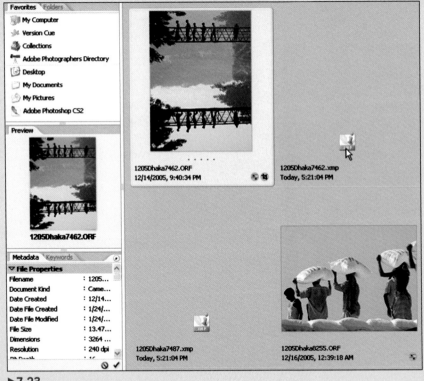

▶7.23

Tip
To view sidecar XMP files in image folders, choose View ➤ Show Hidden Files in Bridge. Also ensure that Show All Files on the View menu is selected as well. If the XMP files become a distraction, you can repeat this process to hide the files.

3

In Bridge, choose Tools ➤ Photoshop ➤ Web Photo Gallery. Photoshop launches and displays the Web Photo Gallery dialog box. Click the Styles drop-down menu to display a list of page templates. Type your e-mail in the E-mail field.

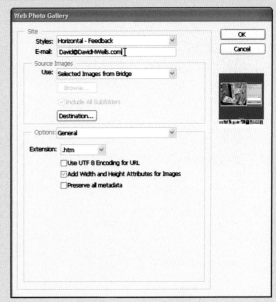

►7.24

4

From the Use drop-down menu, choose Folder or Selected Images from Bridge. If you choose Folder, then click Browse. In the Browse For Folder dialog box, navigate to the folder with the images, and then click OK. If you don't want to include images in subfolders, or if there are no subfolders, click to clear the Include All Subfolders check box. If you choose Selected Images from Bridge, the gallery is created using images you selected in step 2.

Click Destination, and then navigate to a destination folder where the images and the HTML pages will be stored.

►7.25

5

The Options drop-down menu contains a number of individual elements that appear on the Web pages. Go through each one that applies to your needs and make your selections.

- **General.** You can specify encoding, whether to Add Width and Height Attributes for Images, and whether to Preserve all metadata. Ensuring that metadata is preserved is always a good idea.

- **Banner.** Here you can enter the Site Name, Photographer, and Contact Info, and then modify the default Date. In this example, the Security option is selected.

- **Large Thumbnails.** If you want to specify the display size and JPEG quality level, add a border, or use a title for the large thumbnails, use this option to make the changes you want.

- **Thumbnails.** This option allows you to specify the size, layout, border size, titles, font, and font size for thumbnail images.

- **Custom Colors.** As the name implies, you can set Background and Banner colors using this option.

- **Security.** Use this option to add a security or other notice (such as your copyright notice) and specify how the element appears. Security is one area to pay special attention to. I usually use the Filename option from the Content drop-down menu so the exact image name is visible to clients, who then tell me which image(s) they want to use. If you choose Custom Text, the Custom Text field becomes active, and you can include any text you want. I occasionally include both my copyright notice and the filename in the image.

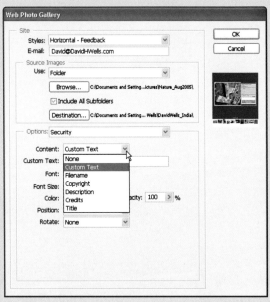

►7.26

6

Click OK in the Web Photo Gallery dialog box, and then sit back as Photoshop creates the gallery. When the processing is complete, Photoshop automatically displays the home page (ending in index.html) in the browser. The destination folder includes the following:

- **A home page, or index.html, file.** The file extension may differ depending on the options you chose. You can open the file in any Web browser to preview the home page and the gallery. In addition, Photoshop adds photos.jpg, photos.xml, ThumbnailFrame, and UserSelections files, which are script and code files that are necessary to order and browse through photos. If you are experienced in editing HTML code, you can open the files in a text editor and customize the files.

- **A subfolder that contains JPEG images.**

- **A subfolder that contains individual gallery pages.**

- **A subfolder that contains JPEG thumbnail images.**

You can upload the package to your Web site. In my case, the final Web link that I send to the client is something like www.davidhwells.com/FolderThat HoldstheSiteName/index.htm.

►7.27

SB Sidebar

Experiment with Templates

You can also try out different Web page looks using any of the 20 templates that Photoshop offers. A good way to do this is by putting a few images in a folder and using different templates. I prefer the Horizontal – Feedback style, but because many different options exist for layouts, colors, security, image sizes, and so on, spending time comparing different styles and deciding which one suits your work, your personality, and works well with the rest of your Web site is worthwhile.

Posting work on your own Web site is an efficient way to show your work to potential end users. Typically after a shoot, I post a set of images going through the process described in this technique. I FTP the completed images to my Web site, and then send a link to the client. The client can immediately evaluate the work by looking at the low-resolution files via the Web and tell me which image(s) he or she wants to use. I can then prepare high-resolution files and send them to the client via FTP or by mailing a CD.

Section 3

Add Finishing Touches in Photoshop

Final Editing in Photoshop

Chapter 08

In this chapter

Cleaning Up Images

Contributor: Charlotte Lowrie ■ **Specialty:** Editorial and Stock
Primary Tool Used: Photoshop Healing and Cloning

Photographers approach image cleanup with approximately the same amount of anticipation as they have at the prospect of a root canal. The advent of digital image sensors—with their unique propensity to gather dust—has resulted in photographers logging countless hours spotting images in Photoshop.

Of course, the best solution is prevention—keeping the image sensor sparkling clean and using immaculate backgrounds. But if your image sensor and backgrounds fall shy of being spotless, then cleanup continues to require attention. This technique shows you how to use various tools to clean up images.

▶8.1

1

Open the image you want to clean up, and make adjustments in Camera Raw. This image of garlic was shot on an obviously well-used, white seamless background. And it provides endless opportunities for clean up. Of course, before cleaning up the image, I have to convert the image and open it in Photoshop. Adjustments to this image included tweaks to Temperature and Exposure, as well as slight adjustments to the tone curve.

When you finish making adjustments, save the image if you want, and then click Open. The image opens in Photoshop.

▶8.2

2

If you didn't crop the image in Camera Raw, now is a good time to crop it so that you don't spend time removing spots from areas that will be cropped. If you want to keep corrections on a separate layer, choose Layer ➤ Duplicate Layer. In the Duplicate Layer dialog box, type a name for the layer in the As box, and then click OK.

For most corrections, I use adjustment layers, but when spotting dust or smudges in non-critical areas, I sometimes edit the original pixels. Later in this technique, you learn how to use an adjustment layer and mask to clean up larger areas.

Select the Zoom tool, or press Alt/Option+V+A to zoom the image to 100 percent.

Scroll through the image from top to bottom and side to side and use the Healing Brush, Clone Stamp, and the Patch tools to remove defects.

These tools are accessible in the Toolbox. Here is a short overview of when to use each tool and what to expect:

- **Healing Brush tool.** This tool works well for most dust spots and other imperfections. It copies a clean area of the image onto the problem area of the image. Its algorithm evaluates both the clean part of the image and the dirty area so that it can make a smooth transition of tones and replaces the dirty area by removing only the dirty pixels. To use the Healing Brush tool, select the tool, press Alt/Option and click a clean area, and then click the defective area to replace it. It's best to make single clicks instead of dragging the tool—a method that can produce noticeable patterns. Also resample from clean areas often. The downside of the Healing Brush tool are the smudges it creates when you use it in areas close to where the color or contrast is different from the sampled area.

- **Clone Stamp tool.** This tool works well for areas where the Healing Brush tool fails, such as around high-contrast edges. The Clone Stamp tool copies the clean area onto the problem area, but it does not evaluate both areas to calculate a smooth transition; rather it makes an exact copy. To use the Clone Stamp tool, select the tool, press Alt/Option and click a clean area, and then click the defective area to replace it.

- **Patch tool.** This tool works much like the Healing Brush and is most useful for irregularly shaped spots. Unlike the Healing Brush and Clone Stamp, you use the Patch tool by first selecting the defect and then selecting the clean area that will replace the defect. You can also use the Patch tool to draw a selection around the defect area. Then you move the tool inside the selection and drag the selection over a clean area of the image. The selection you make with the Patch tool stays selected, so deselect it by pressing Ctrl/⌘+D before moving on to other tasks.

In this image, I used a combination of these tools to spot specific areas in the garlic clove and to remove large smudges on the seamless paper. The Patch tool is being used in the figure.

▶8.3

3

A range of other techniques for cleanup include converting the image to LAB Color, applying a Gaussian Blur to the Lightness channel, or creating a mask and applying the Dust & Scratches filter. Much depends on the type of areas that you want to clean up. Applying the Dust & Scratches filter works well for large areas of continuous tones such as skies and out-of-focus backgrounds. Because this image contains large areas of continuous color, the Dust & Scratches filter is useful for illustration purposes.

To create the layer, choose Layer ➤ Duplicate Layer. In the Duplicate Layer dialog box, type a name for the layer in the As box. Naming layers offers the advantage of being able to quickly identify individual adjustments if you need to go back and tweak them. Click OK. Be sure the image is zoomed to 100 percent. Then scroll to an area in the image with larger-sized spots.

▶8.4

4

Choose Filter ➤ Noise ➤ Dust & Scratches. Drag the Radius slider until the spots disappear. For this image, a radius of 5 is enough to eliminate background spots. Click OK. Photoshop applies the Dust & Scratches filter to the duplicate layer.

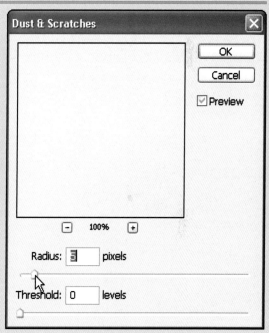

▶8.5

5

Choose Layer ➤ Layer Mask ➤ Hide All. Photoshop creates a black mask that hides the dust layer. Click on the black layer mask thumbnail to select the mask. Be sure that white is set to the foreground color in the Tools palette. If black is in the foreground, click the Switch Foreground and Background Colors double-headed arrow, or press X.

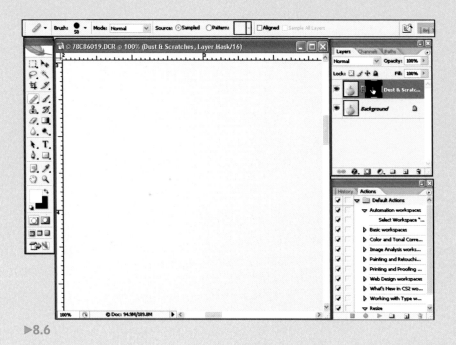

▶8.6

6

Select the Brush tool, and set the brush size to be larger than the average size spot. In this case, a brush size of 20 is adequate to paint over most of the background spots. Paint over the spots. As you paint with white on the layer mask, your Dust & Scratches layer is revealed covering the spots.

With the image spots, you can go on to complete edits on the image and save it in a format that supports layers, such as Photoshop PSD or TIFF.

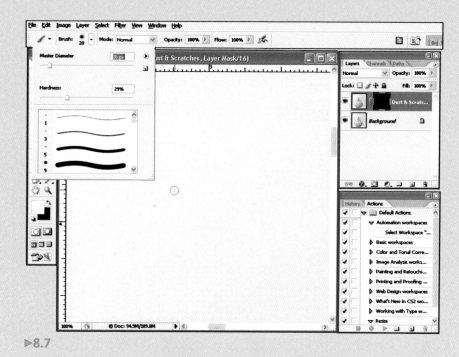

▶8.7

SB Sidebar

A Clean Image Sensor is Next to Godliness

Few early digital photographers managed to escape tedious hours spent spotting images. Regardless of how careful they were when changing lenses, photographers inevitably had to deal with the dust particles—some rivaling the size of digital meteors—that would quickly accumulate on the sensor. At the same time, keeping the sensor clean required shipping the camera body back to the manufacturer where technicians cleaned the sensor. In the meantime, the photographer was minus one camera body for days or even weeks. Today dust and water still accumulate on image sensors but photographers can now safely clean the sensors themselves.

Dust and other spots come from external dust and clothing particles that fall into the chamber while changing lenses, from dust or lubricants within the camera body that are dislodged by carrying the camera, and from changes in air pressure.

Regardless of the source, the task of cleaning the image sensor is easier than ever before. Using the mirror lock-up function and any of several excellent cleaning products available, photographers can clean the image sensor in a few minutes' time. Of course, the best practice is to first check your camera manual to see what cleaning methods and products the camera manufacturer recommends.

To clean the sensor on my camera, I use the VisibleDust products available on www.visibledust.com. The company offers cleaning solutions, swabs, and state-of-the-art soft brushes designed to gently clean or lift dust and spots without damaging the sensitive sensor surface.

Regardless of what product you use, you'll spend more time shooting and less time spotting if you clean the sensor when dust begins to show up in images. The frequency depends on how much you use the camera and in what conditions you shoot. Always follow the manufacturer's instructions and precautions when cleaning the image sensor. The sensor can be scratched and otherwise damaged, so use caution when cleaning it.

Retouch Blemishes and Wrinkles

Contributor: Bob Coates ■ **Specialty:** Weddings and Portraits
Primary Tool Used: Photoshop Healing Brush, Clone Stamp, and Patch tools

Retouching blemishes and wrinkles is the finishing touch to portraits. The trick is to balance the retouching so that the subjects look their best and can still have their character shine through in the final image. As a general rule, judicious choices on how much to retouch and a gentle hand are all that's needed to provide pleasing results.

▶8.8

1

Convert the file you want to retouch in Camera Raw. Because this image was a studio shot, I made very few adjustments to the RAW file, only increasing the Exposure by 0.10, increasing Shadows to 5, and slightly tweaking the Brightness and Saturation.

When you finish making adjustments in Camera Raw, click Open. The image opens in Photoshop.

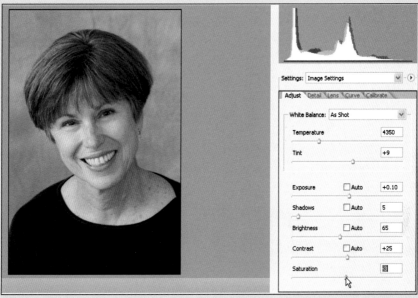

▶8.9

The first step is to remove some of the lines around the subject's eyes and along the upper lip. Zoom in on the areas you want to work on by clicking the Zoom tool or by pressing Ctrl/⌘++. Choose Layer ➤ Duplicate Layer or press Ctrl/⌘+J. In the New Layer dialog box, type a name for the layer in the As box (Wrinkles Adjustment in this example), and then click OK.

To reduce wrinkles in this image, I chose to use the Patch tool. In the Toolbox, click and hold the Healing Brush tool, and then select the Patch tool from the flyout menu, if it isn't the active tool. To use the Patch tool, select the area you want to change, and then select a clean area to replace the area to be changed. Alternatively, you can place the Patch tool pointer inside a selection you've made and drag to the area that you want to use for replacement texture. Then press Ctrl/⌘+D to deselect.

To clean up the next area, move the curser to and select the area. Repeat the process for each area you want to clean up. When you finish making changes, click the Opacity drop-down menu in the Layers palette, and drag the Opacity slider to your chosen adjustment.

Usually I use an Opacity setting for younger clients of 68%, but I chose a lower setting of 40% here to avoid taking away from this person's character.

When you know that you have what you want, you may want to merge this layer down by choosing Layer ➤ Merge Down or by pressing Ctrl/⌘+E.

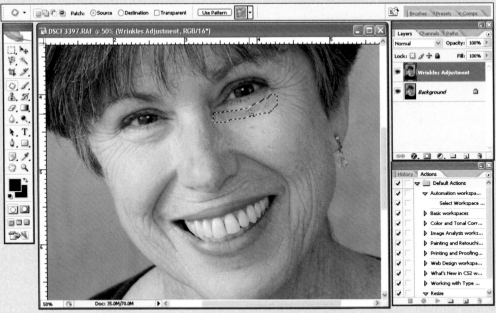

▶8.10

Choose Layer ➤ Duplicate Layer or press Ctrl/⌘+J, and then type a name for the layer. Select the Clone Stamp tool from the Toolbox. From the Mode drop-down menu on the Options toolbar, choose Lighten. Also in the Options toolbar, choose an Opacity of 10 percent. You may want to lessen the Opacity in some cases to 5 percent.

Press Alt/Option and sample an area on the subject that is brighter than the shadow area that you're working on and make strokes to ease the shadows in these areas. To check your work, click the Eye icon next to the adjustment layer to see the image with and without adjustments.

▶8.11

4

To remove brown spots, which are on the subject's neck in this example, select the background layer, and then create and name a duplicate layer (I've called it Heal Brown Spots). Drag the new layer to the top in the Layers palette. In the Toolbox, click and hold the Patch tool, and then select the Healing Brush tool from the flyout menu. The Healing Brush tool works similarly to the Clone Stamp tool. Just Alt/Opt+click a clean area to sample, and then click the area you want to correct. For the best results, don't drag the Healing brush tool; instead click each area you want to correct, sort of like dotting an *i*.

This tool is also great for removing blemishes on younger clients.

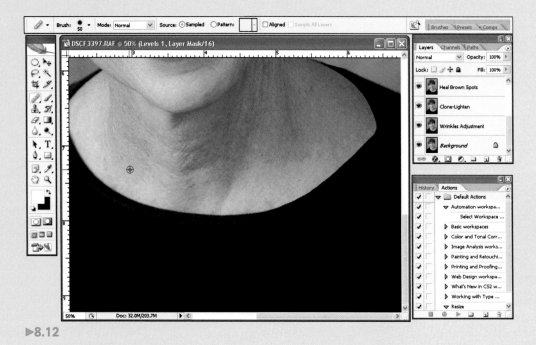

▶8.12

5

In this image, one side of the subject's top moved a bit during the shoot. Noticing and correcting these types of problems while you are shooting is best, but the second best option is to fix it in Photoshop. Create and name a duplicate layer for the adjustments, here simply called Move Top.

Click and hold the Lasso Tool in the Toolbox, and then select the Magnetic Lasso tool from the Toolbox. Make a selection of the edge of the object; in this case, the subject's top. Select the Move tool from the Tools palette and move the selection in. Choose Edit ➤ Free Transform or press Ctrl/⌘+T, and then drag the edges to blend them into the rest of the top. You can use a layer mask to remove any hard line that may have appeared from adding the layer.

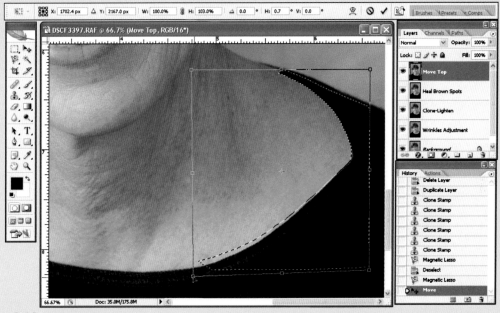

▶8.13

6

Scroll through the image looking for other areas that need retouching. In this image, I retouched a couple of areas where stray hairs were visible using a duplicate layer I called Fix Stray Hairs and the Clone Stamp and Patch tools.

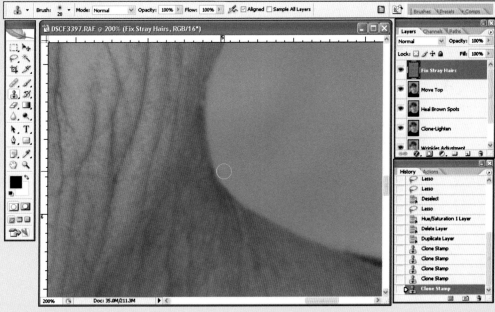

▶8.14

7

The next step in this example is to reduce the appearance of red on the nose. Instead of using the Clone Stamp or Patch tools, select the Lasso tool from the Tools palette, and then make a loose selection around the red areas. To feather the selection, enter the amount on the Options toolbar you want to Feather. For this image a feathering setting of 3 pixels works well.

From the bottom of the Layers palette, click the Create new fill or adjustment layer icon (the icon is a half black and half white circle), and then choose Hue/Saturation from the dropdown menu. In the Hue/Saturation dialog box, choose Reds from the Edit drop-down menu. Drag the Saturation slider to the left slightly. Be gentle when desaturating an image because you don't want an obvious line to show. A slight desaturation allows you to reduce the redness without losing skin texture, as you can see in the figure. Click OK. Choose Select ➤ Deselect or press Ctrl/⌘+D.

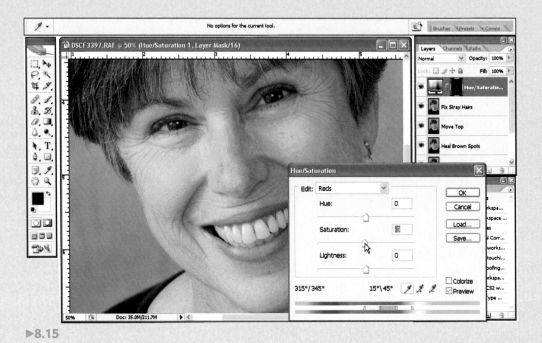

▶8.15

8

If you did not crop the image in Camera Raw, select the Crop tool and drag to crop the image, and then press Enter/Return. Finally, if you didn't add a vignette in Camera Raw, you can do so now to direct the viewer's eye to the subject. Create another duplicate layer. In the toolbox, click and hold the Rectangular Marquee tool and select the Elliptical Marquee tool from the flyout menu. Make a selection with the elliptical Marquee tool. Choose Select ➤ Inverse, or press Ctrl/⌘+Shift+I. On the Options toolbar next to Feather, type **150** pixels for a high-resolution image.

▶8.16

9

From the bottom of the Layers palette, click the Create new fill or adjustment layer icon (the icon is a half black and half white circle), and then choose Levels from the dropdown menu. In the Levels dialog box, drag the left slider, and then the middle slider to the right to darken the image slightly. Click OK in the Levels dialog box. There will already be a selection made in the mask on this layer, and you can refine it using the Brush tool.

Remember to save the final file. You can save the file in PSD, or TIFF format to retain the layers (provided you specify a layered TIFF—actually, layer compression is the TIFF default in the TIFF Options dialog box, so I don't think we have to specify it).

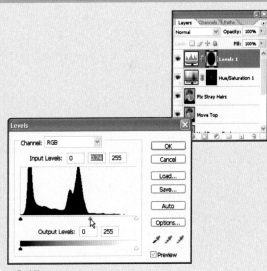

▶8.17

Convert 16-Bit Images to 8-Bit Images

Contributor: David H. Wells ■ **Specialty:** Photojournalism and Editorial
Primary Tool Used: Photoshop Convert Mode

High bit-depth images offer many advantages, including more subtle tonal gradations and a higher dynamic range than low bit-depth images. High bit-depth images also provide much more latitude in editing images. For these reasons, doing as much editing in 16-bit mode as possible before converting the image to 8-bit mode is best.

The process of converting from 16 bit to 8 bit is simple in either Camera Raw or in Photoshop. In most workflows, the conversion to 8 bit is the very last step in Photoshop before sizing the image—even after converting the color space to the target output and sharpening the image.

▶8.18

1

If you want to use RAW images for display on a Web site, you can convert them to 8-bit mode in Camera Raw. In this scenario, you can set all the Show Workflow Options for Web display as well. For example, you can set the Space to sRGB, the Depth to 8 Bits/Channel, downsample the image by choosing a smaller size, and set the resolution to 96 pixels/inch.

If you choose this route, you may want to process and save these images in JPEG format in a subfolder to keep the images separate from the high-resolution images.

X-Ref More automated methods exist for using RAW images for display on a Web site. See Chapter 7.

►8.19

2

Alternatively, you can process the file in Camera Raw, and then click Open. The image opens in Photoshop. Edits in Camera Raw to the image in this example included tweaks to tonal adjustments using Curves, and cleanup of the sky using the Dust & Scratches filter with a Layer mask, which are explained earlier in the chapter.

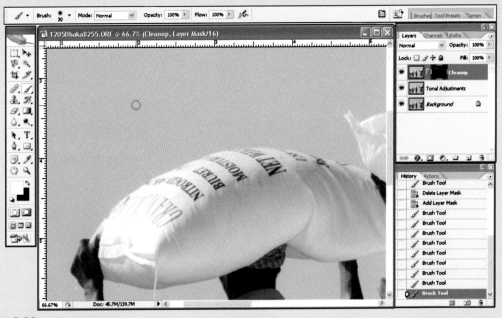

►8.20

Tip

To convert to a different color space in Photoshop, choose Edit ➤ Convert to Profile. In the Convert to Profile dialog box choose the color space you want from the Destination Space Profile drop-down menu. Click OK. For printing images, Adobe RGB (1998) is a good choice. For online display, sRGB is the ticket.

3

Now you can complete adjustments such as sizing the image and converting to the appropriate color space for printing or Web display. For more information on those tasks, see the next technique in this chapter. When you finish editing in Photoshop, convert the image to 8-bit mode. Choose Image ➤ Mode ➤ 8 Bits/Channel. Photoshop converts the 16-bit image to 8-bit mode.

Remember to save the image with a new name if you want to keep it distinct from the 16-bit image.

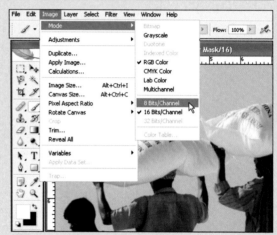

▶8.21

What is High Bit-Depth and Why Should I Care?

SB Sidebar

Because digital images are based on the Red, Green, Blue (RGB) color model, an 8-bit digital image has eight bits of color information for red, eight bits for green, and eight bits for blue. These values make a total of 24 bits of data per pixel (8 bits × 3 color channels). Because each bit can be one of two values, either 0 or 1, the total number of possible values is 2 to the 8th power, or 256 per color channel.

In the RGB color model, the range of colors is represented on a continuum from 0 (black) to 255 (white). On the continuum, an area of an image that is white is represented by 255R, 255G, and 255B. An area of the image that is black is represented by 0R, 0G, 0B.

An 8-bit file offers 256 possible colors per channel equaling potential combinations of 256 × 256 × 256. A 16-bit file provides 65,000 colors per channel—the potential for all colors is 65,000 × 65,000 × 65,000, and a 24-bit file (common on some film scanners) provides 16.7 million colors per channel. There is, of course, an upper limit on bit-depth because the human eye can detect hundreds of thousands of colors whereas printers can reproduce far fewer distinguishable colors.

As you can see by these numbers, you have many more pixels to work with in high bit-depth images than you do in 8-bit images. Every pixel counts toward smoother gradations, increased detail, and more editing latitude as you make the final edits in Photoshop.

Size and Sharpen Images for Specific Uses

Contributor: Charlotte Lowrie ■ **Specialty:** Editorial and Stock
Primary Tool Used: Photoshop Image Size and Unsharp Mask

The final steps for preparing images for printing or for online display is sizing and sharpening, which is what this technique is all about. The most important aspects for these steps is following a careful workflow that includes file renaming to ensure that you don't overwrite the high-resolution files, as well as avoiding oversharpening images. But with the new Photoshop CS2 Unsharp Mask filter or other sharpening programs and plug-ins, you can get beautifully sharpened images with little effort.

▶8.22

1

Open the image you want to size and sharpen in Camera Raw and convert it. In this example, tonal adjustments included increasing contrast and straightening the image.

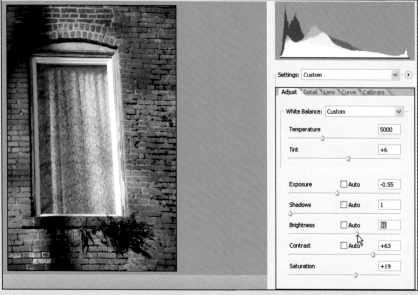

▶8.23

2

Click Open to open the image in Photoshop and make the edits you want using adjustment layers. Because this is a final source file that you can copy and use for a specific use such as printing, you can flatten layers and save the file using a different name. To flatten layers, choose Layer ➤ Flatten Image.

If you save separate versions of the image for different output uses, create a naming scheme and folder structure for each version. For example, if you save a low-resolution version for use on the Web, you can create a subfolder for JPEG images. If you are creating versions sized for printing, create a subfolder for the sized and sharpened images.

Choose File ➤ Save As. In the Save As dialog box, modify the name in the File name field, and choose the format you want from the Format drop-down menu. Click Save. If you save in TIFF format, choose the options you want, and click OK in the TIFF Options dialog box.

▶8.24

Before making a copy of the file for a specific use, determine what size you need for the intended output. If you are sizing an image for printing, know the dimensions that you want to print; if you're sizing an image for the Web, know what display size you want.

Choose Image ➤ Image Size to open the Image Size dialog box. For images that you intend to print, you can

- **Set both the Width and Height.** Type the dimensions that you want in the Width and Height fields in the Document Size section of the dialog box.

- **Set one dimension and have Photoshop set the other dimension proportionally.** To set one dimension, deselect the Constrain Proportions option. (Actually it is a function of the Constrain Proportions check box.) In the Height or Width field, type the size you want in inches. Photoshop automatically sets the other dimension.

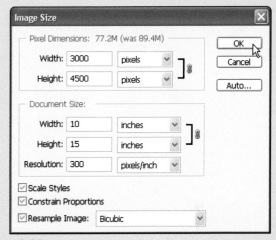

The Resolution automatically reflects the changes made to the image size. It is not a problem if the image resolution exceeds the resolution of the output device. Click OK.

▶8.25

4

Now that the image is sized, you can sharpen it for printing or online display. Choose Filter ➤ Sharpen ➤ Unsharp Mask. In the preview window, move to an area of the image that is most likely to show the effects of oversharpening. In this example, the brick areas around the window can be overly done if the sharpening adjustments are not exact.

In the Unsharp Mask dialog box, the Amount you set depends on several factors, including the sharpness of your camera in general, the sharpening preferences you've set in Camera Raw, and your personal preferences for sharpness. You need to experiment to find the best settings for prints and other output. For this image, a setting of 200 works well.

The Radius setting determines how many pixels around the edges are affected by the sharpening. Usually a setting of 1 or 2 is enough.

The Threshold setting determines how different from surrounding pixels the edge pixels must be to be considered as edge pixels. For example, a setting of 3 means those pixels that differ by a value of 3 are included in the sharpening. A setting of zero means that all pixels are sharpened. For this image I chose a setting of 3.

Click OK, and the image is now ready for printing or for online display.

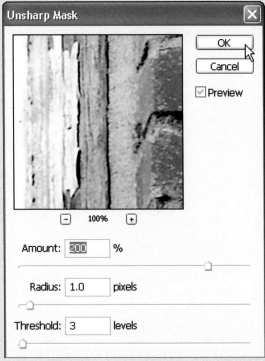

▶8.26

Glossary

Aberration   A deviation from a perfect image caused by the lens. Aberrations happen because lenses are constructed of spherical surfaces and light rays from a single subject point are not formed in the image as a perfect point; because the focal point position differs for different types or wavelengths of light; and because one or many requirements related to changes in angle of view were not met. Types of aberrations include astigmatism, barrel distortion, chromatic aberration, coma, field curvature, pincushion distortion, and spherical aberration.

Adobe RGB (1998)   A color space profile with a color gamut that is often considered the best for output devices, including inkjet and commercial printers.

Additive color   A method of producing colors of light by mixing three primary colors: red, green, and blue.

Algorithm   A mathematical formula that produces results in relation to defined values and issued in programs to process data. For instance, algorithms are used to calculate pixel values for highlight recovery. Generically used as a step-by-step procedure to solve a problem.

Aliasing   A jagged effect seen along lines in an image or graphic when the resolution is too low or when the camera cannot resolve fine detail in a diagonal line.

Artifact   An unintentional or unwanted element in an image caused by an imaging device or as a byproduct of software processing such as compression, flaws from compression, color flecks, and digital noise.

Assigning a profile   Refers to attaching a specific color space or space profile to an image. The profile translates the color numbers of an image and assigns them to specific colors in the profile. Different profiles are used for different devices, such as display and output devices. For example, sRGB is the profile of choice for electronic display devices, including monitors, whereas Adobe RGB is preferred for print output devices.

Banding   Visible tonal lines caused by converting continuous gradations in an image into too few tonal levels.

Barrel distortion   A lens aberration resulting in a bowing of straight lines outward from the center.

Batch processing   Editing multiple images simultaneously and in sequence and applying the same settings to or performing the same actions on all images.

Bit   The smallest unit of information used by computers, or a shortened form of binary digit.

Bit depth   The number of bits used to represent each pixel in an image that determines the image's color and tonal range.

Black point   The darkest area of an image. Setting the black point in Photoshop assigns tones at and below the specified darkest value to the darkest value. For example, if you set the black point setting to 10, Photoshop assigns tonal values from 0 to 10 to black, or 10.

Black-point compensation   An option in a color profile that maintains the darkest tonal value (black) between the source space and the destination space if a difference exists between the two. This feature allows the full tonal range of the destination space to be used.

Blocked up   Describes areas of an image lacking detail due to excess contrast.

Blooming   Bright edges or halos in digital images around light sources, and bright reflections caused by an oversaturation of image sensor photosites.

Bracket   To make multiple exposures, some above and some below the average exposure calculated by the light meter for the scene. Some digital cameras can also bracket white balance to produce variations from the average white balance calculated by the camera.

Brightness   The perception of the light reflected or emitted by a source. The lightness of an object or image. See also *luminance*.

Burn   In traditional photography, to darken an area of a photographic print by giving it additional exposure. In digital photography, to darken by adjusting Levels or Curves and selectively applying the darkened areas via a mask or other methods.

Byte   A unit of digital information that contains 8 bits.

Cache   Holds preparsed thumbnails, metadata, and file information for the most recently accessed files, which speeds loading time when returning to previously viewed images or folders.

Calibration   In hardware, a method of changing the behavior of a device to match established standards, such as changing the contrast and brightness on a monitor. Calibration should occur before a device is profiled, which reduces the amount of compensation the profile must include for the device. In software, calibration corrects the color cast in shadows and allows adjustment of non-neutral colors that differ between an individual camera and the camera's profile used by Camera Raw.

Camera profile   A process of describing and saving the colors that a specific digital camera produces so that colors can be corrected by assigning the camera profile to an image. Camera profiles are especially useful for photographers who often shoot under the same lighting conditions, such as in a studio.

Chroma noise   Extraneous, unwanted color artifacts in an image.

Chromatic aberration   A lens phenomena that bends different color light rays at different angles thereby focusing them on different planes. Two types of chromatic aberration exist. Axial chromatic aberration shows up as color blur or flare. Chromatic difference of magnification appears as color fringing where high-contrast edges show a line of color along their borders. The effect of chromatic aberration increases at longer focal lengths.

Clip   (As in color clipping.) Shifting of out of range pixel values to the highest or lowest value. Clipped areas are fully saturated with no detail.

Clone   A tool in image-editing software that allows you to replace or cover over a flaw by copying one area of the photo into the flawed area.

CMYK   An abbreviation for Cyan, Magenta, Yellow, and Black (K), the four colors used in commercial offset printing.

Color balance   The color reproduction fidelity of a digital camera's image sensor. In a digital camera, color balance is achieved by setting the white balance to match the scene's primary light source. You can adjust color balance in image editing programs using the color Temperature and Tint controls.

Color cast   The dominance of one color over others in an image. A color cast appears as an incorrect overall color balance often caused by an incorrect white-balance setting.

Color gamut   The range of colors that a device can capture or produce.

Color space   In the spectrum of colors, the subset of colors included in the chosen set or space. Different color spaces include more or fewer colors.

Color temperature   A numerical description of the color of light measured in degrees Kelvin. Warm, late-day light has a lower color temperature. Cool, early-day light has a higher temperature. Midday light is often considered to be "white" light (5,000°K). Flash units are often calibrated to 5,000°K.

Compositing   The process of combining all or part of two or more digital images into a single image in an image-editing program.

Compression   A means of reducing file size. *Lossy* compression permanently discards information from the original file. *Lossless* compression does not discard information from the original file.

Continuous tone   An image with smooth gradation of tones from black through gray to white.

Contrast   The range of tones from light to dark in an image or scene.

Contrasty   A term used to describe a scene or image with great differences in brightness between light and dark areas.

Cool   Describes the bluish color associated with higher color temperatures. Also used to describe editing techniques that result in an overall bluish tint.

Crop   To trim or discard one or more edges of an image. You can crop when taking a picture by changing position (moving closer or farther away) to exclude parts of a scene, by zooming in with a zoom lens, or via an image-editing program.

Daylight-balance   General term used to describe the color of light at approximately 5,500°K—such as midday sunlight or an electronic flash.

Depth of field   The zone of acceptable sharpness in a photo extending in front of and behind the primary plane of focus.

Destination profile   The color profile used to interpret colors after a profile conversion.

Dithering   Arranging pixels or dots of colors to simulate colors that are outside the color gamut of a device or color space.

Digital Negative   Abbreviated as DNG, Adobe's proposed standard format for Camera Raw image files that contains the raw camera sensor data as well as data stored in the DNG file that specifies how the image should look as adjusted in Camera Raw.

Dodge   To give less exposure to an area to lighten it.

DPI   An abbreviation for dots per inch. DPI is a measure of printing resolution.

Dynamic range   The difference between the lightest and darkest values in an image. A camera that can hold detail in both highlight and shadow areas over a broad range of values is said to have a high dynamic range.

Exposure   The amount of light reaching the light-sensitive medium—the film or an image sensor. It is the result of the intensity of light multiplied by the length of time the light strikes the medium.

Exposure compensation   Applying a plus or minus exposure factor to make images lighter or darker.

Flare   Unwanted light reflecting and scattering inside the lens causing a loss of contrast and sharpness in the image.

Flat   Describes a scene, light, photograph, or negative that displays little difference between dark and light tones.

Focus   The point at which light rays from the lens converge to form a sharp image. Also, the sharpest point in an image achieved by adjusting the distance between the lens and image.

Gamma   The relationship between tonal values and perceived brightness. A gamma of 2.2 is considered to be perceptually uniform and is recommended as a target for monitor calibration.

Gigabyte   The usual measure of the capacity of digital mass storage devices; slightly more than 1 billion bytes.

GPS   An acronym for global positioning system. GPS-enabled cameras include positioning information in file metadata.

Grain   A speckled appearance in photos. In film photographs, grain appears when the pattern of light-sensitive silver halide particles or dye molecules becomes visible under magnification or enlargement. In digital images, grain appears as multicolored flecks, also referred to as noise. Grain is most visible in high-speed film photos and in digital images captured at high ISO settings.

Gray-balanced   The property of a color model or color profile where equal values of red, green, and blue correspond to a neutral gray value.

Gray card   A card that reflects a known percentage of the light that falls on it. Typical grayscale cards reflect 18 percent of the light. Gray cards are standard for taking accurate exposure-meter readings and for providing a consistent target for color balancing during the color correction process using an image-editing program.

Grayscale   A scale that shows the progression of tones from black to white using tones of gray. Also refers to rendering photo images in black, white, and tones of gray.

Halos   Light or white around distinct edges of an image that has been oversharpened.

HDR   An acronym for high dynamic range. In Photoshop, a 32-bit HDR image is comprised of a series of bracketed images that are composited so that the final image represents the entire dynamic range in a high dynamic range scene.

Highlight   A term describing a light or bright area in a scene, or the lightest area in a scene.

Histogram   A graph that shows the distribution of tones in an image.

Hue   The color of a pixel defined by the measure of degrees on the color wheel, starting at 0 for red depending on the color system and controls.

ICC   An abbreviation for International Color Consortium, a group of companies devoted to developing industry-wide standards for color management. See www.color.org.

ICC profile   A standard format data file defined by the ICC describing the color behavior of a specific device. ICC profiles maintain consistent color throughout a color-managed workflow and across computer platforms.

Interpolation   An algorithm to increase or decrease the size of an image by adding or removing pixels of similar values throughout the image.

IPTC   Acronym for the International Press Telecommunications Council, established to safeguard the telecommuications interests of the world press.

IPTC Core   Editable metadata fields where the photographer or others can enter the photographer's name, copyright, address, a description of the image, captions, and other descriptive details.

ISO   A rating that describes the sensitivity to light of film or an image sensor. ISO in digital cameras refers to the amplification of the signal at the photosites. Also commonly referred to as film speed. ISO is expressed in numbers, such as ISO 125. The ISO rating doubles as the sensitivity to light doubles. ISO 200 is twice as sensitive to light as ISO 100.

JPEG   Acronym for Joint Photographic Experts Group. A lossy file format (it compresses data by discarding information from the original file).

Kelvin   A scale for measuring temperature based around absolute zero. The scale is used in photography to quantify the color temperature of light.

Keyword   A word describing the image content. Keywords are often used to organize and find images with specific content.

Latitude   The amount of overexposure or underexposure possible without a significant loss of image quality.

Layer   In image-editing programs, a method of isolating image elements that require specific work or adjustments. Layers enable corrections to be made without directly affecting the original image pixels.

Lightness   A measure of the amount of light reflected or emitted. See also *brightness* and *luminance.*

Linear   A relationship where doubling the intensity of light produces double the response, as in digital images. The human eye does not respond to light in a linear fashion. See also *non-linear*.

Lossless   A term that refers to file compression that discards no image data. TIFF is a lossless file format.

Lossy   A term that refers to compression algorithms that discard image data, often in the process of compressing image data to a smaller size. The higher the compression rate, the more data that's discarded, and the lower the image quality. JPEG is a lossy file format.

Luminance   The light reflected or produced by an area of the subject in a specific direction and measurable by a reflected light meter.

Luminance noise   Extraneous visible artifacts in digital images that look similar to grain in film photos.

Manual exposure   A mode on cameras where the photographer sets both the aperture and shutter speed.

Mask   Isolating and protecting parts of an image from editing changes. Non-selected areas are protected from the effects of changes. With masks and channels, areas that are painted in black are protected from edits while areas that are painted white are editable.

Megabyte   A size measure of electronic data. Slightly more than 1 million bytes.

Megapixel   A measure of the capacity of a digital image sensor. One million pixels, which are sometimes referred to as picture elements.

Metadata   Data about data, or more specifically, information about a file. Data embedded in image files by the camera includes aperture, shutter speed, ISO, focal length, date of capture, and other technical information. Photographers can add additional metadata in image-editing programs including name, address, copyright, and so on.

Middle gray   A shade of gray that has 18 percent reflectance.

Midtone   An area of medium brightness; a medium gray tone in a photographic print. A midtone is neither a dark shadow nor a bright highlight.

Moiré   Bands of diagonal distortions in an image caused by interference between two geometrically regular patterns in a scene or between the pattern in a scene and the image sensor grid.

Mottle   An uneven gray area of a photographic print.

Nanometer   One-millionth of a millimeter; a measure of wavelengths of visible light.

Noise   Extraneous visible artifacts that degrade digital image quality.

Nonlinear   A relationship where a change in stimulus does not always produce a corresponding change in response. For example, if the light in a room is doubled, the room is not perceived as being twice as bright. See also *linear*.

Overexposure   Exposing film or an image sensor to more light than is required to make an acceptable exposure. The resulting picture is too light.

Perceptually uniform   A property where the distances between two colors in a color space relate to the perceived differences between those colors.

Pincushion distortion   A lens aberration causing straight lines to bow inward toward the center of the image.

Pixel   Abbreviation for picture element. The smallest unit of information in a digital image. Pixels contain tone and color that can be modified. The human eye merges very small pixels so they appear as continuous tones.

Plane of critical focus   The most sharply focused part of a scene.

Plug-in   Programs with additional image-editing tools that can be installed for use within other image-editing programs. Adobe Camera Raw is a plug-in.

PPI   Acronym for pixels per inch: The number of pixels per linear inch on a monitor or image files. Used to describe overall display quality or resolution.

Profile mismatch   A condition where the embedded profile does not match the destination or working space profile.

Proof   A test print made to evaluate color, contrast, saturation, and so on.

PSD   Photoshop's native file format that supports layers and lossless compression.

RAW   A proprietary file format that has little or no in-camera processing. Processing RAW files requires special image-conversion software such as Adobe Camera Raw. Because image data has not been processed, you can change key camera settings including exposure and white balance in the conversion program after the picture is taken.

Reflected light meter   A device, usually a built-in camera meter, that measures light emitted by a photographic subject.

Rendering intent   A method of dealing with out-of-gamut colors when colors are translated between two color profiles. The four ICC rendering intents are Absolute Colorimetric, Relative Colorimetric, Perceptual, and Saturation.

Resampling   A method of averaging surrounding pixels to add to the number of pixels in a digital image. Sometimes used to increase resolution of an image in an image-editing program to make a larger print from the image.

Resolution   The number of pixels per side of a 1mm x 1mm square, or the number of pixels in a linear inch. Resolution is the amount of information present in an image to represent detail in a digital image.

RGB   An acronym for Red, Green, Blue, a color model based on additive primary colors of red, green, and blue. This model is used to represent colors based on how much light of each color is required to produce a given color.

Saturation   As it pertains to color, a strong, pure hue undiluted by the presence of white, black, or other colors. The higher the color purity, the more vibrant the color.

Selects   Photos chosen as the best from among a group of photos. In Adobe Bridge and Camera Raw, you can designate selects by numeric star ratings and color labels.

Sharp   The point in an image at which fine detail and textures are clear and well defined.

Sharpen   A method in image editing of enhancing the definition of edges in an image to make it appear sharper. See also *unsharp mask*.

Silhouette   A scene where the background is much more brightly lit than the subject.

SLR   An acronym for Single Lens Reflex, a type of camera that enables the photographer to see the scene through the lens that takes the picture. A reflex mirror reflects the scene through the viewfinder. The mirror retracts when the Shutter button is pressed.

Spot   To remove individual imperfections in an image-editing program.

sRGB   A color gamut that encompasses a typical computer monitor.

Subtractive color   A method of creating colors by mixing dyes with varying proportions of three subtractive primary colors: cyan, magenta, and yellow.

TIFF   Acronym for Tagged Image File Format, a universal file format that most computers can read. Commonly used for images, TIFF supports 16.8 million colors and offers lossless compression to preserve all the original file information.

Tonal range   The range from the lightest to the darkest tones in an image.

Tungsten   Common household lighting that uses tungsten filaments. Without filtering or adjusting to the correct white -balance settings, pictures taken under tungsten light display a yellow-orange color cast.

Unsharp Mask   In digital image editing, a filter that increases the apparent sharpness of the image. The unsharp mask filter cannot correct an out-of-focus image. See also *sharpen*.

Value   The relative lightness or darkness of an area. Dark areas have low values and light areas have high values.

Vignetting   Darkening of edges on an image that can be caused by lens distortion, using a filter, or using the wrong lens hood. Also used creatively in image editing to draw the viewer's eye toward the center of the image.

Warm   Reddish colors often associated with lower color temperatures.

White balance   The relative intensity of red, green, and blue in a light source. On a digital camera, white balance compensates for light that is different from daylight to create correct color balance. In image editing, an adjustment that compensates for the illumination color temperature so that white objects appear neutral in color.

Workspace   In Adobe Bridge, the configuration of the work area.

XMP   Abbreviation for Extensible Metadata Platform, a standardized method of encoding metadata in a file so that it isn't lost through the use of different programs. In Adobe Bridge and Camera Raw, adjustments are stored in individual sidecar XMP files.

Appendix A

Adobe Bridge: An Electronic Light Table

Adobe Bridge is the electronic equivalent of the traditional photographic light table. In Bridge, you can view, sort, find, and manage images and folders of images all within a relatively uncluttered space. Getting acquainted with Bridge is a first step toward mastering the tools and being able to customize Bridge to better suit your work style.

Here is a quick overview of Bridge.

1

To start Bridge, from Photoshop CS2, choose File ➤ Browse. You can also set Bridge to start automatically when Photoshop starts. In Photoshop, choose Edit ➤ Preferences ➤ General (on the Mac choose Photoshop ➤ Preferences). On the General tab in the Preferences dialog box, select Automatically Launch Bridge, and then click OK.

The Adobe Bridge window opens in the default workspace view, which is what is shown here.

Preview panel   Look In menu   Content panel

Favorites and Folders panels   Shortcut buttons

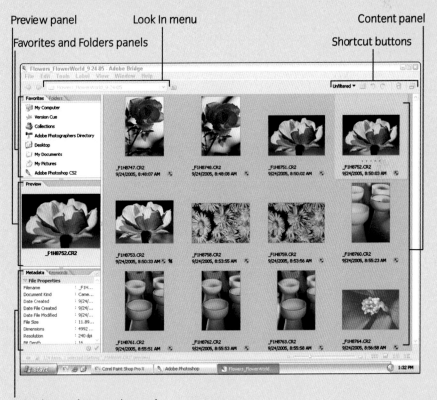

Metadata and Keywords panels

▶A.1

Tip

You can open additional Bridge windows by choosing File ➤ New Window. Starting new instances of Bridge is often a good way to compare images from different folders.

The Bridge window includes the following:

- **The Look In menu.** This menu drops down to display the folder hierarchy, Favorites, and Recent Folders.
- **The Favorites and Folders panels.**
- **The Preview panel.** This panel displays the currently selected image.
- **The Metadata and Keywords panels.** These panels display information about the selected image and keyword set and keywords.
- **Shortcut buttons.** These buttons allow you to perform routine tasks quickly.
- **The Content pane.** This pane displays thumbnail previews and details about the images, and, (7) a thumbnail size slider, and buttons to change the type of display in the content area.

2

To move to a different folder in Bridge, click the drop-down arrow next to the Look In menu. The menu shows the hierarchy of files on your computer, the Adobe Bridge Favorites folder, and a list of Recent Folders. The same options are available in a more graphic fashion on the Favorites and Folders panels at the top left of the Bridge window.

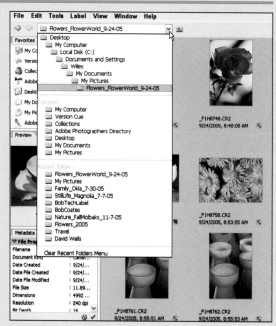

▶A.2

Tip

You can set the number of folders that appear in the Recent Folders list. Choose Edit (Bridge on the Mac) ➤ Preferences, and then choose Advanced. Type a number in the Number of Recently Visited Folders to Display in the Look In menu.

3

The Preview pane displays the selected image, albeit in a smaller-than-useful size. To increase the size of this panel and all panels on the left side of the window, drag the vertical divider bar to the right.

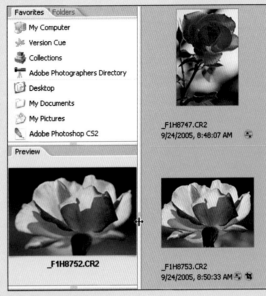

►A.3

4

The Metadata panel includes file information and keywords for the selected image. The metadata display includes the name, kind, dates created and modified, and so on, as well as the EXIF information recorded by the camera.

In addition, Bridge adds an IPTC (International Press Telecommunications Council) section where you can add data that's useful in tracking important aspects of the image. IPTC fields include the photographer's name, contact information, copyright status, and usage information.

For a better view of metadata, switch to the Metadata workspace. Choose Window ➤ Workspace ➤ Metadata Focus. To increase the size of the panels on the left side of the window, drag the vertical divider bar to the right and the horizontal divider bars up or down.

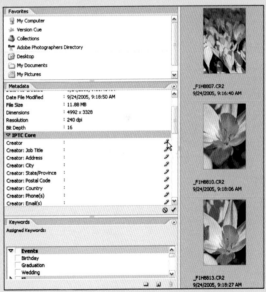

►A.4

5

The content area shows thumbnails with the default image settings and Camera Raw automatic adjustments applied. In the default view, two lines of information are also displayed under each thumbnail.

_F1H8751.CR2   _F1H8752.CR2   _F1H8753.CR2
9/24/2005, ...   9/24/2005, ...   9/24/20...

▶A.5

6

The Unfiltered/Filtered drop-down menu on the Bridge Shortcut toolbar offers a quick way to display rated and labeled photos. Two-level filtering is also possible by selecting both a rating option and a label option from the Filtered menu.

▶A.6

X-Ref

For details on rating and labeling images, see Chapter 3.

Retaining Ratings and Labels

SB Sidebar

Labels and ratings are a handy way to sort through images and indicate keepers from non-keepers. They also provide a quick way to sort through large numbers of images. For these reasons, retaining ratings and labels is important.

Labels and ratings are saved with metadata if you chose to save image settings in a Sidecar XMP file (choose Edit [or Bridge on Mac] ➤ Camera Raw Preferences). If you save files in DNG format, sidecar XMP files are unnecessary and the information is saved automatically. Otherwise, the ratings and labels are saved in a cache, a file that contains the thumbnail and preview, metadata, and sort order for the folder. If you're not using the DNG format, be sure to specify that metadata is saved in sidecar XMP files. Appendix B provides more information on Sidecar XMP files.

Set Bridge Preferences

Although Bridge performs well with the default installation, you can tweak its performance. In addition, you can also make useful changes to other default settings to better suit your workflow preferences. Taken together, these changes ultimately make the Bridge display more useful and can save time throughout the workflow.

1

You can add or subtract the amount of information displayed under thumbnails. Bridge automatically displays the filename and creation date under each thumbnail. You can choose to show two more lines of metadata if you want, or show only the filename. Choose Edit (or Bridge on Mac) ➤ Preferences to open the Preferences dialog box. In the General category, under Additional Lines of Thumbnail Metadata, select the Show options to add up to three additional lines of metadata. Then select the information you want to display in each additional line from the drop-down menu. If you want less information displayed, clear these options.

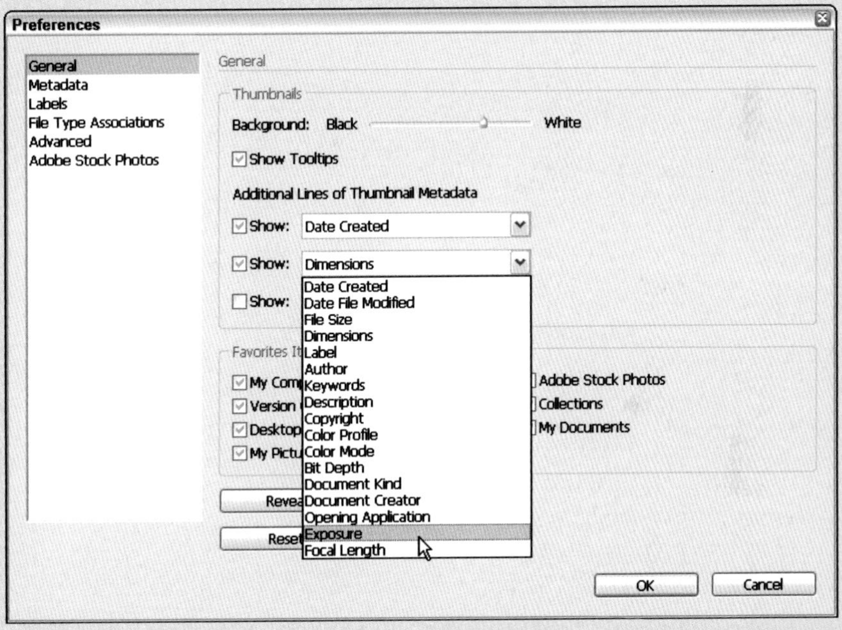

▶A.7

You can also streamline the items shown on the Favorites panel in Bridge. Choose the General category. Under Favorites Items, select or clear the items you want to add to or remove from Favorites.

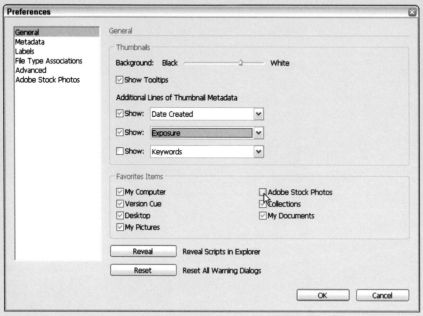

►A.8

Tip

You can add items to the Favorites panel by dragging them from the content area to the Drag Favorites Here entry at the bottom of the Favorites panel. If the Drag Favorites Here entry isn't visible, scroll down in the Favorites tab to display it. If you change your mind, you can right-click (Ctrl+click on Mac for single-button mice/laptops) the item, and then choose Remove from Favorites from the menu that appears.

3

The Metadata category in the Preferences dialog box includes fields that may or may not be useful to you. You can choose to show or hide the fields displayed in the Metadata panel. Choose Metadata in the Preferences dialog box and select the check mark next to the fields that you don't want displayed to deselect it. Or to display a field, select the checkbox to the left of the field.

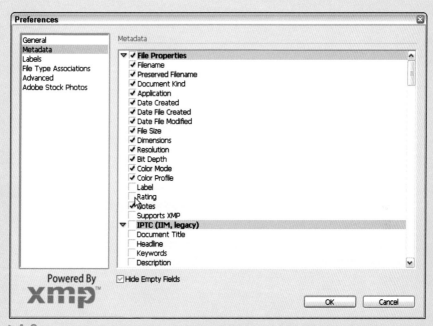

►A.9

4

In the File Type Associations category of the Preferences dialog box, you can set the default program that opens RAW files. Click the drop-down menu to the right of a field type to select from a menu. Choose Browse if you want to open RAW files using the manufacturer's proprietary program. You can also choose Adobe Photoshop CS2. If you choose the Photoshop CS2 option to open proprietary RAW files, Photoshop starts first (if it isn't already running), and then Photoshop opens and hosts Camera Raw.

Note
The changes you make to file associations do not affect the file association settings in Windows Explorer or Finder.

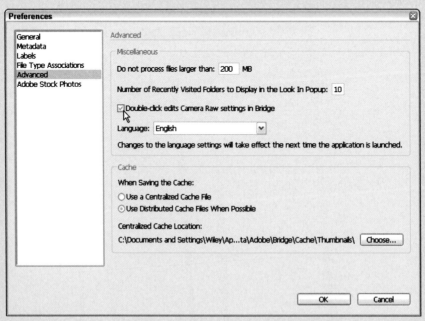

Preferences

General
Metadata
Labels
File Type Associations
Advanced
Adobe Stock Photos

File Type Association

Alias (.pix)	Adobe Photoshop CS2 ▾
ASP (.asp, .aspx)	None ▾
AutoCAD (.dwg, .dxf)	None ▾
Bitmap (.bmp, .rle, .dib)	Adobe Photoshop CS2 ▾
BPDX (.bpdx)	None ▾
Canon Camera Raw (.crw, .cr2)	Adobe Photoshop CS2 ▾
CGI (.cgi)	**Adobe Photoshop CS2**
Cineon (.cin, .sdpx, .dpx, .fido)	**Explorer Settings: Adobe Photoshop CS2**
CompuServe GIF (.gif)	**Browse...**
Computer Graphics Metafile (.cgm)	
Corel Draw (.cdr)	None ▾
CSS (.css)	None ▾
Desktop Color Separation (DCS) (.dcs)	Adobe Photoshop CS2 ▾
Digital Negative (.dng)	Adobe Photoshop CS2 ▾
Electric Image (.img, .ei, .eiz, .eizz)	Adobe Photoshop CS2 ▾
Encapsulated PostScript (.eps, .ai3, .ai4, .ai5, ...	Explorer Settings ▾

☐ Hide Undefined File Associations   Reset to Default Associations

OK   Cancel

▶A.10

If you prefer for Bridge to host Camera Raw when you open RAW files, you can set this option in the Advanced category of the Preferences dialog box. Select the Double-click edits Camera Raw settings in Bridge option to edit without opening Photoshop.

Preferences

General
Metadata
Labels
File Type Associations
Advanced
Adobe Stock Photos

Advanced

Miscellaneous

Do not process files larger than: 200 MB

Number of Recently Visited Folders to Display in the Look In Popup: 10

☑ Double-click edits Camera Raw settings in Bridge

Language: English ▾

Changes to the language settings will take effect the next time the application is launched.

Cache

When Saving the Cache:
◯ Use a Centralized Cache File
◉ Use Distributed Cache Files When Possible

Centralized Cache Location:
C:\Documents and Settings\Wiley\Ap...ta\Adobe\Bridge\Cache\Thumbnails\   Choose...

OK   Cancel

▶A.11

In the Cache section of the Advanced Preferences, you can choose options for how files store thumbnail, metadata, and file information and how they determine the speed with which previously viewed folders are displayed in Bridge. You can specify where the two cache files, Adobe Bridge Cache.bc and Adobe Bridge Cache.bct, are stored and whether they move with the image files or not. You can choose these options:

- **Use a Centralized Cache File.** This option offers simplicity, but it is both program- and machine-dependent. If you move files in Bridge, the cache link remains unbroken, but if you move files in Finder or Windows Explorer, the connection to the centralized cache is lost. And if you move files to removable media or to another computer, the link is likewise broken unless you use the Export Cache command in Bridge.

- **Use Distributed Cache Files When Possible.** This option saves the cache files in the current folder, which means that when you burn a CD or DVD, or if you move the folder outside of Bridge to another location on the same computer or to another computer, the cache files travel with the folder. Given the high number of backups that most photographers routinely make, this option helps ensure a speedy generation of thumbnails and metadata on different media and computers.

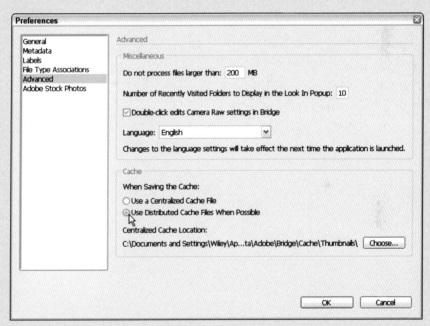

▶A.12

Set Cache Options

You can also control Bridge cache on the fly. For example, you can have Bridge generate folder previews in the background as you do other work, and you can force a refresh of cache. Choose Tools ➤ Cache, and select one of the following:

- **Build Cache for Subfolders.** This option generates the thumbnails, previews, and metadata in the background, allowing you to go on with other tasks while the folder cache is being parsed.

- **Purge Cache for This Folder.** Choose this option when you suspect that the folder cache is out of date and needs to be regenerated.

- **Purge Central Cache.** Choose this option to clear both the central and distributed cache for the current folder to free space on the hard drive.

Purging cache deletes the metadata and thumbnail cache. Also, if you haven't specified DNG format or set metadata to be written to a sidecar XMP file, purging deletes ratings and labels.

Appendix B

Getting to Know Camera Raw

Compared to Photoshop, Camera Raw looks relatively simple. The simplicity belies Adobe's powerful conversion engine and the tools. Getting acquainted with Camera Raw is a first step toward mastering RAW image conversion while maintaining the best image quality.

This section provides an overview of Camera Raw.

1

You can start Camera Raw in a variety of ways, but each technique has different implications. The best practice is to choose a technique based on what you want to do when you finish converting the image(s) and/or based on which program is busy doing other tasks. To open Camera Raw:

- In Adobe Bridge, double-click one or more RAW images. Photoshop opens and hosts Camera Raw, which displays the images. If you select multiple images, Camera Raw opens in Filmstrip mode. The default button to close Camera Raw is Open (in Photoshop). Note that this behavior doesn't apply if you have set Bridge preferences so that double-clicking opens images in Camera Raw.

- In Bridge, choose File ➤ Open in Camera Raw. Bridge hosts Camera Raw without starting Photoshop. The default button to close Camera Raw is Done rather than Open (in Photoshop).

- In Bridge, choose File ➤ Open. Photoshop opens and hosts Camera Raw. The default button to close Camera Raw is Open (in Photoshop).

- In Photoshop, choose File ➤ Open, select one or more RAW files, and then choose Open. The Camera Raw dialog box opens; the default button to close Camera Raw is Open (in Photoshop).

If you select more than 10 images and choose Open in Bridge, Camera Raw displays a message asking whether you really want to open that many images.

Click OK in the message box to open the images. Camera Raw performs well with 10, 20, or many more images open at a time.

> **Tip**
>
> Sometimes you want to see just the selected image. In Filmstrip mode, you can hide the filmstrip by double-clicking the marker on the middle of the vertical bar or anywhere on the divider bar between the filmstrip and preview window, or drag the divider bar to the far left. When you want to redisplay the filmstrip, double-click the marker again.

2

The filmstrip highlights the currently selected image with a border and previews the image in the preview pane. When you select multiple images in the filmstrip, all the images are highlighted and Camera Raw denotes the currently selected image with a heavier border and displays it in the content pane.

> **Note**
>
> An exclamation mark in a yellow triangle in the preview and filmstrip areas means that Camera Raw is busy generating previews. After the previews are built, the icons disappear. Also, as images are processed and cropped, Camera Raw adds icons along the lower thumbnail's border to indicate settings and crop status.

▶B.1

3

The Camera Raw dialog box toolbar includes these tools (left to right):

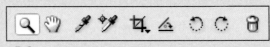

▶B.2

- **Zoom tool.** Use this tool to enlarge the preview up to 400 percent. Press Alt/Option to change the mode reduction. Double-click the Zoom tool icon on the toolbar to return an image to 100 percent, or drag the Zoom tool over the area to enlarge a specific area.

- **Hand tool.** Use this tool to move to different areas of a preview that is enlarged to more than 100 percent. Hold down the spacebar to use the Hand tool with another tool. Double-click the Hand Tool icon on the toolbar to fit an image into the preview area.

- **White Balance tool.** Use this tool to correct color temperature and tint by clicking an area of the image that should be white or light neutral gray. In most cases, this tool is the quickest path to correcting color.

- **Color Sampler tool.** This tool allows you to set up to nine color samples by clicking within the image. Color sample readings appear above the preview window. Use the samples to diagnose shadow color casts, get a read on skin tones, and much more.

- **Crop tool.** This tool allows a freeform crop. Choose the down arrow shown on the bottom right of the tool, and you can crop to one of five preset aspect ratios or set a custom ratio. Camera Raw displays crops with a gray screen, but does not crop the image until you save it. The subsequent image preview in Bridge displays the image cropped. If you select multiple images, all are cropped to the same size and with the crop in the same position.

- **Straighten tool.** Use this tool to straighten horizontal or vertical lines in the image. Just drag within the image to establish what should be horizontal or vertical. Camera Raw straightens the image but changes aren't applied until you save the image.

- **Rotate Image tools.** The two rotate image tools rotate 90 degrees counter-clockwise and 90 degrees clockwise.

- **Delete.** This control marks the currently selected image for deletion.

4

The preview buttons for Preview, Shadows, and Highlights on the toolbar are a good overall indicator of clipping, but a better method is to press the Alt/Option key as you adjust Exposure and Shadow sliders. Regardless, the previews work thusly:

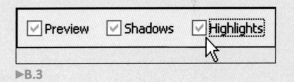

►B.3

- **Preview.** This button toggles between showing the preview at the current and original settings. By default, the preview includes automatic Camera Raw adjustments. As you make adjustments, the preview updates to show the cumulative effect.

- **Shadows.** When turned on, this control displays shadow clipping—when any color channels are saturated to pure black with no detail—as blue on the preview image.

- **Highlights.** When turned on, this control displays highlight clipping—when any channels are saturated to pure white with no detail—as red on the preview image.

5

The main window displays the image preview with controls at the lower left to enlarge or reduce the preview size. In Filmstrip mode, the preview pane displays paging controls to move among open images in the lower right.

▶B.4

6

Selecting the Show Workflow Options check box displays or hides controls for making choices on color space, bit depth, and image size and resolution. Camera Raw sets the workflow options to the default for your camera. You can set different options, depending on how you intend to use the image.

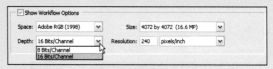

▶B.5

- **Space.** You can choose Adobe RBG (1998), ColorMatch RGB, ProPhoto RGB, or sRGB IEC61966-1. Each color space offers a different gamut, or range of supported colors. ProPhoto RGB offers the widest gamut and can often help prevent color clipping. The second widest gamut is Adobe RGB (1998). If you are converting images for use on the Web, sRGB is the best color space to use.

- **Depth.** For conversion, 16-bit provides the highest resolution. Many photographers recommend keeping images at 16-bit during the editing process to maintain maximum image quality during conversion and subsequent editing in Photoshop.

- **Size.** The default size for your camera is automatically selected. You can upsample or increase the image size by selecting a higher size, or downsample, or decrease the image size by choosing a smaller size.

- **Resolution.** You can set the resolution in pixels per inch or pixels per centimeter. You can also type the resolution. For inkjet printing, 240 is commonly used. For commercial printing, 300 ppi is the standard setting. For Web use, 72 or 96 ppi is acceptable.

7

The R: G: B: controls above the histogram area display continuous color readings for the pixel under the mouse pointer. If the preview is 100 percent or smaller, the RGB values show a 5 x 5-pixel sampling from the preview. At higher zoom settings, the RGB values sample from actual image pixels.

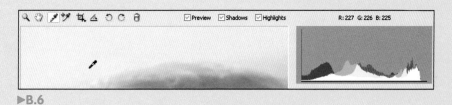

▶B.6

8

The histogram shows tonal distribution and relative number of pixels at each level.

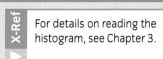

X-Ref

▶ For details on reading the histogram, see Chapter 3.

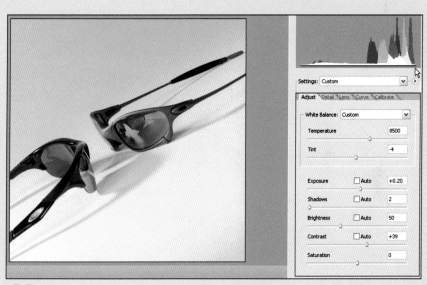

▶B.7

9

The Settings drop-down menu offers four options:

- **Image Settings.** Applies the original image settings if the image has not been previously edited. If the image was previously edited, it displays those settings.

- **Camera Raw Defaults.** Applies the saved settings for a camera, or the Camera Raw Auto Adjustments.

- **Previous Conversion.** Applies the settings from the most recent image conversion to the current image.

- **Custom.** Displays the settings that you've made to the image since opening it.

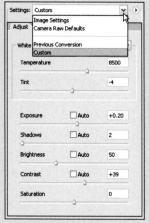

▶B.8

10

The Camera Raw menu is available by clicking the right-pointing arrow next to the Settings drop-down menu.

▶B.9

X-Ref
▶ Chapter 7 provides details on the Settings menu.

Five tabs offer access to specific image conversion adjustments. Each of these tab panels is covered in the technique chapters throughout this book, but here are some of the highlights of each tab panel:

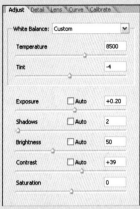

- **Adjust.** This panel, which is shown here, offers the essential image conversion controls including white balance, exposure, shadows, brightness, contrast, and saturation in a central location. You can adjust settings and watch the interaction with other controls to make judicious tradeoffs as you work. Here is where you make overall color correction, set white and black points, and adjust midtones.

▶B.10

- **Detail.** Offers controls to adjust sharpening, set luminance smoothing, and to tame color noise.

- **Lens.** Offers controls to compensate for lens aberrations including color fringing and vignetting.

- **Curve.** This panel tab offers three preset tonal curves that you can tweak to your liking and a custom option.

- **Calibrate.** Offers controls for correcting color casts in shadows and fine-tuning color to compensate for the difference between Camera Raw's built-in camera profile and the behavior of your camera. You can save adjusted settings as the new default and apply them to other images.

12

The Save, Open, Cancel, and Done buttons are the default buttons located at the bottom right of the Camera Raw dialog box. These button choices change depending on whether one or multiple images are open and whether the Alt/Opt key is held down. Also the default button depends on whether Camera Raw is hosted by Bridge or Photoshop.

Here is a rundown of the functionality. In this figure, I have three images selected in Camera Raw, so the button choices reflect my selections.

- **Save... or Save x Image(s).** This option opens the Save Options dialog box where you choose the location, naming convention, and format for saving the image(s). You can choose from Photoshop-supported formats including DNG, .JPG, .TIF, and .PSD. In the Format section, you can choose from Photoshop-supported formats for Digital Negative, JPEG (and choose a quality level from low to maximum), TIFF (and choose either no compression or ZIP), or Photoshop.

  If you save files in DNG format, you can choose from the following:

  - **Compressed (lossless).** Saves the image with lossless compression.
  - **Convert to Linear Image.** Saves the file in an interpolated or demosaiced format which is useful if you want to use another RAW conversion program that recognizes the DNG format to process the file.
  - **Embed Original Raw File.** Embeds the original RAW file in the file that you can later extract. This option is great but produces very large files.

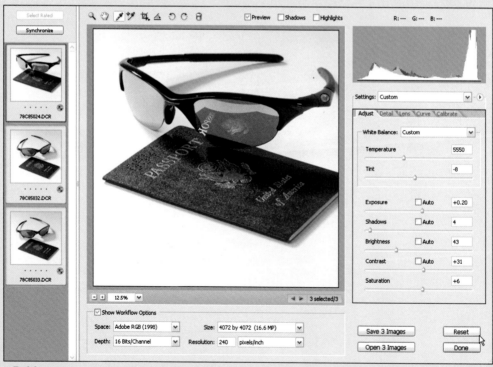

▶B.11

- **JPEG Preview.** Options include None, Medium Size, and Full Size. Choosing an option embeds a JPEG preview image in the DNG file.

- **Save.** Camera Raw saves files in the background, which allows you to continue working on additional images. Pressing the Alt/Option key toggles the Save... button to Save, which saves the image without opening the Save Options dialog box.

- **Open or Open x Image(s).** Opens the selected image or selected images in Photoshop, saves the Camera Raw settings, and updates the image preview and thumbnail in Bridge.

- **Open Copy.** If Camera Raw is hosted by Photoshop, and if you press the Alt/Option key, Open changes to Open Copy, which opens a copy of the image in Photoshop with the Camera Raw settings applied. This option is great to use when you want to process an image multiple times for compositing in Photoshop.

- **Cancel.** Dismisses the Camera Raw dialog box without saving adjustments to the image.

- **Reset.** Pressing the Alt/Option key toggles the Cancel button to Reset, which returns the image to the settings applied when you opened the image.

- **Done.** Applies changes, dismisses the Camera Raw dialog box, and returns to the host program.

Setting Up Camera Raw

Setting up Camera Raw is quick and relatively straightforward, and it is a very important process to do. Some setup options, such as workflow, are on the top-level of Camera Raw's dialog box. You'll find other setup options in Preferences. These options affect whether Camera Raw image settings travel with the images when you burn a CD or DVD or move images to another computer.

This section walks you through the most important setup options for Camera Raw.

1

In Camera Raw, click the right-pointing arrow next to the Settings menu in Camera Raw, and then choose Preferences. Camera Raw displays the Camera Raw Preferences dialog box.

Click the Save image settings in drop-down arrow. Two options are offered, and your choice affects whether image settings get moved to CD or DVD or to another computer when you move or archive the images.

> **Note**
> Camera Raw saves image settings applied during the most recent editing session, but it does not save image attributes, including color space, bit depth, size, and resolution settings.

Camera Raw Preferences (Version 3.1)

Save image settings in: `Sidecar ".xmp" files` ▾

> Camera Raw database
> Sidecar ".xmp" files

Apply sharpening to:

OK

Cancel

Camera Raw Cache

Maximum Size: `1.0` GB   [Purge Cache]

[Select Location...]   C:\Documents and Settings\Wiley...on Data\Adobe\CameraRaw\Cache\

DNG File Handling

☐ Ignore sidecar ".xmp" files

☐ Update embedded JPEG previews: `Medium Size` ▾

►B.12

Be sure you understand that Camera Raw treats the original RAW files as read-only. As a result, the changes you make to files in Camera Raw are saved, but they are not applied to the original file—the original file remains untouched. To retain your work in Camera Raw, you must choose where the settings are stored. Here is an overview of the two options for saving Camera Raw settings:

- **Camera Raw database.** This option saves the image settings you make in the Camera Raw database on your computer. The database is indexed by file content, which means that if you move or rename the image, the link to the settings is not broken. However, if you move the images to another computer or burn them to CD or DVD, the link to the database is lost, along with the changes you made in Camera Raw. To move the settings with the files, you have to use the Export Settings command in Camera Raw to either export the settings to a sidecar XMP file or embed them in DNG files.

- **Sidecar ".xmp" files.** This option stores settings in a separate XMP file that is created with the same base name as the image and is stored in the same folder as the RAW file. An XMP file is simply a small code file that stores Camera Raw settings and can also store image metadata and IPTC information. If you move or rename the images in Bridge, the sidecar XMP files are automatically updated and moved. But if you move or rename the files in Explorer or Finder, remembering to move or rename the XMP files is up to you.

2

From the Apply sharpening to drop-down menu, you can choose to apply Camera Raw's default sharpening to the converted image or only to preview images. For most workflows, image sharpening is the last step in the process—occurring after the image is edited, sized, and ready for printing or online display. In this scenario, applying sharpening to the preview provides a somewhat better view of what the image will ultimately look like with sharpening applied in Photoshop.

The choice is yours and should be based on your overall workflow. If you decide you don't want sharpening after it's applied to the image, you'll need to reprocess the RAW file again. It's better to decide what you want up front and stick with the plan throughout.

►B.13

3

In the Camera Raw Cache section, type the size you want in the Maximum Size box. The default of 1GB is enough to manage approximately 200 images. If your folders are routinely larger than 200 images, increasing the cache is worthwhile. The maximum size is 50GB. You can also change the location where cache is stored by clicking the Select Location button to open the Select Cache Folder dialog box.

Click Purge Cache when the cache becomes excessively large or needs to be refreshed. The Camera Raw cache holds the preparsed RAW image data for recently accessed files. Ample room in the cache lessens the amount of time it takes to load the Camera Raw dialog box and to subsequently display updated image previews in Bridge.

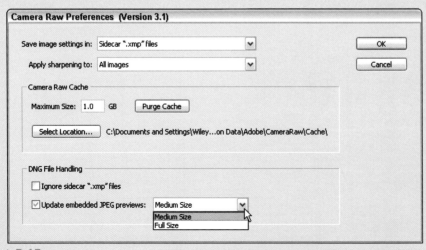

►B.14

4

If you save files in Adobe's DNG format, you can set options for handling in the DNG File Handling section. Here are the options:

- **Ignore sidecar ".xmp" files.** For DNG format files, settings and metadata are stored directly within the file, making Sidecar XMP files unnecessary. Selecting this option tells Camera Raw to ignore the sidecar XMP file and to not update the DNG file.

- **Update embedded JPEG previews.** You can choose this option to ensure JPEG previews are always updated when you edit a DNG file. You can also set the JPEG preview size to Medium or Full Size.

►B.15

In Camera Raw, the Show Workflow Options section offers controls that are generally considered part of setup. Workflow options include the following:

- **Space.** Determines the color space that the image is converted to. Choose an option from the drop-down list to choose one of four color space profiles: Adobe RGB (1998), ColorMatch RGB, ProPhoto RGB, and sRGB IEC61966-1. Each color space has a range of supported colors, some larger than others. ProPhoto RGB supports the widest range of colors and sRGB supports the smallest range of colors. The best practice is to choose the same space here that you use in Photoshop.

- **Depth.** Specifies whether the image remains 16- or 8-bit. If you choose 16-bit, and then open the image in Photoshop, only a subset of Photoshop commands is available.

- **Size.** Camera Raw opens images at the original size expressed in pixels. You can upsample or downsample images.

- **Resolution.** This control allows you to specify the printing resolution. Many inkjet printers use 240 ppi, whereas commercial printers use 300 ppi.

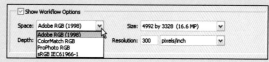

►B.16

Appendix C

Stay Current with Adobe Updates

Adobe periodically updates its products including Adobe Bridge, Camera Raw, and the DNG Converter. As most Camera Raw users know, Adobe updates the plug-in soon after a new digital SLR camera is introduced. If you are using one of the newest cameras, check the Adobe Web site at www.adobe.com/products/photoshop/cameraraw.html to see whether support for the camera has been added to Camera Raw.

If you want to stay current with updates, Web sites such as Rob Galbraith's site www.robgalbraith.com post notices when updates are available.

To download the latest updates to Adobe Bridge and Camera Raw, go to the Adobe Web site at www.adobe.com/support/downloads and find the update that you want to install. You can also choose Help ➤ Updates in Bridge to install the latest updates.

Specific installation steps depend on the computer operating system that you use. But the general process for uploading Camera Raw includes the following steps.

Before You Begin

Before you begin, be sure you have programs to expand compressed downloaded files.

▶ **Windows.** You can uncompress the files using Windows or using WinZip (www.winzip.com) or PKZIP (www.pkware.com).

▶ **Macintosh.** You can expand files on the Mac without a separate program, or you can use StuffIt Expander (www.stuffit.com/mac/expander/index.html or ftp://ftp.stuffit.com/archive/mac/StuffIt_Expander).

You must close Photoshop, Bridge, and Camera Raw. Then, on your computer, navigate to

▶ **Windows Systems.** Program Files/Common Files/Adobe/Plug-Ins/CS2/File Formats

▶ **Macintosh Systems.** Library\Application Support\Adobe\Plug-Ins\CS2\File Formats

Download and Install the Camera Raw Plug-In Update

1

Go to www.adobe.com/support/downloads/ and select the Camera Raw plug-in update for your computer's operating system.

▶C.1

2

Scroll to and click the ReadMe file link, and then read the details of the update, noting any installation precautions.

3

Click the Download button on the left side of the Web page, and then click the Download button on the next Web page. The File Download dialog box appears depending on the operating system and browser that you're using.

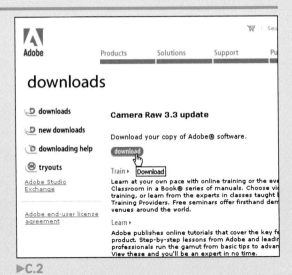

►C.2

4

Click Open in the File Download dialog box. The updates download to your computer as zipped or stuffed files. Using the program appropriate for your system, expand the files.

> **Note**
>
> For Macintosh systems, double-clicking uncompresses the .dmg file and mounts the contents of the file as a disk image on your desktop.

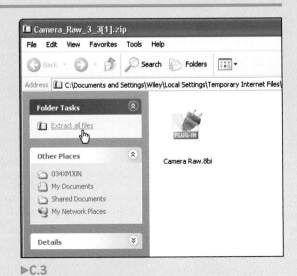

►C.3

5

Copy the Camera Raw plug-in, Camera Raw.8bi, from the unzipped, downloaded files to:

- **Windows Systems.** Program Files/Common Files/Adobe/Plug-Ins/CS2/File Formats
- **Macintosh Systems.** Library\Application Support\Adobe\Plug-Ins\CS2\File Formats

6

Move the existing plug-in to another folder. Retaining the previous plug-in ensures that you can revert to it if you encounter any problems with the updated plug-in.

7

Launch Camera Raw via Photoshop CS2 or via Adobe Bridge.

Appendix D

A variety of professional organizations offer support and training for photographers. Here is a selection of some of the most respected organizations by category.

Aerial

Professional Aerial Photographers' Association
www.papainternational.org

Architectural

Association of Independent Architectural Photographers
www.aiap.photographer.org

Camera Manufacturers

Canon
www.usa.canon.com

FujiFilm
www.fujifilm.com

Hasselblad
www.hasselblad.se

Leaf America
leafamerica.com

Mamiya
www.mamiya.com

Nikon
www.nikonusa.com

Olympus
www.olympusamerica.com

Pentax
www.pentax.com

Sony
www.sony.com

Commercial

Advertising Photographers of America
www.apanational.org

Editorial/Photojournalism

American Society of Media Photographers
www.asmp.org

Editorial Photographers
www.editorialphotographers.com

National Press Photographers Association
www.nppa.org

Fine Art

College Art Association
www.collegeart.org

Photo Imaging Educators Association
www.pieapma.org

Society for Photographic Education
www.spenational.org

General

Professional Photographers of America (PPA)
www.ppa.com

Association of Photographers (UK)
www.the-aop.org

Professional Photographers of Canada Inc.
www.ppoc.ca

PIC - Professional Imagers Club
www.pic-verband.de

The American Society of Picture Professionals
www.aspp.com

Nature and Wildlife

Lepp Institute
www.leppphoto.com; www.leppinstitute.com

Nature Photographers Network
www.naturephotographers.net

North American Nature Photography Association
www.nanpa.org

Photoshop

Adobe Tips & Tutorials
http://studio.adobe.com/us/

Photoshop Support
www.photoshopsupport.com

The National Association of Photoshop Professionals
www.photoshopuser.com

Software Cinema
www.software-cinema.com

Portrait/Wedding

Wedding and Portrait Photographer International
www.wppi-online.com

Society of Wedding and Portrait Photographers (UK)
www.swpp.co.uk/

Stock

Adobe Stock Photos
www.adobe.com/adobestockphotos/

Stock Artists Alliance
www.StockArtistsAlliance.org

Workshops

Anderson Ranch Arts Center
www.andersonranch.org

Ansel Adams Gallery Workshops
www.anseladams.com

Brooks Institute Weekend Workshops
http://workshops.brooks.edu

David Wells
www.davidhwells.com/PublishedWork/Workshops/index.html

Eddie Adams Workshop
www.eddieadamsworkshop.com

Eddy Tapp Workshops
www.eddietapp.com/seminars.html

Ellen Anon
www.sunbearphoto.com/instruction.html

John Paul Caponigro
www.johnpaulcaponigro.com/workshops/index.html

Katrin Eismann
www.photoshopdiva.com/classes.html

Kevin Ames
www.amesphoto.com/training.html

Macduff Everton
www.macduffeverton.com/html_pages/workshop.html

Maine Photographic Workshops
www.theworkshops.com

Mentor Series
www.mentorseries.com

Missouri Photo Workshop
www.mophotoworkshop.org

Mountain Workshops
www.mountainworkshops.org

Nikon School
www.nikonschool.com

Palm Beach Photographic Centre Workshops
www.workshop.org

Photography at the Summit
www.richclarkson.com; www.photographyatthesummit.com

Rob Sheppard
www.robsheppardphoto.com/workshops.html

Rocky Mountain Photo Adventures
www.rockymountainphotoadventures.com

Santa Fe Workshops
www.santafeworkshops.com

Sean Duggan
www.seanduggan.com/training/index.html

Toscana Photographic Workshop
www.tpw.it/

Woodstock Photography Workshops
www.cpw.org

Index

Index

Index

RAW files, compositing *(continued)*
        versus other techniques, 229
        overview, 65
        shots in ambient light, 156–157, 159
        using Smart Objects, 116–122
    three or more exposures, 97, 229
    two-exposure technique, 64–65, 229
    using HDR tool, 229
Reduce Noise filter, 167
resampling images
    defined, 305
    overview, 78
    using Image Size and actions, 81
    using Size option, 72, 79–80
Reset button in Camera Raw, 324–325
resolution, 305
Resolution options in Camera Raw,
    72, 320, 329
retouching portraits. *See* Photoshop
    adjustments
RGB controls in Camera Raw, 52, 321
RGB hue/saturation sliders, 181, 189–192,
    207–208, 224, 248
RGB (Red, Green, Blue) color model, 294, 305
Rotate Image tools in Camera Raw, 319

S

saturation, 305. *See also* hue
Saturation sliders on Adjust tab, 59, 133
Save As dialog box in Photoshop, 296
Save button in Camera Raw, 88, 324–325
Save Collection dialog box, 50
Save Image Settings In options, 325–326
Save Metadata Template dialog box, 17
Save Options dialog box in Camera Raw
    Destination options, 34
    Format options, 28, 34–36, 324–325
    naming images, 159
    opening, 88, 324
    overview, 209, 324
Save Raw Conversion Settings dialog box,
    254, 256
Save Settings Subset dialog box, 255
Save Workspace dialog box, 15
saving images
    in DNG format, 34–36, 324–325
    as JPEG, 28, 265
    JPEG previews within DNG files, 36, 325
    in Photoshop, 296
    as PSD, 265
    retouched in Photoshop, 291

    as TIFF, 265
    using Image Processor, 39–40, 265
saving settings. *See also* Camera Raw
    adjustments; Settings drop-down menu
    adjusting settings, 253
    applying saved settings, 254
    in Camera Raw database, 325–326
    and copying/pasting to multiple images,
        89–93
    made in Image Processor, 266
    overview, 193, 252
    in Save Settings dialog box, 254, 256
    settings subsets, 255–256
    in sidecar XMP files, 325–326
Scruggs, Brantlea, 70
searching images in Bridge, 22, 48–50
sensors, cleaning, 283
sepia tone simulation. *See also* color
    Adjust tab in, 205–206, 208
    Calibrate tab in, 207–208
    overview, 204
    refining in Photoshop, 209
    and saving, 209
Settings drop-down menu in Camera Raw.
    See also saving settings
    defined, 322
    Image Settings, 37
    Preferences, 174
    Save New Camera Raw Defaults, 125,
        148, 256
    Save Settings, 254
    Save Settings Subset, 255–256
    Use Auto Adjustments, 73, 256
shadow tint correction. *See also* tinting
    images
    Adjust tab in, 178–179, 182
    Calibrate tab in, 180–182
    Curve tab in, 179
    overview, 177
    refining in Photoshop, 182
Shadow Tint slider on Calibrate tab,
    180, 189, 207
Shadows button in Camera Raw, 319–320
Shadows slider on Adjust tab, 53, 57, 75
shadows threshold screen, 62
sharp, 306
sharpening images. *See also* color/detail
    correction
    in Camera Raw
        checking for noise, 175
        deciding when to apply, 172–173
        setting preferences for, 174, 327

IN Index

Index